The End

NAPOLEON AT SAINT HELENA
(1815-1821)

EDITOR'S NOTE

All photos were taken at Saint Helena in 2007.

L. Bombled's illustrations are carefully restored versions from the original ones produced by the artist for the 1895 edition of Las Cases' "Mémorial de Sainte-Hélène".

All K.G.M. illustrations were produced especially for this work.

Napoleon's words and utterances are printed in bold letters all along the book.

ISBN: 978-84-96658-60-8

DL: M-27610-2017

Published by
ANDREA PRESS
C/Talleres, 21 - Pol. Ind. de Alpedrete
28430 Alpedrete (Madrid) SPAIN
Tel.: (34) 918 570 008 - Fax: (34) 918 570 048
www.andreapresspublishing.com
sales@andreapresspublishing.com

Author: Lee Preston

Editor-in-Chief: Raúl Rubio

Proof Reading: Simon Wintle

Book Design: Andrea Press

Printed in Spain

Distributed in the EU by:

ANDREA EUROPE S.L.

C/Talleres, 21 - Pol. Ind. de Alpedrete
28430 Alpedrete (Madrid) SPAIN
Tel.: (34) 91 857 00 08
Fax: (34) 91 857 00 48
orders@andreaeurope.com
www.andreaeurope.com

Distributed in USA and Canada by:

ANDREA DEPOT USA, INC

2000 Windy Terrace,
Bldg 20 Suite A
Cedar Park, Texas 78613
Phone: 512-766-5641
orders@andreadepotusa.com
www.andreadepotusa.com

To the pursuers of the impossible

(Bombled. ©Andrea Press)

CONTENTS

(KGM. ©Andrea Press).

INTRODUCTION

erhaps because History has been traditionally told and written mostly as a gigantic epic starred but a scarce handful of men that make his will on billions of anonymous human beings –that seem to play no other role that simple clay in the hands of a modeller– great men's biographies have always intrigued me.

What was the real essential difference –if any– that makes these rare men protrude above their contemporaries? Did they really belong to a 'superior breed' as stated in some way by many western historiographers in late 19th century, or were they no more than the visible instrument of economic and sociological forces and tensions moving the development of the humanity as a whole as suggested by Marxist historians? Whatever the answer to these questions may be, the mystery is still to be solved but the truth remains that no sound understanding of human history can be reached if names like Alexander, Caesar, Hannibal... or Napoleon, are omitted in the telling.

It has been said by Napoleon's detractors that he is the idol of the uneducated[1] and probably this is true, if only because he is possibly the most popular political or military leader in world history. In my opinion admiration is difficult to avoid when learning on Napoleon's incredible life, and indifference almost impossible. Apart from that, the truth remains that the books, paintings, plays, movies and even great musical pieces on the personage began to amount during his life and have not ceased to enlarge since.

The curiosity to know the reasons able to explain such a phenomenon led me to my first approach to the character in my early childhood and have kept me intrigued to this very same day, in which I really think not feasible explanation can be found, perhaps because fascination and mystery are always deeply interwoven.

The intention behind this book consequently, is not to judge or even explain Napoleon's life or personality, but simply following him into his long demise at Saint Helena as close as possible in the attempt to 'meet the man'.

---

1. *Referred by Jean-Paul Kauffmann in the prologue of his book 'The Black Room at Longwood' as said by the French historian Jules Michelet.*

One of the most astonishing facts in Napoleon's life is his fall: a man that held such an enormous power, who ruled over most of Europe, finished his amazing career in one of the remotest places of the world then and now: Saint Helena, an island in the middle of the south Atlantic, thousand of miles from shore. There the successor of Charlemagne, the emperor of the modern age, spent the last years of his life withstanding inconveniences bordering humiliation, while stubbornly building his own legend that, likely, would have been pretty different without this exile.

At Saint Helena it was Napoleon alone, devoid of the power he had been so used to. No great palaces anymore; just a mediocre, *'petit bourgeois'* lodging and a retinue composed by a variety of personages ranging from self interest to real loyalty: a stiffing little world pathetically clinched to the etiquette of a court existing never more; living on a glorious past and denying a painful present...

So Saint Helena doubles as a romantic epic and 'laboratory' to study the behaviour of the exiles under pretty odd circumstances. Among them, and very especially, is Napoleon; finally exposed to the observation of all the people around. Friends and foes, partial or impartial; many of them –fortunately enough– left a huge variety of memoirs and reports on the fallen emperor so exposing to critical analysis and investigation the nature of this exceptional being and making possible an intriguing approach to the man and his personage almost two centuries since, what, in its turn, may be the best opportunity to learn what is lying behind these great personalities of human history or –even if it will remain veiled forever– get closer to the mystery...

Lee Preston

(KGM. ©Andrea Press).

NAPOLEON THE MAN: A PORTRAIT IN DETAIL

uriously enough a feasible and generally agreed depiction of Napoleon, both from the physical and psychological point of view is difficult to fix up, despite (or perhaps because of) the prolific source of pictorial, sculptural or written depictions flowing unceasingly since the earliest times of his fame. On the other hand, the highly controversial nature of the character have inspired –now and then- some myths backing an almost grotesque picture that, surprisingly, is naturally supported by many people even nowadays. Kind of example Napoleon is almost universally depicted as a ridiculous short man while the truth is that he was probably slightly above the average height for the period.

Constant, his faithful *'valet de chambre'* told us[1] that *'Sa taille était de cinq pieds deux pouces trois lignes'* what would be the equivalent to 5 feet 6 inches (169 cm.). This measurement is well backed for a number of sources with very slight variations; the last of them being perhaps the measurement of the corpse after his death[2]. Hatred, political propaganda and the fact that many of Napoleon's generals and marshals were unusual tall men (Murat is reported to be 6 feet tall (183 cm.) are probably lying behind this misconception.

His most prominent physical feature would be the head. Again according to Constant: *'Sa tête était très forte, ayant vingt-deux pouces de circonférence'*[1] that is almost 7½ US hat size (60 cm.). Certainly a notorious head for a man his height though it is interesting to notice those measurements taken by Antommarchi during the autopsy tell that *'the circumference of the head was twenty inches and ten lines[3]...'* that is 7⅛ US hat size (56'7 cm.), what makes a significant difference. Two hats at the Musée de l'Armée in Paris[4] are reported to be 7¼ (58 cm.) and 7⅛ size. So, even though Napoleon's large head seems to be a clear prominent feature remarked in more period reports, a size of 7⅛ or 7¼ seems far more feasible than Constant's estimation that, on the other hand, would render a monstrous big head in a man his height...

1. *Mémoires de Constant, premier valet de chambre de l'Empereur. Napoléon. An intimacy account of the years of supremacy 1800-1804. Proctor Patterson Jones.*
2. *The Last days of the Emperor Napoleon. Doctor F. Antommarchi. London 1825.*
3. *Old English unit of uncertain length most frequently understood as 1/12 of an inch.*
4. *Napoléon et Ses Soldats. L'Apogée de la Gloire 1804-1809. Paul Willing. Collections Historiques du Musée de L'Armée.*

At the time of his arrival at Saint Helena, young Betsy Balcombe wrote:

> '...he was deadly pale, and I thought his features, though cold and immovable, and somewhat stern, were exceedingly beautiful ...his fascinating smile and kind manner removed every vestige of the fear with which I had hitherto regarded him. While he was talking to mamma, I had an opportunity of scrutinizing his features, which I did with the keenest interest; and certainly I have never seen anyone with so remarkable and striking physiognomy. The portraits of him, give a good general idea of his features; but his smile, and the expression of his eye, could not be transmitted to canvas, and these constituted Napoleon's chief charm. His hair was dark brown, and as fine and silky as a child's, rather too much so indeed for a man, as its very softness caused it to look thin. His teeth were even, but rather dark, and afterwards found that this arose from his constant habit of eating liquorice, of which he always kept a supply in his waistcoat pocket.'[1]

Betsy's remarks are important because unlike many other depictions produced by followers and detractors render a fresh impression of a child who met the Emperor unexpectedly and was strongly conditioned by tales about 'a huge ogre or giant, with one large flaming red eye in the middle of his forehead, and long teeth protruding from his mouth, with which he tore to pieces and devoured naughty little girls, specially those who did not know their lessons.'[1]

Also in Betsy's account we find two crucial elements to understand Napoleon's personality: his smile and 'the expression of his eye that could not be transmitted to canvas'. To have Napoleon posing for portraits was certainly a difficult achievement. He was not really interested in leaving an accurate depiction of Napoleon the man for posterity but rather the personification of his political system and thought. In fact he can justly be considered as an early forerunner of political propaganda. In spite of the huge and mass produced pictorial and sculptural representations released during his life to furnish all kind of governmental offices, the real man seems to vanish when trying to get closer to him, perhaps because his main instruments to seduce people around were his glance and smile... and they can 'not be transmitted to canvas'.

As probably all the great leaders, Napoleon possessed a magnetic and chameleon like personality. Through Betsy's narration a mild, almost sweet facet of an incredible kaleidoscopic nature emerge catching Betsy's sympathy forever.

---

1.   *To Befriend an Emperor. Betsy Balcombe's Memoirs of Napoleon on St. Helena. (Originally published in 1844). Ravenhall Books.*

Let´s Constant describe another impression:

    '...when excited by any violent passion his face took on a stern and even terrible expression. A sort of revolving movement very visibly produced itself on his forehead and between his eyebrows; his eyes flashed fire; his nostrils dilated, swollen with the inner storm. He seemed to be able to control at will these explosions, which, by the way, as time went on, became less and less frequent. His head remained cool. In ordinary life his expression was calm, meditative and gently grave'[1].

Even though Constant's memoirs should be handled with care, the fact that he was serving Napoleon for 14 years and sharing his intimacy gives us an invaluable insight into the understanding of Napoleon.

These 'flashing' eyes are reported to be grey or blue; sometimes grey-blue. The mouth was *'perfectly modelled, the upper lip slightly drawn towards the corner of the mouth and the chin slightly prominent'[2]*. So wrote Napoleon's secretary Meneval who, like Constant, spent many years besides the Emperor, perhaps missing the detail that the upper lip protruded slightly from the lower one, but rendering a general depiction of Napoleon's body in concordance with many others given by people who knew him:

    '...well built, though the bust was rather long. His head was big and the skull largely developed. His neck was short and his shoulders broad. His legs were well shaped, his feet were small and well formed...His forehead was high and broad, his eyes grey, penetrating and wonderfully mobile; his nose was straight and well shaped. His teeth were fairly good... His skin was smooth and his complexion pale, but of a pallor which denoted a good circulation of the blood. His very fine chestnut hair, which until the time of the expedition to Egypt, he had worn long, cut square and covering his ears, has clipped short. The hair was thin on the upper part of the head, and left bare his forehead... The stoutness, which grew upon him in the last years of his reign, developed his trunk more than the lower part of his body'.[2]

Another significant part of Napoleon's anatomy playing a foremost role in body language were his hands of which he felt very proud and probably he was right as they are repeatedly remarked in many contemporary accounts. Let's Betsy Balcombe tell us about them once again:

    'His hand was the fattest and prettiest in the world; his knuckles

---

1.   *Mémoires de Constant, premier valet de chambre de l'Empereur. Napoléon. An intimacy account of the years of supremacy 1800-1804. Proctor Patterson Jones.*

2.   *Baron de Méneval´s memoirs. Napoleon. An intimacy account of the years of supremacy 1800-1814. Proctor Patterson Jones.*

dimpled like those of a baby, his fingers taper and were beautifully formed, and his nails perfect.'[1]

Though he was lean and rather drawn in his youth, Napoleon started to gain weight around 1806, probably reaching the peak of 90 kg in 1820.[2]

From the psychological point of view there may be little doubt in nominating Napoleon's more outstanding feature, one on which followers and detractors all agree: his intellect. An incredible powerful, restless mind able to deal with several complex matters simultaneously (it is well know how the Emperor dictated to different secretaries at the same time at a very fast speed). A perfectly organized brain suited with the gift of discernment indispensable for all those who have to decide on the most serious matters. ***'Rien de plus difficile que de se decider'*** *(Deciding is the most difficult thing).*

Napoleon was always eager to learn about everything. According to Meneval: *'The contradictory opinions pronounced by Napoleon's schoolmasters, or school inspectors, go to prove that as a boy he gave no signs of what he was to be one day. As a matter of fact, it was not until he left the military school that he gave himself up with ardour to study. He often told me that since that date he has constantly worked sixteen hours a day. His dominating qualities were pride and a sentiment of his dignity, a warlike instinct, a genius for form, the love of order and discipline'.[3]*

The fact that he suffered from insomnia and slept around just four hours a day surely should have given him a good surplus of time to read and study because he was a truly consummate reader who, even when travelling, had always a large library on a variety of topics ranging from classical and contemporary literature to military, political or geographical works directly related with his campaigns or his prominent political role. His curiosity about practically everything seemed to have no limits. A true man from the Enlightenment who gave an extraordinary impulse to the development of science and general knowledge. At the same time he set the path for many institutions and infrastructures that were to shape the modern world emerging

---

1. *To Befriend an Emperor. Betsy Balcombe's Memoirs of Napoleon on St. Helena. (Originally published in 1844). Ravenhall Books.*
2. *Napoleon's autopsy: New perspectives. A. Lugli MD, A. Koop Luigi, M. Horcic. Human Pathology (2005) 36, 320-324. A study of 12 different pair of trousers worn by Napoleon between 1800 and 1821, year of his death suggested a weight increase form 67 to 90 kg falling to 79 kg during the last year of his life.*
3. *Baron de Méneval's memoirs. Napoleon. An intimacy account of the years of supremacy 1800-1814. Proctor Patterson Jones.*

from the extraordinary catharsis that the French Revolution meant for Western civilization.

Napoleon had and incredible capacity for hard work that he displayed in an amazingly organized way. Still this exceptional brain was not exempt of some flaws, for example his poor aptitude for languages as told by his minister Chaptal:

'Napoleon couldn´t speak properly any language. His mother tongue was the Corsican that is an Italian dialect, and when he spoke French it was quite apparent that he was a foreigner. He couldn´t read English nor German. He had no learned any word from this last language even though he had been many times in that country'[1].

Writing did not count among the Emperor's abilities either, as unanimously reported by many and sufficiently proved by endless surviving letters and documents that in some cases are illegible. It is said that he even had difficulties sometimes to understand his own writing.

Powerful imagination and memory reinforced Napoleon´s analytical mind but all these gifts would had been not enough at all in the accomplishment of the gigantic works undertaken through his unbelievable life, should an extraordinary temper and character not have supported him even in the most difficult hours. Coolness is perhaps one of the key words to understand his many successes in war and peace. An almost perfect mind control even in the moments of annoyance that more often than not were surely but a kind of theatrical effect: ***'Un homme, véritablement homme, ne hait point; sa colère et sa mauvaise humeur ne vont point au-delà de la minute.'*** *(A man, a real man, never hates. His wrath and bad temper last no more than a minute).*

A paramount feature of Napoleon's personality was surely his uncontrollable ambition. When masterfully forging his legend during his long stay at Saint Helena, Napoleon managed to picture the English government as the main instigators and direct culprit of his demise, it is a fact that he was drawn mostly by the kind of chronic ambition for power and glory as ambition only can explain some of the bigger mistakes that in the long term led him to Saint Helena long before Waterloo as – arguably– the invasion of Spain in 1808 and of Russia in 1812.

But Napoleon was the man who said that ***'la mort n'est rien, mais vivre vaincu et sans gloire, c'est mourir tous les jours'***. Glory, an empty word nowadays for most people but an indispensable term to a reasonable understanding of Napoleon and many other men of

---

1.   *Quoted by Alain Fillion in his book 'Napoléon'. Dictionnaire Intime.*

his kind because perhaps 'Glory' was the only thing, the sole goal beyond power at the beginning of 19th century. Glory is one of these words with an abstract, ample and ambiguous meaning. Still, though difficult to define, it seems clear that there is no glory without risk, without gamble, without adventure. It is here, in the unlimited field of 'adventure' where the deepest nature of our man lays and perhaps the only label that - very cautiously- could be given to him. *'On ne monte jamais si haut que quand on ne sait pas où l'on va'* (*One never goes higher than when destination is not known*).

Napoleon´s entire life is an incredible novel that cannot be reasonably explained but in terms of chance at least in the most crucial moments of his existence. He, apparently, fought for France, the Frenchman and even the high ideals deriving from the French Revolution but, in fact, he was not really French at all but a Corsican-born despised by his classmates when a child because he couldn't speak French in a proper manner (in fact he never did). Perhaps it would be better to say that he 'had France working for him' instead of the opposite. Was he then European in the modern sense of the term? He might be; but then: what about his incredible expedition to Egypt, his dreams of dominating the Far East in emulation of Alexander? When making Saint Helena out for the first time on October 14th 1815 he exclaimed while leaning his spy glass on Marchand´s shoulders: *'Ce n´est pas un joli séjour! J´aurais mieux fait de rester en Égypte. Je serais aujourd´hui empereur de tout l´Orient'.* (*This is not a jolly destination! I would rather remain in Egypt. I would be now Emperor of the whole East!*).

Indeed Napoleon was an adventurer in the most meaningful and deepest sense of the word that, just like many other men of his kind, was 'dragged' from the very beginning of his epic life to a dramatic end. This end 'had' to arrive sooner or later as the only thing –besides death- able to stop him. Even if he had won the campaigns of Russia and Spain, wouldn't he have followed to the East irremissibly attracted by an inner dream of infinite glory...? *'Une puissance supérieure me pousse à un but que j'ignore; tant qu'il ne sera pas atteint je serai invulnérable, inébranlable; dès que je ne lui serai plus nécéssaire, une mouche suffira pour me renverser'* (*A superior force pushes me towards an uncertain end. As long as this is not reached I would be invulnerable, unshakeable; when I am no longer necessary a fly will be enough to knock me down*).

Nepotism has been often cited as a major drawback in Napoleon's character. Surely it is true and very specially when considering the poor human and personal quality of his family (with the important exception of his mother Mme. Leticia) but, on the other hand, how could he have managed to achieve his dream of an imperial monarchy without counting on his family? Here lies a paradox of rather difficult concealing. He perfectly knew his brothers´ and sisters´ limitations but chose them as the lesser of all possible evils. That is to mention another significant feature in Napoleon's character: pragmatism **'Quand il le faut, quitter la peau du lion pour prendre celle du renard'** *(when required, remove the lion´s skin and take that of the fox).*

The above remarks should be enough for a first approach to the man who boarded the Northumberland on August 4th 1815 and set the course to Saint Helena but perhaps there is still a final, indispensable feature that is common to the true great men in history: nobility in the sense of magnanimity. Despite his many errors and weaknesses there is little doubt that one important reason explaining the durable fame and prestige of Napoleon Bonaparte is his nobility of character, largely credited in uncountable contemporary rapports. *'At Saint Helena, deprived of any prestige, powerless, not having over his unfortunate companions but the influence of his spirit and his character, dominates absolutely winning them by his immutable goodness up to the point that, having feared him for most of their lives, they loved him for the rest of it'*[1].

---

1.   *Thiers, Histoire du Consulat et de l´Empire. Quoted by Alain Fillion in his book 'Napoléon'. Dictionnaire Intime.*

Napoleon at the end of the battle of Waterloo. (Bombled. ©Andrea Press).

THE ROAD TO SAINT HELENA

n June 25th 1815 Napoleon is at the Malmaison, the charming chateau in which he and Josephine had possibly enjoyed the sweetest moments of a time of no return. He has been defeated at Waterloo so putting an end to his extraordinary career and has decided to abdicate the throne to his son Napoleon II just a few days ago.

What could be his deepest feelings at that moment? It was just one year since Josephine had passed away... surely the house would stir up so many memories... Even today there is something touching when walking across the park and the empty rooms. This building personified Josephine in many ways.

Much later, at Saint Helena, in the course of a 'candid' conversation on the true nature of love he appears to have admitted to not ever really being in love with the possible exception of Josephine, and that just to some extent and because of the fact he was so young[1] (see page 231). Notwithstanding a simple view at any of his passionate love letters to her, wildly refutes such an assertion, probably pronounced to keep a difficult psychological balance during his long, suffering '*tour de force*' at the island.

He is now 46 years old, healthy and spirited enough to keep fighting on for '*la France*', '*pour l´Empire*', but the high risk of civil war in the country, exhausted after so many years of struggle and wars against growing overwhelming odds, and the lack of elementary support by his Marshalls and ministers, have pushed him to desist. He knows that a solution like the retirement to Elba is no more feasible for the allies who would never risk a new Waterloo. Then Fouché suggests a fair solution: the United States of America providing the pertinent safe conducts. After some last minutes at Malmaison with his brother Joseph, Napoleon leaves the place for the last time. He has taken off his uniform and is wearing a grey or brown morning coat. General Becker joined him to travel in his barouche with General Bertrand and the duke of Rovigo[2]. Colonel Gourgaud, Montholon, Las Cases and Lallemand ride in another carriage. The destination is Rochefort, where they are supposed to get aboard a ship set off to the United

---

1   *Général baron Gourgaud. Journal de Sainte-Hélène 1815-1818.*
2.   *General Savary.*

States, but on arriving at the shore it becomes clear enough that Fouché has succeeded in deceiving Napoleon one last time: the safe conducts are not accepted by the Americans. The trap is closed...

At the isle of Aix, the last French place he would ever see, he is forced to make which is apparently, his last great decision: to put and end to his life; to deliver himself to the royalist or to give himself up to British honour. Did he 'really' ever think the British would let him rest in a pleasant domain in their island? Suicide was of course not considered (he had attempted it in 1814, at the time of the first abdication and completely disregarded it after the poison failed). The second option barely could be an alternative as he would have been sentenced to death and executed in reprisal for the death of the duke of Enghien. So, there only remained the English but Napoleon should have known that they were not free to decide alone on his future and, even if they were, how could he expect them risking any further evasion? Always the gambler, he probably thought his only feasible chance was to gain time while entertaining negotiations with the English.

On July 8th he was aboard the 'Saale', moored near L'Ile d'Aix from which he sent General Savary and Comte de Las Cases to the British HMS Bellerophon –then sailing between the islands of Olerón and Ré– to check if a permit to sail to the United States could be granted. Not surprisingly the Bellerophon's captain, Frederick Lewis Maitland, made clear that no trip to freedom would be allowed. Then some bizarre choices to break the English blockade and sail to the United States were still pondered. Especially when Napoleon's brother Joseph, who had arrived at Rochefort on the 12th of July and had a brig ready to conduct him to that country, offers Napoleon to take his place, but the idea is finally discarded probably upon considering the craftiness of this plan would be hardly compatible with imperial dignity.

The die was finally cast. At 4:00 AM on July 14th, Las Cases and General Lallemand board the Bellerophon once again and attempt to get from Captain Maitland full guaranties that Napoleon could live in Britain as a private individual and not as a war prisoner. There has always been much controversy about the terms of the conversation that followed, as Napoleon would always blame the English to have deceived him by giving through Maitland full assurance that he was going to England as a 'guest' that *'throw myself upon the hospitality of the British people'* and *'under the protection of their laws'* as stated in the letter Napoleon had written to the prince regent the day before[1]. However, and in all probability, Maitland dodged the issue by just assuring them that he *'would convey Napoleon to England but that the ex-Emperor would be entirely at the disposal of the British government'*. How could the Emperor expect anything else? He was defeated and cornered; with no other choice than deliver himself to his archenemy: the British.

Obviously being no fool, he must have known perfectly well that living peacefully in England, only a stone's throw from the continent was an impossible choice; especially after his flight from Elba and the subsequent extreme political agitation leading to Waterloo. In addition, letting him escape close to British control was no choice either... this was a poor set of cards. A final meeting among Napoleon, Bertrand, Savary, Montholon, Las Cases, and Gourgaud took place later that day to decide on the final course of action resolving that going to England aboard Maitland's ship was the less bad move[2]. Interestingly, the fact that the famous letter to the Regent Prince had been produced the day before, suggests that Napoleon had made his mind earlier and perhaps this meeting was just aimed to check the disposition of his entourage... and save time. Because only time could modify his desperate position amidst the turbulent European politics of the moment.

On the other hand, it is hard to believe he was thinking of the idiotic Prince Regent (future George IV) or any member of the British ruling class when writing his rather bombastic pleading to British hospitality. Rather it seems addressed to the common people of England and the continent as the first foundation stone of what –eventually– would be the last of his great deeds: the creation of his own, everlasting legend and the beginning of a personal calvary.

1.   *Your Royal Highness,*
     As a victim to of the factions which distract my country, and to the enmity of the greatest powers of Europe, I have terminated my political career, and I come, like Themistocles, to throw myself on the hospitality of the British people.
     I put myself under the protection of their laws; which I claim from your Royal Highness, as the most powerful, the most constant, and the most generous of my enemies. Rochefort 13 July 1815, Napoleon.
2.   *There seems to be some disagreement on how this decision was made according to Montholon and Gourgaud, as stated in there their respective memoirs: 'July 14th..The grand Marshal, the duke of Rovigo and the count of Las Cases favoured the option of boarding the Bellerophon preceded by an aide de camp that would deliver a Napoleon's autographed letter to the prince regent. General Gourgaud and I were the only ones opposing that (...). After all, in case we weren't able to reach the American coast; going to England would be still and option. (Charles de Montholon, Récits de la captivité de l'Empereur Napoléon à Sainte-Hélène). However, Gourgaud's version says on the same date that 'His majesty summoned us and demanded our opinion. Everyone –with no exception– advocated for surrendering to the British ships.' Général baron Gourgaud. Journal de Sainte-Hélène 1815-1818.*

The HMS Bellerophon –nicknamed 'Billy Ruffian' by its sailors– was a 75 gun ship with a gun deck length of 168 ft (51 meters). It had been laid down in 1782 and served on blockade and escort duties during the Revolutionary and Napoleonic wars. It would be broken up in 1836 after serving as a prison ship for some years. That was the cruiser that would take the Emperor to Britain...

On the morning of July 15th at 6 a.m. the brig l'Epervier, flying a truce flag, conveyed Napoleon, who dressed his legendary uniform of *'Colonel de Chasseurs de la Garde'*, on board the Bellerophon. On leaving the French brig he was greeted with the last cheers of *'Vive L'Empereur'* he would ever hear... Cheers that faded into a wail as his boat reached the Bellerophon, where Las Cases was waiting for him on top of the stairs. When finally on board the British ship he was introduced to Captain Maitland waiting for him on top as he came **'to place myself under the protection of British laws'**. He was treated with respect, but there was no salute...

Napoleon, always displaying a cheerful mood, was introduced to the ship's officers, inspected the quarters assigned to him and visited all parts of the ship giving compliments to everything he saw; including a portrait of Maitland's wife. In all probability Maitland and his companions were not indifferent to the seductive power of this great conductor of men.

A small number of persons boarded the Bellerophon too forming a last, rather pathetic, expression of the fallen emperor's court: the Grand- Maréchal Bertrand and his wife; General Montholon, his wife and their little boy; count Las Cases and his adolescent son; Savary and Lallemand (who would soon part company); surgeon Maingault and head valet Marchand, Ali and a number of servants.

Gourgaud, who was commissioned to deliver Napoleon's letter to the prince-regent would board the Slaney on the 14th setting course to England but would be never allowed to land there and would rejoin the others when both ships met at Torbay on July 24th.

By keeping the court etiquette and protocol running around Napoleon as if they were still at the Tuileries they would fight a peculiar war of formalities against the English that soon would be determined to deny the Royal character of Napoleon by simply addressing him as 'General Bonaparte'.

They started sailing for Britain on the same evening. The Emperor

Napoleon inspecting British infantry troops aboard the Bellerophon.
(Bombled. ©Andrea Press).

was lodged in the spacious room on the upper deck that was preceded by a dinning room and then a drawing room in which one his ADC's slept. Marchand stayed beside him in the night and Ali would rest lying across the doorway. All the rest were hosted in cabins in the gun battery[1]. They could be not fully aware of the real situation at that difficult moment in which, apparently, there could remain some hope, but the fact was that they were in prison from the very moment they boarded the Bellerophon...

Also that evening the Superb, commanded by Admiral Hothman, dropped anchor alongside the Bellerophon and the admiral came on board to pay his respects to the Emperor and invited him next morning

1. *Mémoires de Marchand d'après le manuscrit original par Jean Bourguignon. Plon, Paris 1952.*

to visit the Superb, which he did receiving there the honours due to his rank... If Napoleon was really still fooling himself about his future, this splendid reception by Hothman should have fuelled his hopes.[1]

After some days of navigation, upon arriving at Torbay, Napoleon learned the bad news about Gourgaud and the impossibility to deliver his letter to the prince regent but, perhaps for the last time, seemed to cherish the dream of living in England. According to Marchand[2], while dressing, he looked through the porthole of his bed room to the charming houses on the coast and said he would be pleased to live there anonymously under the name of Murion or Duroc; both old comrades of moving memories.

During the night of the 25th to the 26th the Bellerophon set course to Plymouth where they dropped anchor 27 days after they left Paris and 10 days from Rochefort. There was great expectation at the port upon their arrival, with many small boats crowded with people eager to catch a view of the great man, but they were soon harshly moved away and the Emperor and his companions were kept aboard waiting for further notice. At this time the first rumours of a deportation to Saint Helena begun to circulate. In fact the capture of Napoleon had been mandatory for the British government from the very moment he had left Paris and intended to sail to the United States. Clear instructions were issued then to the English ships to patrol the French coast and impede Napoleon's evasion.

As early as July 8th Maitland was ordered to detain any suspicious ship in order to seize the Emperor and his party and transport them to Torbay or Plymouth, which he finally did even though –funnily enough– it was Napoleon who delivered himself to Maitland as a 'guest' of the British government.

---

1. *'Next morning the Emperor descended into a boat to reach the Superb for breakfast. I followed him. The admiral received him with distinction; the troops in formation and the sailors on the yardarms and rigging. His majesty reviewed the troops and then the admiral, who speaks French very well, led him to every place in the ship. The greatest order and cleanness reigned everywhere. All below the water line was sanded: it was marvellous. Once the visit over, we went back up to the bridge and the admiral took the Emperor to the poop deck where a proper and carefully prepared -tough still simple- breakfast had been arranged. The admiral, who was a man of good manners, admirably rendered the honours at the table. The repast lasted quite a long time. Once it was finished, the Emperor took farewell from the Admiral and the Superbe and sailed back to the Bellerophon. He enjoyed this reception very much as premonitory of a favourable future.'* Souvenirs du Mameluck Ali (Louis-Étienne Saint-Denis) sur L´Empereur Napoléon. Payot, Paris 1926.

2. *Mémoires de Marchand d'après le manuscrit original par Jean Bourguignon. Plon, Paris 1952.*

Napoleon aboard the Bellerophon at Plymouth. (Bombled. ©Andrea Press).

For the English there was no question about Napoleon's future. According to a letter dated the 15th of July from the Prime Minister Lord Liverpool to Castlereagh[1] they considered themselves as the more suitable partner to arrest Napoleon. On his side Castlereagh, upon knowing of Napoleon's capture, expressed the feeling of most of the members of his government by saying that *'after 20 years fighting the Emperor they had won the fight to hold him as a war trophy...'*

Castlereagh was a well known foe of Napoleon. He had played a significant role to decide on the English intervention in the Peninsular War in 1808 and favoured the idea of confining Napoleon to a Scotland fort. There were no doubt about seclusion, and only the place remained

---

1. *Principal British diplomat at the Gongress of Viena.*

to be settled. Gibraltar, Malta, Saint Helena and even Great Britain were considered but finally, on the 21st, Saint Helena is designated as the future home for Great Britain's defeated, but yet frightening, enemy[1]. Saint Helena: one of the most isolated islands in the world, more than 1200 miles (2000km) from the nearest continental coast and a natural fortress measuring just 10 by 5 miles (16 by 8 km).

On the morning of the 27th the frigate Eurotas dropped anchor next to the Bellerophon[2] and all the officers not directly attached to the Emperor were ordered to tranship while the rest of the French remained expectant in great anxiety the arrival of Admiral Keith, an old sea wolf and fierce enemy of Napoleon and the man commissioned with delivering to Napoleon the British ministry decision and his fate on the 31st, when he came on board the Bellerophon in the company of Sir Henry Bunbury[3] and had a private meeting of half an hour with the Emperor to give him the following letter that was first read in French:

'As it is appropriate for General Bonaparte to learn, without any further delay, the intentions of the British government toward him, Your Lordship (Admiral Keith) conveys the following information to him:

It would be little in keeping with our duty toward our country and the allies of His Majesty that General Bonaparte retains the means or opportunity to again disturb the peace of Europe. This is why it is absolutely necessary that he is restrained in his personal freedom, insofar as this primary and important goal requires.

The island of Saint Helena has been chosen as his future residence; its climate is healthy and its location will allow him to be treated with more indulgence than would be possible elsewhere, in view of the mandatory precautions that would have to be employed to secure his person.

General Bonaparte is authorized to choose among the people who accompanied him to England –with the exception of Generals Savary and Lallemand– three officers, who along with his surgeon and twelve servants will be permitted to follow him to Saint Helena, and will never be allowed to leave the island without the approval of the British government.

---

1. *In a letter from July 21th Liverpool wrote to Castlereagh: 'We are all of the same opinion: we must not let Napoleon reside in this country. The very delicate questions that would be raised on this subject would be highly embarrassing' Marchand Memoirs. Proctor Jones's first English edition.*
2. *The Eurotas had left Torbay on August 8th with Lallemand and Savary on board. They expected to be delivered to the French and shot, but were later taken to Malta, where they remain until 1816. Both lived quite adventurous lives before returning to France and die in 1839 and 1833 respectively.*
3. *Sir Henry Bunbury, general and historian, was a secretary in Lord Liverpool's cabinet.*

Rear Admiral Sir George Cockburn[1], who is named commander in chief of the station at the Cape of Good Hope and the adjacent oceans, will take General Bonaparte and his retinue to Saint Helena, and will receive detailed instructions governing the execution of this duty.

Sir George Cockburn will probably be ready to leave in a few days, therefore it is desirable that General Bonaparte immediately choose the people who are to accompany him.'[2]

Apparently, the Emperor reacted to this news with the impassibility one can expect from great men in such occasions but, according with Gourgaud[3] he '*déclare qu'elle n'ira pas, que son sang rougira plutôt le Bellérophon (declares that he won't go, that his blood would rather redden the Bellerophon) (...) qu'elle préfère la mort à Sainte-Hélène (that he prefers dying to Saint Helena)'* and that he '*ne veut point aller à Sainte-Hélène, que ce serait mourir d'une manière ignoble (by no mean want to go to Saint Helena, that it would be to die in an ignoble way)'*. Did the terrible news take him really by surprise? From the British point of view taking him to Saint Helena –or any other similar place– was the best practical solution and Napoleon couldn't ignore that. In addition, rumours about Saint Helena had been around before this official declaration took place. Wasn't he just staging surprise and anger...?

Immediately after Keith and Bunbury departed, Napoleon – perfectly unruffled– started making preparations for the imminent trip. He would write two reiterative letters addressed to Admiral Keith on July 13th and August 4th claiming on the 'violation of his rights' and the profound injustice exerted upon him. These letters received of course no response and seem rather written for posterity as another step in the reaffirmation of his own legend. If, as stated before, the idea of Napoleon sustaining any reasonable hope about escaping British grip and seclusion is hardly feasible, the same cannot be sustained for his companions in exile, whose reactions ranged from depression to extreme despair as was the case of Countess Bertrand who would have jumped into sea through the porthole of his cabin had she not been stopped in time.

On the night of the 4th, the Bellerophon left Plymouth towards Start Bay to await the Northumberland that would take them to Saint Helena. Once arrived at Start Bay they had to spend some days yet till the Northumberland was ready for the long trip. By this time no

---

1. *Sir George Cockburn (1772 –1853) was a prestigious naval officer who had fought during the French Revolutionary Wars and in America in the War of 1812.*
2. *Marchand Memoirs. Proctor Jones's first English edition.*
3. *Général baron Gourgaud. Journal de Sainte-Hélène 1815-1818.*

little doubt about their real situation was left: they were prisoners, and as such submitted to restrictions, orders and inspections. All of them unfitting to imperial dignity and humiliating.

Napoleon's baggage aboard the Bellerophon at Start Bay being inspected.
(Bombled. ©Andrea Press).

On the arrival of the Northumberland on the 6th Admiral Keith came again to the Bellerophon to introduce Admiral Cockburn and instructed that a general search of belongings was required before coming on board the Northumberland. But that was not all, as also according with Keith's instructions to Captain Maitland: '*All weapons of any kind shall be taken from the Frenchmen of all ranks who are on board the vessel (...)*'[1]. This was a pretty unnecessary and –for that reason– insulting request, and thus Maitland decided on his own to take just the firearms and forget the swords.

1.   *Marchand Memoirs. Proctor Jones's first English edition.*

Cockburn had been of course instructed in detail by his government on how to proceed before transferring the 'General' on board the Bellerophon; very especially concerning his valuables, money and jewellery; this should be inventoried and confiscated. In addition, he was also informed that any letter should be delivered open and warned that any evasion attempt could be punished with jail. When Lord Keith and Cockburn, clearly uneasy with a most unpleasant duty, arrived to Napoleon's quarters and muttered: '*England requests your sword*' the Emperor, his hand resting on the hilt of the Austerlitz's sword, just gave them a terrible and defiant look that made these two gentlemen desist from their ignoble task on the spot. They just saluted respectfully and left.[1]

With the transfer to the Northumberland now a matter of hours, the loyal Marchand managed to hide some money and valuables from the British while everybody made their best to get ready and set their minds for a long journey of unforeseeable return.

A late, unexpected problem arose when Napoleon's surgeon Maingault refused to go to Saint Helena and had to be substituted by the Bellerophon's doctor Barry Edward O'Meara; an interesting character, then aged 33, who would play a significant role in the future events (see page 86).

August 7th was a moving, sad day. Very especially at the moment of parting with those who would not accompany the Emperor into exile. Napoleon got into the boat that would take him to the Northumberland amidst other boats loaded with onlookers eager to get a last view of the legendary man. When 'General Bonaparte' was finally on board the boat that would take him to Saint Helena he was received in a correct but cold manner...

---

1.   *Marchand Memoirs. Proctor Jones's first English edition. According to Marchand this scene was witnessed and referred to him by Saint-Denis.*

The Emperor, after the usual remarks on the weather, the course of the ship or the wind, entangled in some theme of conversation, or retrieved some of the previous days. Then, after strolling ten or twelve times across the bridge, he used to lean over the penultimate gun on the left of the ship, besides the rail. Such practice didn't pass unnoticed to Midshipmen and soon everybody aboard referred to this gun as the 'Emperor's gun'. Memorial of Saint Helena. Las Cases. (KGM. ©Andrea Press).

ABOARD THE NORTHUMBERLAND

he vessel HMS Northumberland was an imposing 74 gun, third rate ship launched in 1798 that had served in the Egyptian campaign in 1801. Gun deck length was 182 feet (55 m) and beam 48 feet 7½ inches (almost 15 meters). Crew was nominally of 640 men, but Marchand says in his memoirs that there were 1080 people on board at the time of Napoleon's arrival[1]. It was commanded by Captain Charles Bayne Hodgson Ross. This was the vessel that, accompanied by seven more and an additional store ship was to convey the former emperor to Saint Helena.

Lord Bathurst[2] gave detailed instructions to Cockburn about how Napoleon should be treated and, accordingly, the latter would make a point in checking Napoleon in what he thought to be a battle to hold the moral superiority befitted to an Emperor in an obvious situation of captivity. This essential contradiction would be the main cause in a pugnacious conflict between Napoleon and his jailers all during his exile, and even after his death. As the title of Emperor would have been clearly incompatible with his condition of prisoner, it was always firmly denied to him.

Consequently Cockburn was ordered to avoid any acknowledgment of his imperial rank. Napoleon on his side had no other choice than 'playing the Emperor' to the end for the sake of his dynasty and the future of France and even Europe; at least in the light of his own conceptions derived from the experience of his hazardous life.

According to Keith, the Emperor 'appeared to be in perfect good humour' aboard the Admiral's barge that took him to the Northumberland, *'talking of Egypt, St. Helena, of my former name being Elphinstone, and many other subjects and joking with the ladies about being seasick'*[3]. So, when climbing to the ship that would take him to his prison and final destiny, he sported perfect mind control and good spirit. When he finally set foot on the desk a total hush came over the crew.

---

1. *Marchand Memoirs. Proctor Jones's first English edition.*
2. *Barthurst was Secretary for War and the Colonies until 1827 and, as such, instrumental concerning the treatment given to Napoleon.*
3. *The Life of Napoleon I. John Holland Rose, M.A. George Bell and Sons 1902.*

Then, when he received the uncovered salute said loud and clearly to Cockburn *'Here I am, General, at your orders'*[1]. Immediately after Keith and Cockburn accompanied him to his cabin of 12x9 feet (366x274 cm.) which he accepted *saying* **'the apartments are convenient, and you see I carry my little tent-bed with me'.**[2]

Not surprisingly, the Emperor's presence aboard the Northumberland roused great excitement and curiosity among the men during the first days. (Bombled. ©Andrea Press).

He was lodged in the quarter deck, next to the admiral. According to Saint Denis, always ready to consign any minute detail[3]:

1. *Napoleon's Last Voyage. Extract from a Diary of Rear-Admiral Sir George Cockburn. Simpkin, Marshall & Co. 1888.*
2. *The Life of Napoleon I. John Holland Rose, M.A. George Bell and Sons 1902.*
3. *Souvenirs du Mameluck Ali (Louis-Étienne Saint-Denis) Sur L'Empereur Napoléon. Payot, Paris 1926.*

'The Emperor used to wake up at 7 or 8 in the morning. He had his breakfast between 9 or 10 and rested just wearing a robe or in shirtsleeves until 3 or 4 in the afternoon, when he dressed. Then he went into the after or great cabin to play checkers with some of his generals until the admiral appeared to announce dinner was served.

In the morning he used to call some of these officers for chatting and updating himself with the last news aboard. Most of the time however he would be reading seated on his armchair.

The quarterdeck comprised a dining room with two entrance doors to port and starboard. Just in the centre of the room was a large square table fitted with two round side tables hanging from its left and right sides. A third one (perhaps just one of the other two) could hang under the centre.

To port, next to the partition wall of the Emperor's cabin was placed a big sideboard serving as a buffet.

The door was built inside a huge recess measuring some feet with two small doors built-in left and right, leading to two cabins: the Emperor's to port and the admiral's to starboard. Both cabins were cut irregularly as to keep the main room squared.

The after or great cabin was of common use. Two small doors opened to the two cabins and each one was furnished with a bed hanging from two iron forks. The admiral tried to convince the Emperor that he would find this bed comfortable. It was fitted with a kind of canopy made with a white cotton fabric decorated with red foliage.

I don't remember whether the Emperor did ever use that bed. He rather favoured his iron portable bed despite the fact that it was fitted with wheels and was certainly not the best choice in a ship.'

In contrast with the rather hagiographical memories left by Napoleon's French companions, Cockburn's diary[1] portraits our man under a quite different light in which the almost cheerful mood of the first days would alternate with periods of deep sulkiness or even depression. Cockburn pictures the Emperor as always keeping a polite, sociable façade with the English but, at the same time, struggling to maintain the psychological game alluded to before. One good example of this would be Cockburn's account of Napoleon's behaviour of one night in which *'heavy rain and the wind gradually died away until it failed us altogether and was succeeded by a southerly wind. To my great surprise, after General Buonaparte had eaten his dinner he got up to take his walk as usual, and upon my remarking to him that it was still pouring with rain, and therefore advising him not to go out in it, he treated it lightly and said it would not hurt him more than the sailors he observed at the time catching*

---

1.   *Napoleon's Last Voyage. Extract from a Diary of Rear-Admiral Sir George Cockburn. Simpkin, Marshall & Co. 1888.*

water, working and running about in it. Of course I no longer opposed his whim. And out he went in the rain accompanied by two French friends, who, though obliged to attend him, seemed by no means to enjoy the idea of the wetting they were doomed to get par complaisance. *I have no doubt General Buonaparte intended this dash of his should give us a great idea of his hardiness of character; as, however, no further particular notice was taken of it by any of us, and finding it, I suppose, more unpleasant than expected, he was inevitably, perfectly wet through, he, immediately on quitting the deck, went into his own cabin, from whence he did not rejoin us during the evening.'*

Notwithstanding, the idea of a man like Napoleon playing ridiculous games like that is hardly feasible. He was by then well known for spending little time at the table and he was certainly not a courteous man; especially when feeling ill at ease. In any case Cockburn and Napoleon got along fairly well despite some tug-of-war episodes like this.

A great myth looks much better in the distance, and even if there is no doubt that Cockburn was a respected senior naval officer and a gentleman, his unexpected closeness to Napoleon during two months aboard the Northumberland obviously produced a debased rendition of the great man in sharp contrast with Las Cases' account of Napoleon´s demeanour aboard the ship as follows:

'The Emperor had his breakfast at irregular hours during the morning; while the French and the English had it customarily at 10 and 8 AM respectively. He would call one of us by turns to learn about the logbook, the leagues covered, the state of the wind and the news. He read a lot and get dressed around 4PM before going into the common room to play chess with some of us. At 5PM the admiral, just upon leaving his cabin, announced that dinner was served.

Everybody knows that the Emperor took no more than 15 minutes for eating, but here the two services lasted between one and one and a half hours; which drove him extremely uncomfortable, even though this was never reflected in his behaviour or attitude. His countenance, his gestures; all of him remained perfectly impassible. The new cooking; different flavours or quality were never approved or censored. At the beginning the Admiral tried to offer him other things but, by simply expressing his thanks in a most sober manner, the Emperor stopped any further insistence. Notwithstanding the admiral remained always very attentive; even if he would only address the servants to procure what he thought was more suitable or preferable.

The emperor kept an absent mood; not seeing, asking or remarking anything. He was generally silent in the middle of the conversation —mostly in French and very tactful. He only would speak to produce some scientific or technical questions or to address some words to those that were incidentally invited. Most of the time he had me translating these questions.

As we know, the English are fond of long postprandials at the table chatting and drinking. But the Emperor, already weary after the long services, was not prepared to stand for these soirées. Accordingly, right from the first day, he left the table immediately after the coffee and went to the bridge. As the Grand Marshall and I followed him, the admiral was mystified and uttered some flippant remarks to his people. To which countess Bertrand, whose mother language was English, replied heatedly: 'Do not forget, sir, that you are dealing with who was the master of the world, to whose table kings sought to be invited'. 'That's right' –replied the admiral. From this point on, this officer, that is a fair man sporting correct manners and not exempt of certain grace, stressed

Napoleon at the table next to Mme. de Montholon aboard the Northumberland. (Bombled. ©Andrea Press).

to facilitate this custom of the Emperor by accelerating the services and asking in advance for the Emperor's coffee and for those expected to leave in his company.

Once done the Emperor left and all of us stood up until he was outside while the rest remained drinking for one hour more. Then the Emperor strolled across the bridge till the night came in the company of the Grand Marshall and me, which soon became customary. Later the Emperor would be back in the salon to play 21 and generally retired half an hour later.'[1]

The Emperor, who had to live confined to a small cabin all during the long voyage to Saint Helena, surrounded by his tiny 'court' and watched by his ever- present English 'hosts', was determined to keep being the Emperor till the end in almost perfect ataraxia. Cockburn was wrong when supposing he was simply acting a farce. He had been crowned by the Pope as the last of the European emperors and, indeed, this was not a futile question but one of the highest political and historical significance; at least in Napoleon's view.

Again according to Cockburn[2], Napoleon's retinue aboard the Northumberland accounted for (sic):

'**Grand Márechal Comte de Bertrand.**
    Madame Bertrand.
    3 children of ditto.
    1 female servant with her child.
    1 man servant.
General Comte de Montholon.
    Madame de Montholon.
    1 child.
    1 female servant.
Le Comte de Las Cases.
    1 son (a boy about 13 years of age)

    General Gourgaud.
    3 valets de chambre.
    3 ditto de pied.
    1 maître d'hotel.
    1 chef d'office.
    1 cook.
    1 huissier.
    1 lampiste.

---

1.   *Le Mémorial de Sainte-Hélène. Le Comte de Las Cases. Garnier Frères. Paris 1895.*

2.   *Napoleon's Last Voyage. Extract from a Diary of Rear-Admiral Sir George Cockburn. Simpkin, Marshall & Co. 1888.*

Of which:
7 grown-up, to be at my table.
2 maid servants
1 young gentleman } At a separate table.
5 children
12 domestics, with my servants

27 in all.'

Among all the high officers it was probably Las Cases who would enjoy Napoleon's company most of the time while engrossed in writing his personal account of the voyage, taking the first dictations of the Emperor's memories started aboard on September 9th or even giving some English lessons to the fallen monarch, who became tired of it just after a few days[1].

It was a long and boring voyage before arriving at Saint Helena on October 17th 1815; seventy days after their departure from the coast of England and one hundred and ten days after leaving Paris. Napoleon, tightly constricted to the narrow room of the British war vessel, scrutinized by friends and foes always at close range, obviously set his mind unwaveringly and prepared for a most uncertain future probably discarding any further release from his captivity....

Logbook to Saint Helena

(Extracted from Napoleon's Last Voyage. Extract from a Diary of Rear-Admiral Sir George Cockburn. Simpkin, Marshall & Co. 1888.)

1815
August

9th   *Proceed the way down the Channel.*
10th   *Latitude at noon 49°41' N.*
11th   *Blew very fresh all day from the N. W. Latitude and longitude this day at noon 48°48' N., 5°58'W.*
12th   *Weather more moderated though the west wind and swell continued Latitude and longitude this day at noon 46°30' N., 8°2' W.*
13th   *Calm most of the day but still a disagreeable swell.   and longitude at noon being 45°42' N. and 8°10' W.*
14th   *Continuation of fine weather and light wind. Latitude and longitude at noon: 45°13'N., 9°5' W.*

---

1.   *Le Mémorial de Sainte-Hélène. Le Comte de Las Cases. Garnier Frères. Paris 1895.*

15th *Napoleon's birthday. Still light wind and fine weather with less swell than usual. Latitude and longitude at noon: 43°51' N. and 10°21' W.*

16th *Fine weather but light winds with calms. Latitude and longitude at noon: 42 59', and 10°42' W.*

17th *We had light baffling weather. Latitude and longitude at noon 41°57'N. 11°11' W.*

18th *We had fine weather with light winds form the westward. The brig I sent to Guernsey joined us again this day, which enabled me to give General Buonaparte some French papers and gazettes which she brought. Latitude and longitude at noon 40°50'N., 11°20' W.*

19th *Our weather was moderate with a pleasant breeze from the N.W. Latitude and longitude at noon 39°9'N. and 11°26'W.*

20th *The weather continued fine, and would have been pleasant but for the swell. Latitude and longitude at noon 37°19' N. and 12°14'W.*

21st *Our weather continued much the same, but rather more thick and cloudy, and the wind, though light, veering to the N.E. Latitude and longitude at noon were 35°56' N. and 13°16' W.*

22nd *On the 22nd August we got the N.E. wind which usually prevails in these latitudes, with fine weather, though unpleasantly hazy. General Buonaparte requested me to write home from Madeira for some books for him, which I promised to do. Latitude and longitude at noon were 34°58'N. and 13°31' W.*

23rd *Our N.E. wind veered to E., freshened, and the weather became hot, hazy and unpleasant. Soon after noon we made the Island of Porto Santo and afterwards Madeira. We were this day at noon about nine leagues E.S.E. of Porto Santo.*

24th *We remained lying –to off the town of Funchal. I sent the frigate and troopships to the anchorage with my letters for England and to procure water and refreshments. We were unfortunate in having a very strong and unpleasant siroc (sic) wind which kept the thermometer above 80°.*

25th *We had a continuance of the violent and disagreeable siroc. The heat of this day and the (...) nature of the wind, added to the motion of the ship, which was considerable, evidently affected General Buonaparte very much.*

26th *Though the wind continued from the E. its siroc qualities had quitted it (to our great relief) and this proved a pleasant cool day in comparison with what we had experienced off Madeira. Latitude and longitude at noon 30°53' N., 17°22' W.*

27th *We had a fine breeze form the N.E., but the weather became more than usually foggy and hazy, which I the more regretted as, General Buonaparte having expressed some curiosity respecting the peak of Tenerife and the Canary islands, I caused the squadron to be this day* *steered between the Islands of Gomera and Palma for the purpose of gratifying his curiosity; but though we passed close to Gomera about mid-day, yet the haze continued so thick that we obtained but bad views of the land, and could only make it out very imperfectly and with much difficulty. Today at noon we were about four leagues W. from Gomera, with a fresh breeze fro the N.E., running between the Islands at the rate of about eleven miles an hour. To-day (sic) we were about four leagues W. from Gomera, with a fresh breeze from the N.E., running between the Islands at the rate of about eleven miles an hour.*

On August 31st 1815, at 11 PM a drunken black man falls into the water. Despite the fact that he can swim pretty well and that a rescue boat is launched he is finally lost. (Le Memorial de Sainte-Hélène. Le Comte de Las Cases. Garnier Frères. Paris 1895.) (Bombled. ©Andrea Press).

28th   *Our N.E. trade continued, but not so fresh as yesterday, and the weather became hot, thermometer being form 78°to 80°. Latitude and longitude at noon were 26°2' N., 19°9' W*

29th   *We had a moderate trade wind with a good deal of swell. Latitude and longitude at noon were 24°23' N., 20°23' W.*

30th   *Latitude and longitude at noon 22°27' N. and 22°12'W.*

31st   *The fresh trade wind and swell continued; the General, however, appeared better, though the rolling of the ship seemed still to affect him considerably. Latitude and longitude at noon 19°53'N., 25°42'W.*

1815
September

1st   *We had a fresh trade wind accompanied by uncommonly thick weather, which prevented our making out the Island of St Antonio so soon as we expected. Latitude and longitude at noon 17°45'N., and 25°4' W.*

2nd   *About 1 A.M., the trade wind, which had been for some time strong, freshened to a perfect gale of wind, bringing with it a very heavy sea and violent rain. We were to-day at noon W.N.W. from the S.W. end of St. Antonio, about seven leagues distance; our latitude 17°6' N.*

3rd   *The wind continued form the S.E. and became light, baffling and calm at times, the weather extremely hot, the thermometer being from 82° to 83° throughout the day. General Buonaparte complained much of the heat, and I saw but little of him and had no conversation with him. Latitude and longitude at noon were 16°15'N., and 26°30'W.*

4th   *The calm weather which continued a little after daylight was succeeded by a moderate breeze from the N.E., and though we had much swell form the S.W. the ship proceeded forward on her course pleasantly. Latitude and longitude at noon were 15°34' N. and 26°36' W.*

5th   *We had a moderate trade wind but excessively hot weather, and nothing occurred during the day with regard to General Buonaparte worthy of notice. Latitude and longitude at noon was 13°58' N. and 25°30' W.*

6th   *Our trade wind continued till about four in the evening, when we experienced excessively heavy rain, and the wind gradually died away until it failed us altogether and was succeeded by a southerly wind Latitude and longitude at noon were 12°41' N. and 23°55' W.*

From the 6th to this day, the 23rd September (on which we crossed the Equator about the meridian of Greenwich), General Buonaparte, continuing to keep nearly the same hours, and following the same routine of eating, drinking and sleeping, as before noticed, and my usual conversations with him after dinner having suffered considerable interruption from the shortness of the evenings and from his own people keeping more closely about him during his evening walks than formerly, so little variety of material for detailing on each successive day that I have been induced to merge this period. It is worthy of remark that this day we have passed zero of latitude and zero of longitude, and the sun the zero of its declination.

Some day in between Tuesday 26th and Saturday 30th, September 1815 the sailors of the Northumberland catch an enormous shark. When the Emperor approaches, the fish gives a strong jolt that almost broke Napoleon's legs. There is no real damage but his left stocking resulted covered with a lot of blood from the animal to the dismay of his companions. (Le Memorial de Sainte-Hélène. Le Comte de Las Cases. Garnier Frères. Paris 1895.) *(Bombled. ©Andrea Press).*

1815
October

From the 23ʳᵈ September to this day, the 6ᵗʰ October (which period, like the preceding, I combine to avoid uninteresting monotonous details), we have had the wind with little or no variation from the S.W., accompanied by a heavy swell from the westward, the weather being cloudy and very cool, almost indeed amounting to cold, but without rain.

From the 6ᵗʰ October the wind, remaining from S.S.W. to S., allowed us to continue on the larboard tack without losing ground to the northward, until we got at last the S.E. Trade on the 11ᵗʰ inst., having, however, previously passed the thirteenth degree S. latitude; and even then the Trade hung considerably to the southward, but the ship being so much to windward this became immaterial to us, and with a fine, strong, fair wind we made between two and three hundred miles a day until we reached Saint Helena this morning (the 15ᵗʰ), the sixty-sixth day since we quitted the Lizard.

The Northumberland arrives to Saint Helena. (Bombled. ©Andrea Press).

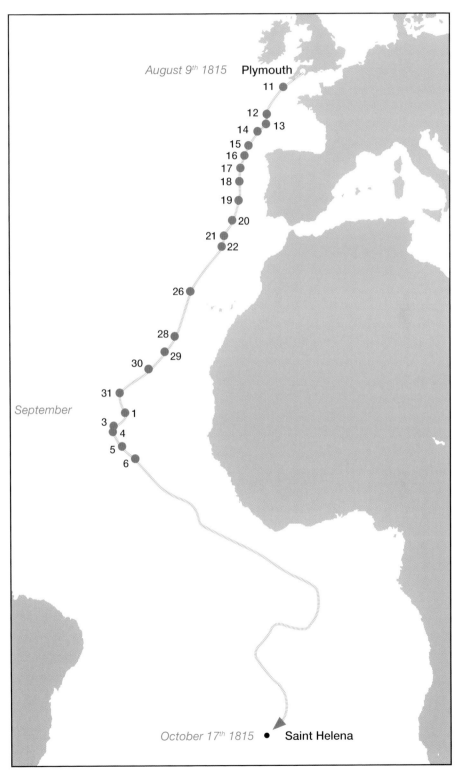

Napoleon´s route to Saint Helena according to Sir George Cockburn´s diary

THE ISLAND

 laced in the middle of the South Pacific Ocean, about 1,200 miles (2,000 km) and 2,175 miles (3,500 km) from the African and Brazilian coasts respectively, is Saint Helena: Napoleon's final destination.

Saint Helena is a volcanic island of 30,146 acres (122 km^2) inside a perimeter of about 24.5 miles (40 km.), just measuring 10 by 5 miles (16 by 8 km.) and thought to have erupted from the sea 15 million years ago. It was discovered by the Portuguese in 1502 and alternatively occupied by these and the Dutch before being finally seized by the British in 1651, being a British dominion ever since. It is still today one of the most remote places on the planet. The nearest port is in Namibia in Southern Angola, from where the Royal Mail Ship Saint Helena departures twice a month to drop anchor at Saint Helena after four or five days of navigation. There are no other means to reach the island as –up to this day- no way to build a practicable airport has been found due to the rugged topography of sharp peaks and deep ravines[1]. While the center is covered by exuberant vegetation, and thus well protected from the trade winds that blow almost continuously, that is not the case of the highland areas –where Napoleon's final lodge would be located. Jamestown, placed between two steep rocky promontories of almost perpendicular sides is the capital –the only city– and port on the island, remaining today quite the same it was in 1815.

At Napoleon's time the isle was still an important meeting point and supply station for vessels navigating from Asia to Europe: a function completely non existent today. Surely for this reason the population is now of just around 4,000; almost half of the people living there in 1815 that comprised '*3,395 whites (military included), 1,218 black slaves, 489 Chinese and 116 Indians and Malaysians and would even grow to a total of 7,998 souls in 1820*'[2].

Throughout Napoleon's stay in Saint Helena, and specially upon the arrival of the new governor sir Hudson Lowe, the whole island was submitted to severe controls and inspections to prevent an eventual escape of the illustrious prisoner. The local Saint Helena

---

1. *An airport was later built. With works starting in 2012 it would finally be operative in 2016.*
2. *Record Book of Saint Helena, 1815. As mentioned in Octave Aubrey's notes to Général baron Gourgaud's Journal de Sainte-Hélène 1815-1818. Flammarion.*

regiment troops were reinforced by regular regimental forces arrived from Britain and it was settled that Saint Helena would remain in the East India Company's[1] possession although the British Government would appoint its own Governor during Napoleon's stay and cover the additional costs implied in guarding the imperial captive. The population's growth, significantly oversized with the coming of the military, civil functionaries and respective families, resulted in a shortage of supplies that, together with the tight surveillance created a stifling atmosphere.

Typically, as any European society of the period, Saint Helena was neatly stratified in classes topped by the military which had arrived with the Northumberland, the Navy and the personnel from the East Indian Company that in some way lived in segregated groups accordingly with their respective regulations and identities. Those belonging to the lower strata simply struggled in more or less degree to make a precarious living always menaced by the spectres of hunger and gallows.

Not surprisingly for a place suddenly converted into a fortified prison, the military would occupy the highest position in the social ladder. A fact never well accepted by the naval elements, used to holding a prevalent position according to the foremost role played by the navy in the British Empire. In a similar way the East Indian Company functionaries would react badly confronted with the arrival of military personnel that rapidly seized the better lodgements and in many cases imposed their authority indiscriminately. Saint Helena living conditions would then be irremediably affected and the combined action of the climate, defective nutrition and hygiene soon became evident.

A silent witness of the past lying on the beach. Quite a few of these abandoned cannons can still be spotted all over the island.

1.   *The East India Company was a joint stock company founded in late 16th century for the development and exploitation of the British commerce in the Far East. It was a strong private lobby controlled by wealthy businessmen and aristocrats in which the British government held no shares but exerted indirect control.*

According to Doctor O'Meara the most common diseases were severe dysenteries, intestinal inflammation, liver complaint and fevers. Only during the first twelve or thirteen months staying on the isle, the 2nd battalion from the 66th foot lost 56 men out of 630 because of all these troubles. Things were certainly no better either aboard the ships of His Most Gracious Majesty King George III, where crews had to live stacked around the batteries and inside narrow compartments, amidst suffocating heat, in ships anchored in spots naturally protected from the fresh winds that could have alleviated their painful situation. For example the flagship HMS Conqueror lost 110 men out of 600 in just 18 months.[1]

Military duty at Saint Helena was in truth no bargain for the other ranks that should bear living in tents or poor quarters, meagre rations, strenuous work and guard duties. Officers of course could enjoy better conditions and even access to certain 'social life' on the island thanks to the balls and parties celebrated now and then, where especially the younger could meet the indispensable feminine element or drink at large and relax.

There could be little doubt that sex has always been a dominant factor in world's history and Saint Helena certainly protrudes as a paramount example. Most new arrivals were men –young men most of them too– eager to have sex after months of navigation and hardships. On the other hand, most females in the island saw these foreigners as their only escape from the claustrophobic site. In consequence there was a licentious mood and little or no trouble at all for sexual intercourse. Marital and extra marital relations popped up everywhere while pregnant ladies were a permanent element in the Saint Helenian landscape.

On the side of the French, Countess Bertrand had 5 or 6 false pregnancies and the flighty Mme. Montholon had her daughter Charlotte Hélène Napoléone in 1817. Gourgaud, the only bachelor among Napoleon's high officers went almost crazy trying to get a convenient lover. Among servants it was the same game all the time with lots of jealousy and squabbling. The Emperor, alone and surrounded amidst the craze of sexual urge, caused not least by the terrible tedium, struggled to keep an imperial indifference, which was not always so easy as we will see later in this book (see page 284).

The British were not lagging behind in this respect either: the strict Hudson Lowe had his younger lady Lowe giving birth to three children in five years, while admiral Cockburn entertained a lover and

1.   *La Vie quotidienne à Sainte-Hélène au temps de Napoléon. Gilbert Martineau. Tallandier.*

Admiral Plampin –probably the hands-down winner in this contest for sexual entertainment– brought his much younger lover with him surreptitiously from England, which eventually caused a true social turmoil in the island.

But, still, there was something reigning all over the island, troops and officers shared it with everybody there: boredom. The impassive, constant boredom of Saint Helena that Gourgaud consigned in so many pages of his diary: '*Ennui, ennui, ennui...*'[1].

Seamen have always been noticed to keep a high and straight sense of military honour to which the Royal Navy, that had been responsible to a great extent for the final victory upon Napoleon and ruled then over the seas for the sake and glory of the British Empire, was no exception. This nobility of character can be well observed in the disposition and treatment given to Napoleon by most of the British seamen.

In fact Napoleon entertained the company of naval officers with pleasure and showed true appreciation for sailors and midshipmen. There were mutual admiration and respect between these men and Napoleon and, perhaps for this reason, it has been argued quite often that had the Emperor been guarded by admirals like Cockburn or Sir Putney Malcolm all during his captivity, things would have run smoother for everybody. Maybe; but the case of Malcolm's successor at the head of the naval detachment, Admiral Sir Robert Plampin should be remarked anyway. Plampin –a notorious outlandish character– detested the Emperor and boasted every time he met him bragging about '*the number of men, women and children he had destroyed à coups de mitraille on the Place d'Armes of Toulon*' or produced statements such as:
> '*There was generally a great deal of trickery and mannerism about Bonaparte in the audiences he gave to individuals, as he mostly placed his back close to a window, so that he could watch, with the greatest ease and minuteness, the persons whom he addressed, whilst they were inconvenienced by the strong light being full in their faces. Although he had not been out of his apartment, nor thought of going, an enormous cocked hat employed his left hand and arm, and the right was put at ease by frequent application to the snuff-box*'[2].

Unfortunately –or not– the military Sir Hudson Lowe arrived on April 1816 to take control of the situation as the new governor and inaugurating a new phase in Napoleon's calvary by imposing additional measures and restrictions that, in Napoleon's view, were

---

1.   *Général baron Gourgaud. Journal de Sainte-Hélène 1815-1818.*
2.   *The Drama of Saint Helena. Paul Frémeaux. New York. D. Appleton and Company, 1910.*

unacceptable and unnecessary but that, on the other hand, were useful to sustain the notion of being treated by the English in the most unjust and humiliating way.

In this little and isolated society dominated by men in uniform, civilians certainly did not enjoy a privileged situation. Whites, Asians and Africans were also duly stratified according to their colour and position. Higher among the whites were of course the functionaries from the Indian Company that included some military elements as well as British officers commanding over 600 men composing the artillery and infantry detachments on the island.

They were mostly seasoned gentlemen that after long years of service in the Far East enrolled in the company to enjoy rather representative posts in almost full idleness while waiting for an upcoming and comfortable retirement in good old England.

The people in the roll of the Indian company formed a compact corporatist group headed by higher administrative officials of British ancestry who had arrived to the island during the previous two centuries. It was indeed a close, endogamous clan holding all significant posts except that of the governor; for which the Company invariably appointed a military who arrived to Saint Helena after long years of service in India and who was not related in any way with the alluded clan, probably to put a brake to their unbridled ambition. Normally these governors ruled gently over the island according to the Company's policy that regarded Saint Helena as just an outpost lost in the ocean.

Major Gideon Gorrequer (see page 88), aide-de-camp and acting military secretary to Sir Hudson Lowe, left us the following account of the Governor's views on Saint Helena:

'There was something in the air of the place that contaminated everybody. In any other place where a word would suffice, here orders upon orders must be given before it was done, and in the end he must do it himself. It was dammed hard to his other duties that he should have this additional labour, but he never saw such a place as this. There was a torpor and indifference, a want of feeling, that he had never seen before'.[1]

Napoleon's coming was certainly a revulsive for this stagnant society. Even though the many controls and restrictions –including pass words and curfews– were received reluctantly and with obvious displeasure, the new situation shook to great extent the tedium and somnolence reigning all over place. Now, provosts and most prominent

---

1.   *The Drama of Saint Helena. Paul Frémeaux. New York. D. Appleton and Company, 1910.*

A view of the Governor´s residence: Plantation House.

citizens would desperately seek to be invited to the regular receptions and balls given at Plantation House –the Governor's residence. Still –and not surprisingly– it would be the French who demanded the maximum attention and provided lots of fresh gossiping. Needless to say, the leading part would be played by Napoleon himself from whom many 'audiences' would be requested by top personalities of the Indian Company, British officers, foreign commissioners and travellers passing by Saint Helena en route to India or Britain. The Emperor would not accede lavishly to these meetings, even though they may obviously represent a refreshing hiatus in his monotonous existence –determined as he was– to keep a convenient distance, fully aware of the fact that excessive exposure would contradict the legendary status he was working on.

Accordingly –and very especially– after his installation in the little cottage that eventually would be revealed as his last dwelling (Longwood) he would carry an increasingly indoor-living style sparing his outings more and more each time and mostly eluding visitors...

Below these high rank functionaries there remained many others placed at the lower steps of the social ladder who had no access to the Governor's classy receptions and had to make do with most popular festivities like that of the Prince Regent on 12th August. At this time the British scattered all around the world joined together in booming celebration for the success of their country personified in the Prince Regent. Saint Helenians were naturally no exception and even had an additional reason to enjoy the feast as now, 'Boney'[1]; England's more redoubtable enemy is, defeated and humiliated, reduced to the category of a 'war trophy' and prisoner in their impregnable little island.

Britain, being an island too, had evolved –at least to some extent– isolated from the continent's social and political tensions. In addition its precocious industrial revolution had greatly boosted the commerce and industry. Last, but not least, it counted with a formidable navy that procured this country the control of the seas; a factor that in the long term has been considered by many scholars as the ultimate reason for Napoleon's defeat.

It was then the most powerful country in the world both economically and militarily and, after Napoleon's fall, its ruling class was dictating European politics; France included. Napoleon, who should have given to these reflections a lot of thought at Saint Helena, is quoted to have said in a clear derogatory mood that the English *'sono mercanti'*[2]. And indeed they were, but considering the fact that economy and military forces always go hand in hand couldn't go unnoticed for such a brilliant mind as his; this remark could only be understood as the bitter expression of a devastating desolation. Now, when hidden behind shuttered windows he uses his inseparable spy glass to watch, unnoticed, the splendorous, cheerful celebrations of the Prince Regent's day, his inner torment should have grown to unbearable levels facing the sarcastic spectacle of a great, successful people that, being ruled by an idiotic Prince of Wales, had been able to wipe from the face of earth his entire political system questioning the very foundations of his convictions and –very especially– the idea of the supremacy of character backing his entire career and persona...

Considering that even nowadays just a limited variety of eatables and beverages can be obtained in the isle; imagine how it would have been two hundred years ago. In addition, the significant increase in population alluded above worsened even more this endemic problem. Food and drinking were in consequence a regular conversational and gossiping topic as reflected by the many remarks on the subject consigned in period memories and chronicles. Not surprisingly, most of them related to eating and drinking habits of the French; who then and now enjoy a sound reputation for having a fine taste at the table and good appetite.

---

1. *Boney. A familiar-scornful nickname given by the English to Napoleon.*
2. *La Vie quotidienne à Sainte-Hélène au temps de Napoléon. Gilbert Martineau. Tallandier.*

On 4th October 1820, Napoleon was on horse back accompanied by Bertrand, Montholon and a handful of servants. They set their course to a cottage called Mount Pleasant inhabited by Sir William Doventon and his family. Doventon was an old 'yamstock'[1] that had been a high rank functionary in the island and –as such– a good representative of the Saint Helena's 'upper' class. When the riders reached Doventon's home he was much honored and excited by the unexpected group and invited them all to share the breakfast the whole family was about to have. This, consisting in a big pat of butter and a bottle of orange shrub was kindly –and proudly– offered by Mr. Doventon's wife: Mrs. Greentree. Instead, the Emperor proposed to lay the table on the lawn in front of the house and use two baskets full of provisions brought by his servants. Then he honoured Doventon by having him seated at this right hand. The 'collation' would consist of potted meat, a cold pie, cold turkey and ham, curried foul, a salad, dates, almonds, coffee and... champagne.[2]

Given the sharp contrast between the breakfast of this high functionary and this last Napoleonic picnic, the many criticisms given to the French party on account of their eating habits –and expenditure– are certainly not surprising. Alluding to Sir William's reaction on account of this episode the marquis de Montchenu[3] would remark that *'the English were much shocked seeing the French having so big variety of cold food and drinking very good wine instead of tea and especially champagne, black coffee and liquors'*.

This Montchenu's comment is just an example among many others in the same tone. The matter of food and drinking supplies to Napoleon's dwelling constituted a major feud between the French and their guardians throughout the captivity. It is not surprising when considering how the population had increased after Napoleon's arrival and the additional supplying difficulties derived from the harsh security measures regulating the access of foreign ships to Saint Helena or the prohibition to fish at night imposed by Hudson Lowe. The result was a severe shortage to which practically nobody escaped, as reflected again by the ever loquacious and whining Montchenu:
   'There is also a big shortage. Even the governor spent fifteen days without a piece of beef and hospitals have to make the broth with salty meat. It is now more than two months with no butter to the sale; no matter

1.   *A nickname meaning yam (or sweet-potato) eater given by the European British to Saint Helenians.*
2.   *The Drama of Saint Helena. Paul Frémeaux. New York. D. Appleton and Company, 1910.*
3.   *Claude Marin Henri marquis de Montchenu was appointed by Talleyrand commissioner at Saint Helena on 22nd September 1817 who, reportedly, remarked on the marquis: 'Montchenu est un sot et un bavard. Il fera mourir le prisonnier d'ennui'. (Montchenu is a stupid and a gossip. He will kill the prisoner from boredom.)*

the price. Mutton is so scarce that we pay three shillings the pound. If this situation persists I don't know what's going to happen; as poultry is now almost exhausted. Despite our penury, Longwood is supplied everyday with sixty pounds of beef and thirty of mouton. However, they even moan that having no butter, no confectionery is possible, while we cannot get the essentials even if we pay their weight in gold.'

At the same time the French complained bitterly of being poorly fed as a major point in Napoleon's tactic against his guardians, once he had definitively set his mind to appear as a modern Prometheus chained to the terrible rock. This rather silly controversy reached its climax when the Emperor had Cipriani[1] (see page 113) destroy many fine pieces of his silverware that were sold in Jamestown and delivered to the English to support the expenditure of his household. It was indeed an exaggerated staging mainly addressed to the European public, stressing on the idea that the exiles were suffering unbearable hardships at Saint Helena. However, the truth –most probably– was that the French should consider themselves reasonably fed according with the prevailing conditions already commented, but this –like many other minor squabbles– were the matter of course for Napoleon and his companions; always prepared to show their disagreement with any measure dictated by Hudson Lowe as reflected in this passage written on 30th November, 1815 from Las Cases' original manuscript that was apparently suppressed in the printed version:

'We are possessed of moral arms only: and in order to make the most advantageous use of these it was necessary to reduce into a system our demeanour, our words, our sentiments, even our privations, in order that we might thereby excite a lively interest in a large portion of the population of Europe, and that the Opposition in England might not fail to attack the Ministry on the violence of their conduct toward us.'[2].

A comprehensive rendition of the Saint Helena ruling class would be certainly incomplete without some words about a major factual power essential to any sociological understanding of the western civilization: the clergy. In 1815 the Anglican Church enjoyed a period of tremendous power after a long process initiated in the 16th century, when Henry the VIII expulsed the Catholic Church from England seizing all its properties and joining church and state in the person of the king. This was a rigid society in moral terms closely watched and constrained by the priests that meddled in divine and material matters and often interfered with the political authorities.

---

1. *Cipriani. An obscure character: officially Napoleon's maître d'hotel but in fact his confident and factotum.*
2. *The Life of Napoleon I. John Holland Rose, M.A. George Bell and Sons 1902.*

Such was the case at Saint Helena at Napoleon's time when the reverend Richard Boys, a notorious intolerant and fanatical chaplain being in his thirties at the time, was always ready to confront Hudson Lowe and the lay authorities of (in his own words) *'an isle abandoned and corrupted'[1]* on account of his spiritual supremacy. This was a state of permanent dispute and Boys would take any opportunity during the mass services celebrated at James Town and Saint-Paul, where the crème de la crème congregated every Sunday, to harass individuals and shake collective behaviours. A good example would be that of admiral Plampin, accused publicly by Boys during his sermons for living sinfully with his young lover to his great embarrassment and the exasperation of Lowe, impotent as he was to stop Boys' diatribes.

Mainly because of the fact that the French were catholic, interaction between them and Boys was little and unclear. It has been said that Boys was the first person to whom Napoleon spoke upon his arrival in Saint Helena, but there is no feasible documentary evidence today. However, it is known that the Emperor showed his gratitude to Boys by presenting the priest with one of this snuff boxes after the latter accepted burying Cipriani –a catholic– in the island graveyard.

Old burial place.

1.   *La Vie quotidienne à Sainte-Hélène au temps de Napoléon. Gilbert Martineau. Tallandier.*

Among the many social affairs that worried reverend Boys during his stay at Saint Helena was the question of slavery; which he would fight with extraordinary zeal. At Napoleon's time Saint Helena was the only spot under the British flag still allowing slavery. Despite Boys' efforts and the existence of a significant anti-slavery group in the island, sales of slaves are reported as late as 1823, despite an official declaration produced in 1818 stating that all children born after Christmas 1818 should be considered free men, even though they must serve their mother's owners until being 18 years old[1]. Actually, black slaves, Chinese and Indians altogether shared the same pitiful conditions; no matter if they were blacks 'belonging' to the Company or the white settlers, or Chinese working as 'freemen'.

In 1820 these unfortunate people numbered above 2000. Even if they were not submitted to the terrible treatment given to slaves in earlier times, they suffered a hard discriminatory treatment and bore a very pitiful life that included ridiculous wages (if any), poor and unhealthy lodging; a scanty diet basically consisting in sweet potatoes or 'yam', rice and some fish, and disproportionate chastisements; as for example two years of hard labour for stealing two glasses of wine from the residence of Hudson Lowe's deputy adjutant Sir Thomas Reade[1].

The phrase '*Quand la Chine s'éveillera, le monde tremblera*' has been quoted as pronounced by Napoleon in 1816. Being not sufficiently documented, it might be apocryphal but, even in this case, this is a surprising premonitory statement of what is going on nowadays ... In any case the situation of these people was of course very different back in the early 19th century. The first Chinese arrived to Saint Helena transported by the East Indian Company in 1810. It was a first party of 50 soon to be followed by another of 150 some months later. They were hard labourers, far more productive than the slaves and highly appreciated by the insulars that would have them coming till numbering 481 in 1820[1]. Their Chinese names being unidentifiable to European settlers they were simply renamed with numbers. Kind of counter part to their great labour capacity, inventiveness and resolution, they were also inclined to drunkenness and robbery and on these grounds submitted to extreme reprisals. Such was the case of Chinese number 265 that was hanged for burglary in 1810 by order of Governor Lowe.

At Longwood House, Marchand was in charge of a group of twenty odd Chinese that worked as carpenters, gardeners or servants. Among the fine works performed by these devoted and anonymous craftsmen

---

1.   *La Vie quotidienne à Sainte-Hélène au temps de Napoléon. Gilbert Martineau. Tallandier.*

was an elaborated wooden bird cage, a replica of which can be admired at Longwood today. Napoleon's attitude to these humble people was extremely considerate and humanitarian; given the circumstances.

A replica of the bird cage made by chinese workers.

There always has been a lively debate about the living conditions at Saint Helena. Almost invariably French chroniclers have produced rather pejorative depictions of the isle as an extremely unhealthy place, constantly whipped by the winds and chastised by an extremely whimsical weather in which a splendid sunny day could change to a completely different scenery; with dark and sombre clouds all over the island delivering heavy and cold rain, in a matter of minutes. On the contrary English accounts usually favour the picture of a luxuriant paradise full of vegetation and pristine streams: a sort of Arcadia amidst the immensity of the South Pacific Ocean.

Persuaded that the real Saint Helena should lie somewhere in between, I travelled there in 2007. My first view of the island brought to my mind the remark made by Walter Henry, surgeon of the 66th foot who would be garrisoned at Saint Helena as a part of the troops watching the fallen Emperor: 'a *black wart rising out of the Ocean*'[1]. Very truly the first view of Saint Helena a voyager has is a terrible one: a mass of black rocks shaped like an impregnable natural fortress of almost vertical walls, often crowned by a mass of heavy, dark menacing clouds.

Despite to its proximity to the Equator where even heat and rather dry and clear atmosphere should in principle reign, this solitary rock rising as a ruined fortress in the middle of the South Atlantic, retains

---

1. *The Life of Napoleon I. John Holland Rose, M.A. George Bell and Sons 1902.*

and condenses all the clouds drifted by the trade winds just over Saint Helena's high lands, that become in this way frequently overcast and chilly. Facing this view for the first time the first words produced by the Emperor on approaching the island resonate: *'Ce n'est pas un joli séjour. J'aurais mieux fait de rester en Egypte; je serais à présent empereur de tout l'Orient'*[1] *(This is not a happy travel. I would have rather stayed in Egypt; I would be now Emperor of the entire East)*. However this very first impression would be soon counter balanced by others of a very different nature. Inside the intimidating rock contour there is a very unique place of unusual beauty. Plenty of vegetation –except on the higher plateau as remarked before– and rare endemic fauna and flora seem to delight a few cultivated, introspective people from abroad that settled their permanent residence in this island.

As stated above there should have been 4,000 inhabitants on the island in 2007. Ethnically the majority of the people seem to be a mixture of a diversity of races with a clear black dominant; peaceful, pleasant and very hospitable people. At the time of my visit to the isle (June) weather was stable and good, but I was told sudden changes happened in fact depending on the season and weather conditions.

A view from Saint Helena´s highlands.

I will always remember the magnificent, extremely beautiful dusks and the quietness and majestic silence reigning all over the place. In fact Saint Helena provides a splendid isolation for anyone devoted to

---

1.   *Général baron Gourgaud. Journal de Sainte-Hélène 1815-1818.*

thinking or writing, or simply tired of mundane life. Apparently, Saint Helena could well have been a fair refuge for a man that had lived through one of the most intense, hazardous and amazing existences in world history. A place for reflection, inner reconciliation and serenity for writing his memories and even perhaps keeping some hope for eventual release after some years of seclusion, when the terrible mayhem and turbulences induced in Europe by the French Revolution and the subsequent Napoleonic wars were finally settled.

But this was not the case for Napoleon Bonaparte. The idea of a melancholic retirement in this remote but in some way pleasant little island was probably never considered seriously by him. When he uttered immediately after the abdication that he just longed for a peaceful life as a land owner in the United States and was interested no more in politics, he was in all probability fooling everybody and perhaps even himself. He was indeed a man of many facets; a sort of 'kaleidoscopic' character so to speak, but if one could use but one single word to describe his essential nature that word would be 'gambler'.

In fact he never stopped gambling one way or the other; in victory or defeat. Had he decided to drop once and forever his title of Emperor and please the British by accepting the simpler –and even nobler– title of 'General Bonaparte' he most probably would have lived peacefully and in relative comfort on the tiny island, but then the game would have been definitively over.

Instead he decided to go ahead staging the 'Emperor', surrounding himself with a rather pathetic bunch of sycophants and setting an impossible battle on the 'field' of Saint Helena for the glory of France and his dynasty. The isle would play then a foremost role in this last imperial battle shaped as the Golgotha of the unfortunate Emperor who would die there after long years of mistreatment and suffering at the mercy of his 'sinister gaolers' and the harsh living conditions offered by the little island...

Magnificent sunset at Santa Helena.

THE ENTOURAGE

round Napoleon were a number of people who would play significant roles in the drama of Saint Helena. Most important among them all are probably those who have left some kind of written account on this story. Not surprisingly the French who lived with or near the Emperor rendered extremely detailed and, in most cases, rather hagiographic accounts. English memoires, on the other hand, are fewer but certainly helpful to get a balanced, unbiased picture. In any case the extraordinary source of first account testimonies of Napoleon's stay make possible the reconstruction of this historical drama day by day with accurate detail, as rarely seen in events that happened two hundred years ago. In fact this abundance of reports and documents relating to the figure of Napoleon can only be explained considering the general perception of the personage as the nearest 'great man' in history who was recognized as such even during his life.

It seems only natural to open this gallery of characters with those that helped to build the legend of Saint Helena by reflecting his experience and views in writing.

FRENCH CHRONICLERS

Las Cases

Emmanuel-Auguste-Dieudonné, count Las Cases (21st June 1776-15th May 1842) was a French noble who received military education in his early years in Paris before entering the navy to participate in some action during the period 1781-1782. At the outbreak of the French revolution in 1789 he emigrated to Germany and England. It is precisely in London where he composed his famous *'Atlas Historique, Généalogique, Chronologique et Géographique'*

(KGM. ©Andrea Press).

under the pseudonym of A. Lesage in 1801. This work had a great and long lasting success that procured the author considerable earnings.

Las Cases would return to France during the Consulate, but it was only in 1810 that he would be appointed chamberlain and count of the Empire. At the time of the first abdication in 1814 he fled to the United Kingdom probably to avoid possible reprisals. However, upon Napoleon's return from Elba, Las Cases would be back in France to recover his post of chamberlain and even be appointed councillor of state. On Sunday 25th June 1815, at La Malmaison, Las Cases, whom the Emperor only scarcely knew, offered himself to accompany him to exile. *'Savez-vous où cela peut vous conduire?'* (*Do you know where this can lead you?*) asked Napoleon. *'Je ne l'ai point calculé'* (*I have not at all worked it out*) answered Las Cases[1].

There has been permanent speculation about the real motives behind Las Cases' determination to join his destiny to Napoleon's. The fact that he was already a successful author before going to Saint Helena works one way and the opposite; in the sense that it may be argued that he decided to go 'despite' being a successful, well-to-do gentleman after the release of his famous atlas or –on the other hand– that he was for the same reason in an excellent position to exploit a book on Napoleon's seclusion in very profitable terms. Whatever the case Las Cases, accompanied by his young son Emmanuel, then just 15 years old, would board the Bellerophon as a main character in the drama of Saint Helena; not the least because of his good command of the English language.

From an intellectual point of view Las Cases' memorial excels far and beyond the others left by his companions in the captivity. He was a cultivated man and a prestigious author and, for this reason Napoleon favoured his company, enjoyed his conversation and entertained a series of works such as writing his own memoires or even learning English, which he tried with poor or none success for a short time.

Las Cases commenced working on his memorial immediately after boarding the Northumberland, constantly writing and taking notes; which passed not unnoticed to the Emperor. He requested to check the writings and, judging the recording of superficial conversations unworthy, decided to initiate regular dictation sessions to Las Cases. So, in September 9th 1815 he dictated for the first time some reflections about the siege of Toulon. That was the first of a series of pieces that would enrich Las Cases' memorial with his exceptional views

---

1.   *Le Memorial de Sainte-Hélène. Le Comte de Las Cases. Garnier Frères. Paris 1895.*

and remembrances. Besides this body of work directly provided by Napoleon, Las Cases offers remarkable renditions of the most diverse scenes that happened during the captivity and even portraits of true literary value; as this one on Hudson Lowe: '(...) *a man of about 45 years, medium height, slim, lean, curt, red haired and with a flushed, freckled face. His slanted eyes look sideways and rarely face to face under prominent, thick, rabid blonde eye brows.* **'He is a hideous man!** *–the Emperor said–* **This is a frightening face. But let us not rush; morality, after all, could rectify this sinister impression; that wouldn't be impossible"**.[1]

Notwithstanding, Las Cases' memorial would be far from being an objective account. Rather it should be classified as a political book aimed to praise Napoleon's virtues and justify his shortcomings with sights set on an eventual restoration in the person of Napoleon II.

Las Cases would leave Saint Helena on December 30th 1816. His memorial covers just 15 months from a total of 68 spent by Napoleon at Saint Helena. Apparently he was forced to abandon the isle after a servant was intercepted with a clandestine letter. This was a rather obscure affair resulting in Las Cases and his son leaving Saint Helena on Las Cases' own decision. The long winded explanations consigned in his memorial backing such a decision are not convincing enough to dispel the idea that Las Cases' ultimate reason for accompanying Napoleon might be the creation of this Memorial of Saint Helena, that would soon prove to be a true 'best seller' rendering fat profits to its author who, after some time living in Brussels would be finally allowed to return to Paris, where he died peacefully in 1842.

Montholon

Charles Tristan de Montholon-Sémonville (1783-1853) was born in Paris and entered the military career at a young age. He became a follower of Napoleon at the time of the coup of Brumarie in 1799 and would later serve with honour in the Napoleonic wars; even though some feats consigned in his record might be false, according to some scholars.

(*KGM. ©Andrea Press*).

1. *Le Memorial de Sainte-Hélène. Le Comte de Las Cases. Garnier Frères. Paris 1895.*

Montholon belonged to an upper class family that boosted him into a fast and successful career. He was aide-de-camp of Berthier in 1807 and in a few years had been appointed Count and chamberlain of the Empress Josephine.

In 1812 Montholon dared to marry a divorced lady; Albine Vassal, against Napoleon's orders, as he regarded Albine unfitting for a dignitary of the Empire, and for this cause Montholon and his new wife fell in disgrace, being estranged from the court. But it would be only temporary, as Montholon's remarkable command of palace intrigues had Napoleon appointing him in charge of the Garde Nationale of the department of La Loire in 1814. He wouldn't pass unnoticed to Louis XVIII during the restoration either, as the king conferred him the rank of field marshal; which in turn did not prevent Napoleon having Montholon serving as a chamberlain of the Emperor during the Hundred Days... Montholon doesn't seem to be a man attached to high moral standards, but rather a cynical, ambitious character whose life is sprinkled with obscure episodes including being suspected of murdering Napoleon by poisoning at Saint Helena.

After Waterloo came the turning point. Montholon decided to follow the Emperor to his uncertain destiny. He took his wife and son with him and would not change his mind even when Napoleon decided to deliver himself to the British against his earnest advice to the contrary (and Gourgaud's). Considering Napoleon's distaste for his wife and the ostracism imposed on the couple after the marriage, if Montholon indeed took this crucial decision out of loyalty to Napoleon and his regime he should be praised as an exceptional man of honour or... as a fool. In all probability Montholon wasn't either, which suggests that there should be at least some 'complementary' reason, such as the fact that after Waterloo was lost the Emperor and his world was sentenced and lost forever too. Obviously Montholon was a significant part of that world and, once the last game was over his future back in Paris, under the Bourbons, was not very promising. Even for a master of intrigue like him the most feasible prospect was a firing squad... In addition he was ruined and pursued by a legion of creditors. So he went aboard the Bellerophon with his family and stayed by the side of the Emperor till the very end, after Las Cases and Gourgaud had left. In fact he was Napoleon´s third and last confident.

It has been argued that the cold, ultimate reason leading the Montholons to Saint Helena was to persuade Napoleon to leave them a fortune big enough as to send them back to the high-life style they had enjoyed in the past... which they really would get as Napoleon's largest beneficiaries. As a part of the 'work' Albine would have been sweetening Napoleon's captivity as his mistress with his husband's acquiescence which, in addition, might add a touch of jealousy reinforcing the theory of the assassination alluded before... but let it suffice for the moment, as we will return to the subject in a subsequent chapter of this book (see page 291).

Back in Paris he could at last enjoy the high life he so much cared for, but in 1829 he was again in bankruptcy and decided to draw lots once more beside the future Napoleon III, whom supported all along the hazardous years of struggle till gaining political power. Once finally crowned, the brand new Emperor would bestow upon Montholon new sinecures in his administration; but this time the good luck arrived too late as Montholon would die shortly after; in 1853.

Regarding Montholon's literary works he signed the first volume of the '*Mémoires pour servir à l'histoire de France, sous Napoléon écrits à Sainte-Hélène*' published by Firmin-Didot et Bossange in 1823, which failed to attract much attention. Some years later, when the coup of Boulogne-sur-Mer in August 1840 failed, Louis-Napoléon was sentenced to life imprisonment and Montholon to 20 years in the fortress of Ham in the department of the Somme. It was there that Montholon wrote his memoirs of Saint Helena: '*History of the Captivity of Napoleon at Saint Helena*' published in London in 1846, which was forwarded by Montholon with the following words:

'During six years I shared the captivity of the greatest man of modern times and relieved the agony of his martyrdom with observant care, which he denominated filial.

The recollections of these years, passed in close intimacy with Napoleon, in conversing with him about the events of his reign, or in writing, from his dictation, the commentaries of this second Caesar the memory of forty-two nights passed in watching by his bedside, upon that political Golgotha of Saint Helena and, finally, the reward granted me by his formally expressed desire that I should be the person who should close his eyes and receive his last sigh, are not only the ruling thought, but continue to be the richest consolation of my declining years.

During the last years passed at Longwood, the Emperor sent for me every night, at eleven o'clock, from which time I never quitted him till six in the morning, when he entered the bath. In his paternal goodness, he was accustomed to say to me every day **'Come, my son, go and repose, and come to me again at nine o'clock. We shall have breakfast, and resume the labours of the night'.** *At nine I* *returned, and remained with him till one, when he went to bed, and received the grand marshal. Between four and five he sent for me again. I had the honour of dining with him every day, and about nine o'clock I left him to return at eleven.*

Count Las Cases only remained thirteen months at Saint Helena, and nevertheless, in the recitals of these thirteen months, he obtained enough material to fill eight volumes of his memorial (sic). *Had I followed his example, I could have written a whole library; but such is not my intention. I wish to consign to these pages such details only as may be useful to history. I therefore relinquish the idea of following the regular order of my journal. Days passed in captivity resemble one another; I shall consult the records of my diary merely as* memoranda (sic), *and give free course to my recollections. I shall detail the facts according to their importance in my memory.*

Everything which I state shall be verified by proof. In my case, especially, the fatalist axiom has become a truth: Destiny is written (sic).

In fact, without having sought it, my destiny brought me into contact with the Emperor in the Elysée Bourbon (and) *conducted me, without my knowing it, to the shores of Boulogne, where honour imposed upon me the necessity of not abandoning the nephew of the Emperor, in presence of the dangers by which he was surrounded. Irrevocably bound to the misfortunes of a family, I am now finishing in Ham the captivity commenced in Saint Helena.*

Erased, as one dishonoured, from the army list in 1816, and having had my good name tarnished by the Chamber of Peers in 1820, half of my life has been spent under the weight of these two sentences of condemnation.

My contemporaries have already avenged me for the former; and I trust posterity will absolve me from the latter.

Montholon.[1]

This work has been ever since a matter of debate and mostly considered as of dubious reliability. Apparently Montholon, who wrote these memoires many years after the facts they account for happened, would have plagiarized the memoires of prior works on the subject

---

1.   *History of the Captivity of Napoleon at Saint Helena. General Count Montholon. Henry Colburn. London, 1846.*

like Las Cases'. In any case, and despite any criticism, it should be taken into account, if only because Montholon was the closest person to the Emperor until the very moment of his death.

Gourgaud

Baron Gaspard Gourgaud (1783-1852) was born in Versailles, the son of a musician of the royal chapel and the nanny of the duke of Berry. He was educated as an artillery officer (like Napoleon) fighting during Napoleonic wars and being appointed ADC to the Emperor in 1811. Being good at mathematics he was sent to the *École Polytechnique* in 1799 in which records he appeared as having brown hair and eyebrows; low forehead; large nose; grey eyes; small chin; filled oval face and being 168 cm. high[1]. He was truly fond of his Emperor and this feeling was in all probability reciprocal by the side of the great man who has been quoted as saying that *'Gourgaud était mon premier officier d´ordonnance; il est mon ouvrage, c'est mon enfant'*[2] (*Gourgaud was my best orderly officer. He is my work, my child*).

(KGM. ©Andrea Press).

Always beside his beloved master Gourgaud was one of the first to enter the Kremlin, discovering a plot to kill Napoleon, and always revealing himself as a brave and resolute soldier, for which he would be given the title of baron and appointed first ADC to the Emperor. Apparently, in 1814, he saved the emperor's life by killing from a pistol shot a Cossack who was about to drive his lance through Napoleon[1].

At the time of the first abdication Gourgaud –following Napoleon's advice– enrolled in the *Louis XVIII's Gardes du corps*, but that would not impede from rejoining the Emperor upon his return from Elba in time for the last battle at Ligny, Fleurus, and Waterloo[1].

1.   *Dictionnaire Napoléon 1999. Baron Gourgaud. Fayard. Paris.*
2.   *Le Memorial de Sainte-Hélène. Le Comte de Las Cases. Garnier Frères. Paris 1895.*

When Gourgaud boarded the Bellerophon he is just 32 years old and unlike his most immediate companions he is a single man. That circumstance would be a determining factor in Gourgaud's mood and behavior during his reclusion, as he wouldn't have been able to find satisfactory relief to the strong sexual appetite normally expected in a man his age that, in Gourgaud's particular case, was exacerbated by his over-sensitive temperament as well as the overwhelming '*ennui*' he so often complained of during his painful stay at Saint Helena. His only amusements were taking notes from Napoleon's dictation and some occasional hunting. Always annoyed, he would spill a series of derogatory epithets on practically everybody around. Such was, for example, the case of Las Cases whom he regarded as a 'jesuit' and petty scribbler or the much hatred Albine de Montholon to whom he plainly refers to as a 'whore'.

Another significant feature was his constant fits of jealousy that, in the case of the Montholons acquired pathological proportion and, in the end, motivated his leaving in February 1818; immediately after challenging Montholon to a duel that could only be avoided thanks to Napoleon's personal intervention, who, in his turn, was extremely relieved upon Gourgaud's departure.

Once back in Europe –and banished from France– he settled initially in England and would later wander around the continental courts in the attempt of improving Napoleon's condition at Saint Helena before being finally allowed to return to France in 1821 where he wrote a series of books including his 'Journal de Sainte Hélène 1815-1818'; that would only be published in 1899.

At the time of the Revolution of 1830 Gourgaud was restituted to the military career enjoying recognition and success and would even return to Saint Helena in 1840 as a significant personality in the expedition to recover Napoleon's corpse. He would live however through a final reversal of destiny when he completely lost his status after the coup of 1851; shortly before dying from a long disease the next year...

Gourgaud's account of the drama of Saint Helena is reputed to be the most sincere –even brutal– of them all. His writing certainly lacks the pedantic literary quality of Las Cases' apologetic work consecrated to immortalize a sublimated version of Napoleon as a political and military genius and one of the greatest men in history. With Gourgaud the situation is very different: it is Napoleon the man day by day; the human being behind the myth. There was a sort of paternal-filial relationship between them and it is quite surprising to read how Gourgaud dared to go so far in this familiarity that no one else 'enjoyed', with the possible exception of Cipriani. A closeness that would grow and degenerate with the passing of time in the boring and constricted space Napoleon was reduced to live in.

The gossiping, jealousy and constant pestering of Gourgaud, always pressing on prosaic, unsubstantial matters, would eventually lead Napoleon's back to the wall to the point at which Gourgaud's unbearable impertinences seriously jeopardized the dignity of the illustrious captive. The following excerpt in connection with the episode of Gourgaud's shooting a Cossack commented above is just an example:

'*Cockburn had told the Emperor on board that he knew well why he was so fond of me, and that it was because I had saved his life; which His Majesty had denied.*

Gourgaud: *I have never boasted that I saved your life and, however, I killed a hussar that was pouncing on His Majesty!*

The Emperor: **I don't remember.**

Gourgaud: *I can't believe it! What, His Majesty does not remember! The staff witnessed it, and even M. Fain[1] asked me that evening if I used the little pistols that I usually kept in my pockets or my saddle pistols. Everybody in Paris knows about that.*

The Emperor: **I should have been told.**

Gourgaud: *Sire, I was convinced that His Majesty had seen it, and I thought that if I were vain about this service rendered to His Majesty, He would be upset. Besides, I just probably acted as any other in my place would have done.*

The Emperor: **I know that you are a brave young man, but it is quite surprising that with your spirit you may be so childish. Let's read the article together[2].**'

---

1.   *The Baron Fain, that succeeded Méneval as 'secrétaire du Cabinet'.*
2.   *Sunday 9th, March 1817. Général baron Gourgaud. Journal de Sainte Hélène 1815-1818.*

Gourgaud saves Napoleon's life by shooting a Cossack during the Battle of Brienne fought on 29 January 1814, and resulting in the victory of the French over the Russian and Prussian forces. (Bombled. ©Andrea Press).

Bertrand

Henri Gatien Bertrand, (1773-1844), was born in Châteauroux to a well settled family. At the time of the French Revolution he would volunteer to the army, being commissioned as an engineer officer in 1793. A colonel during the Egyptian campaign he would also be appointed aide-de-camp to Napoleon after Austerlitz. He was very close to Napoleon, who sincerely trusted and appreciated him conferring Bertrand the title of Count and finally the rank of

(KGM. ©Andrea Press).

Grand Marshal of France in 1813. Bertrand held an impressive military record and was a highly respected and honourable man.

He was indeed an accomplished engineer, as Napoleon would eventually remark in one bulletin of the 'Grande Armée' in 1809: '*The Danube has ceased to exist for the French army: the general Count Bertrand has ordered the execution of works which cause astonishment and inspire admiration*'[1].

Bertrand followed Napoleon to Elba, fought at Waterloo and did not hesitate to go along with him to Saint Helena accompanied, reluctantly, by his wife Fanny Dillon. Madame Bertrand was the daughter of a French general guillotined during the revolution; she had been educated in Britain and kept some kin with the Empress Josephine, which gave her some preferential treatment at the Tuileries. She would become an element of discord all along the seclusion on the isle. In fact she never accepted the harsh living conditions or the reigning boredom so different from the splendor and abundance of the old court. Very especially, Fanny couldn't cope with the oppressive atmosphere reigning at Longwood, refusing to be lodged there and opting for living in a separate cottage with her growing family (she gave birth to three children during her stay on the isle). Even though

1. *Le Memorial de Sainte-Hélène. Le Comte de Las Cases. Garnier Frères. Paris 1895.*

Bertrand turned up to Longwood punctually every day, she always found some reason to excuse her presence, which greatly annoyed the Emperor, embittering even more the rather devious relationship prevailing among them all.

It has been speculated that Napoleon made some advances on Countess Bertrand after his supposed lover Madame Montholon left the island. Theoretically that would be implied in the remark in his diary by Bertrand on September, 29th, 1819 (see page 285). In any case this diary is regarded as invaluable for its honest account of Napoleon's character and his life in captivity. Curiously enough Bertrand wrote it coded –probably lest Hudson Lowe and his acolytes seized it– and it remained undiscovered until the end of the WWII. It would be finally published in 1949 by Fleuriot de Lange under the title of 'Cahiers de Sainte-Hélène, 1816-21'.

Madame Bertrand. (KGM. ©Andrea Press).

Bertrand would only return to France after Napoleon's death. Once back there Louis XVIII dropped the death penalty imposed on the Grand Marshal on 1816 and even reinstated him to his old rank. Like Gourgaud he would board 'La Belle Poule'[1] in 1840 to recover the remains of Napoleon from Saint Helena. A few years later, in 1844, he passed away and was buried under the dome of Les Invalides, near his beloved Emperor.

---

1. The Belle-Poule was a French 60-gun frigate commissioned to recovering Napoleon's remains from Saint Helena and bringing them back to Paris according with the express desire of the long-ago deceased Emperor.

Already a successful General in his younger years, Napoleon would grow used to have quite a few assistants and valets around who shared his intimacy and even in some special cases enjoyed his 'care'. Unlike the ministers and high officers that comprised Napoleon's closest staff, these servants naturally took no part in military or political affairs but, on the other hand, the 'domestic proximity' implied by their work enabled them to get a closer view of the Emperor in those aspects of daily

(KGM. ©Andrea Press).

life common to every man: his habits and his temper or what might please and displease him...

Louis Étienne Saint-Denis (1788-1856) was born at Versailles the son of a couple of servants in the pre-revolutionary court, who managed to procure him a grade of education enabling the boy to be employed as clerk for four years before entering the service of the Emperor as an *élève-piqueur* (stable groom) and finally, in 1811, he would enter the Emperor's personal service as he duly his recounted in his 'Souvenirs':

> *'I learned to set the bed of the lord of Europe, and to have everything that he needed at his disposal and that he might require in his privacy. I served him personally at breakfast and suited the mess pages with the dishes, cutlery and delicacies to be presented. That was an entirely new life for me: instead of walking across the stables, healing horses, transporting –in short, performing the duties of a groom– I sat in an arm chair or canapé, chatting or sleeping beside a good fire waiting to be called. Idleness had overtaken activity.'[1]*

Initially Saint-Denis was an assistant to the Mameluke Roustam, the well known Armenian bodyguard and valet to the Emperor. The Mamelukes were the slave horsemen of the Ottoman Empire that ruled Egypt at the time of Napoleon's invasion in 1798. Impressed by the Mamelukes' military performance, he raised an elite Mameluke company as part of the regiment of Chasseurs-à-Cheval of the Imperial Guard.

---

1.   *Souvenirs du Mameluck Ali sur L'Empereur Napoléon. Payot, Paris 1926.*

Roustam entered the service of Napoleon during the Egyptian campaign and stayed by him until the Emperor's first abdication in 1814. Roustam would not go to Elba, which displeased Napoleon very much and, for this reason, he refused to take him back into service when he returned to power in 1815. As Saint-Denis was as a second to Roustam, Napoleon should have thought it only natural to make Saint-Denis a Mameluke, even insisting in having him dress in full Mameluke fashion and giving him the sobriquet of Ali.

Ali would follow Napoleon all through the Russian campaign and, from then on, he would mostly remain very close to the Emperor until the very moment of his death. During his stay at Saint Helena Saint-Denis married a young British girl named Mary Hall (see page 123), the governess of Bertrand's children who eventually would give birth to three girls. After Napoleon's death, Saint-Denis would return to Paris with his family and took a job at a riding school before finally moving to Sens, in Burgundy. He carried there a peaceful life perhaps only interrupted in 1840, when he took part in the expedition to Saint Helena to retrieve Napoleon's remains.

It seems that Saint-Denis did not produce any notes during his stay at Saint Helena. In all probability it was only when he was living at Sens that he started to write his 'Souvenirs' supervised by his family and Marchand through 321 pages of large size written in small, cramped letters. Ali was still working and perfecting his memories when death visited him...

Saint-Denis was certainly not an illiterate man. Much to the contrary, he found all through his life the means to refine the basic education he was given as a youth by reading and studying the most diverse subjects. The fact that he was appointed by Napoleon as his librarian at Saint Helena speaks by itself. On the other hand the closeness and warm affection between these two men for so many years and, finally, the impeccable loyalty professed by Ali during his whole life, leaves little doubt about the true nature of this man.

Besides his 'Souvenirs' he also worked out a complete catalogue of Napoleon's library at Saint Helena and produced interesting comments on many other works about Napoleon written by renowned authors.

Ali made it clear in his last will that he didn't want his 'Souvenirs' published or accessed by anybody with the sole exception of Marchand. For this reason it would be only in the early twenties of the past century that the 'Souvenirs' would be finally released thanks to

Monsieur G. Michaut, whose mother in law eventually happened to be one of Ali´s last descendants, whose family adamantly refused the publication of his work in strict accordance with Ali's last will. Today, Ali's 'Souvenirs' are mostly regarded as a reliable and indispensable source for the study of Napoleon's life and, very specially, of the long years of seclusion at Saint Helena...

Marchand

Louis-Joseph-Narcisse Marchand was born in Paris in 1791 the son of Marie-Marguerite Broquet, one of the three nurses taking care of Napoleon's only legitimate son; the 'King of Rome'. It was because of his mother's position at the court that Marchand entered the imperial household in 1811 as a servant.

Being just twenty years old, he rapidly made himself out because of his good nature and diligence. At the time of the first abdication in 1814; when Constant and Roustam – Napoleon's closest and trusted

(KGM. ©Andrea Press).

servants– fled away in pretty dishonorable circumstances[1], Marchand would be appointed first valet to Napoleon and followed him to Elba.

He soon gained the Emperor's sympathy, and started an extraordinary relationship of loyalty and love rarely matched in the course of Napoleon's life.

Back to France during the Hundred Days; after Waterloo and all along the long journey and painful years of captivity, Marchand never receded in his love and devotion to the Emperor; just as he had done at the Tuileries during the splendorous years.

Already at Saint Helena, Marchand's activities went far beyond the duties of a servant, as he always did his very best to alleviate the

---

1.   *Mémoires de Marchand. Libraire Plon. Paris 1952.*

suffering of the great man; mitigating the boredom and the idleness by displaying rare conversational and literary capacities much to the pleasure of Napoleon, as proved by the fact that he bestowed on Marchand the title of count on his deathbed and named him a trustee of his will. He was an accomplished painter too, having left some accurate depictions of Longwood house.

Marchand was a honest and sincere man that would die –the last of Napoleon's close companions at Saint Helena– peacefully in Trouville on June 19th, 1876 when he was 85 years old. Like his friend Saint-Denis he would travel one last time to Saint Helena in 1840 even though he did not travel aboard the *Belle-Poule* but in the *Favourite*, another ship part of the same expedition.

Marchand's memoirs were kept in private hands until 1952. They are more a chronicle than a history work; all through which Marchand renders an extraordinary account of his experience beside Napoleon in a laconic, clear style enriched with a series of appendixes containing interesting data and inventories.

Two thirds of the memoirs are dedicated to Saint Helena and it has been speculated whether he took notes during his stay or he started writing at a later moment, once some other memories had been published. This is certainly a point of difficult or impossible settlement but, in any case, considering Marchand's personality and his detailed and well structured work, the fact that he might have taken notes on the spot –at least to some extent– cannot be discarded.

Marchand himself made the following introduction to his memoirs:

'My memoirs reproduce my observations, my feelings, and the emotions that events spurred within me. Much has been written about the Emperor on the island of Elba, during the Hundred Days, and his captivity in Saint Helena. All that has been printed is not always accurate.

I am indebted to the Emperor's memory, not to his dignity, certainly little compromised by manoeuvres due to cupidity or partisan spirit; I am indebted for his kindness toward me and for the honour he has done me in naming me one of the executors of this will, so that I may restore the truth in the facts I am aware of. I shall do so with moderation, often without even referring to the alterations it has suffered, and through the simple recounting of events.

Although I have shared the enthusiasm that Napoleon inspired, I have not ceased to be truthful. During the ten years I spent in his personal service, six were spent in a more special way, during his captivity in Saint Helena and his stay in Elba. I was able to admire such genius, talent and glory on the throne; such courage, resignation and grandeur in adversity; and always and everywhere such sensitivity and kindness for his people! I have but one fear, and shall have but one regret: that my pen might fail my heart.'[1]

Albine de Montholon

Albine de Montholon (1779-1848) was Montholon´s wife and, together with Madame Bertrand, one of the two only women in Napoleon's tiny court. She certainly didn't enjoy a flawless reputation having married two other men before Montholon; a fact that moved Napoleon to forbid their marriage and her husband's dismissal when he found they had secretly married.

Seductive, enticing and scheming, this woman played a significant role around Napoleon, who could even have fathered her daughter Charlotte Hélène, born at Longwood in

(KGM. ©Andrea Press).

1818. Back in Europe in 1819, and probably unable to cope with her husband's dissolute life, she divorced him before finally dying in 1848.

Just like many other of his companions in the seclusion, Albine would produce a sort of memoir that, assembled in 1840, would only be published in 1901.

Mostly dealing with events prior to Saint Helena, Albine's contribution is mostly rated as irrelevant and prissy.

---

1. *Mémoires de Marchand. Libraire Plon. Paris 1952.*

THE ANTAGONIST: HUDSON LOWE

Should the well-known saying 'a man's greatness can be measured by his enemies'[1] be applied to Napoleon, he would fare poorly, as one of the possible reasons explaining his striking success was the mediocrity of most of his political and military adversaries. Once at Saint Helena he was in urgent need of the last of his enemies, a suitable antagonist, naturally a man of some importance but despicable enough; not a fool truly, but

(KGM. ©Andrea Press).

certainly insensible; not a ruffian, but not a gentleman either...

On April 14th Sir Hudson Lowe –the son of an army surgeon and mostly unknown in Britain after he had served 28 years abroad– landed at Saint Helena as the new Governor succeeding Colonel Mark Wilks[2]. Lowe was a lean man, slightly above Napoleon's height. His ruddy, freckled and bony face was adorned with bushy eyebrows, an aquiline nose and a tight mouth: all of that topped by a head of reddish hair. He was a nervous and restless type and even though he was proficient in Portuguese, French, Corsican, Italian and had a good knowledge of Spanish he was never a fluent speaker.

He was born in 1769; early entering the British army; wining his commission by service in Corsica and Elba and soon gaining the command of a corps of Corsican exiles that had enlisted with the British after 1795.

Lowe was certainly respected by his Corsican Rangers and campaigned against the French in Egypt and Capri. In fact he could be

---

1. *Attributed to –amongst others– to the American writer Donn Piat.*
2. *Colonel Mark Wilks (1759-1831) appointed Governor of the island in 1813 and thus predecessor of Hudson Lowe. He was a pleasant man that, together with Cockburn, entertained an affable relationship with the fallen Emperor.*

proud of his service record, festooned with feats of arms such as the seizing of the isle of Santa Marta[1] in 1810, serving in Russia in 1813 or even later attached to Blücher's staff in the advance to the Rhine and the Seine. As the only high ranking British officer with Blücher, Lowe took part in some important decisions such as that of the advance on Paris that he strongly recommended.

Worthy of mention is also the fact that Lowe was the first to bring to London the news of Napoleon's abdication in April 1814 after a daring ride from Paris to Calais; all across hostile territory and escorted by only one rider.

He was honored by the Russians and Prussians for his services. Gneisenau[2] produced the following remark about Lowe:

'Your rare military talents, your profound judgment on the great operations of war, and your imperturbable sang froid *(sic) on the day of battle. These rare qualities and your honorable character will link me to you eternally'*[3].

Wellington, on the contrary, had a pretty different judgment when, reportedly, rated Lowe a *'dammed old fool'* (for hesitating reading a map on the field) when he was serving Wellington as his quartermaster-general in the Netherlands early in April 1815.

Both comments would serve perfectly to represent the two poles of the everlasting controversy about Lowe. Even today, almost 200 years since Napoleon's death the discussion is still going on obstructing a serene, definitive portrait of the 'infamous' governor. However, beyond the many biased, passionate judgments produced over the years the truth is that –from a strictly practical point of view– there is no point in discussing Lowe's efficacy in serving both British and French parties. Indeed he kept Napoleon on the island for the rest of his life (so avoiding any other political or military turmoil in Europe –or even America) and perfectly performed the role of a sinister, mean, imperturbable gaoler in a way probably Napoleon could never have dreamed of. A subtler, more intelligent man would most probably have softened the harsh restrictions and rules imposed by the British government; or even perhaps ignored some of them so increasing the risk of an evasion as had already happened in Elba. But, even though no escape happened, the picture of Napoleon entertaining a pleasant existence on the island,

---

1. *The Greek isle of Léucade nowadays.*
2. *August Wilhelm Antonius Graf Neidhardt von Gneisenau (1760–1831) was a prominent Prussian field marshal in the Napoleonic wars.*
3. *The Life of Napoleon I. John Holland Rose, M.A. George Bell and Sons 1902.*

living in a luxurious residence, enjoying total freedom of movement, unlimited funds, a mistress... is in open contradiction to the drama of Saint Helena as reported by Las Cases' memorial as told by Napoleon in November 1815:

> *'Our situation here may even have its attractions!... The universe is watching us!.... We remain the martyrs of an immortal cause... Millions of men cry for us, the fatherland yearns, and Glory is in mourning!... We struggle here against the oppression of the gods, and the wishes of the nations are for us!...'* And after a pause of some seconds he continued: *'My true sufferings are nothing here!... If it was only me, possibly I would be glad!... Misfortune also has its heroism and glory!... Adversity was missing in my career. Had I died on the throne amidst the clouds of my omnipotence, I would have remained a problem for many people; today, thanks to misfortune, I will be judged bare of all.'*[1]

Lowe was in Marseille in August 1815 where he had the first notion about being designated as Napoleon's guardian, but it was only in September that Bathurst's first instructions about dealing with the Emperor reached him in advance of being appointed lieutenant-general in November and even invested with the coveted British title of 'Knight commander of the Bath' in the first days of 1816.

1815 should have been a most agitated year for the new lieutenant-general as in December that year he married the prolific Susan Johnson; a widow with two daughters from a previous marriage who would present Lowe with three additional children (two boys and a daughter) once at Saint Helena. The whole brand-new family left Portsmouth in January 1816 for Saint Helena, where they arrived on 14th April as the new Governor of the island.

Regular Bathurst dispatches make a point in reiterating Napoleon's status as a prisoner and reflected the ministers' fear of an eventual escapade as he had from Elba. The always pernickety Lowe felt compelled to follow his instructions to the very detail, but he was far from being an evil man. Much to the contrary he had a natural good disposition and, had he enjoyed more freedom of action –or determination– he probably would have relaxed his orders so making life for the French party on the island a little sweeter. In any case, this lack of determination was not Lowe's only –or most decisive– shortcoming. Rather it was his lack of sensitiveness and imagination which impeded a reasonable relationship with the Emperor. If, in general, the British instructions aimed to prevent an eventual escapade are perfectly understandable,

---

1.   *Le Mémorial de Sainte-Hélène. Le Comte de Las Cases. Garnier Frères. Paris 1895.*

the obsession in denying Napoleon his imperial rank addressing him just as 'General Buonaparte' can only be rated as a vexatious measure maintained all along the captivity and even beyond Napoleon's death, whose tombstone at Saint Helena would be deprived of any title and remain unmarked after any inscription short of 'General Buonaparte' was forbidden. Typically, when Lowe first met the Emperor he promptly addressed him as 'General Buonaparte'. They would only meet five times in four months, the last two being especially acrimonious and moving Napoleon to decline any further intercourse with Lowe on August 18th 1816 after stating that:

'I must never more receive this officer: he makes me lose my temper, this is below my dignity: he makes me pronounce words that would have been unforgivable at the Tuileries; if there is any excuse here that is being in his hand and under his power'[1].

Obviously Lowe was no match for the Emperor and, had the ministers at London enrolled a man of substance perhaps the drama could have gained some richer tones derived from a closer interaction between the captive and the jailer. Unfortunately, and not surprisingly, the idea of a superior man playing such a despicable role was not really feasible. Lowe always failed in establishing a closer relationship with his prisoner, who characterized him on his second encounter with the new governor on April, 30th 1816, as being a despicable, sinister figure.

About two months after Napoleon's death on May 5th 1821, Hudson Lowe left Saint Helena and sailed to Britain, where he was cordially received by George IV. He served for some years in Ceylon before returning to Britain for good; then spending his last years in an endless –and fruitless– squabbling for a pension increase with the Colonial Office until his death in 1844.

Lowe left to posterity a collection of written memories and documents that, compiled by William Forsyth would only be published in 1853 under the title 'Captivity of Napoleon at Saint Helena, from the Letters and Journals of Sir Hudson Lowe' including this excerpt on the first meeting between the two men on April 14th 1816 narrated by Lowe:

'Had my first interview with him at four o'clock in the afternoon; was accompanied to his house by Rear- Admiral Sir George Cockburn. General Bertrand received us in his dining-room, serving as an ante-chamber, and instantly afterward ushered me into an inner room, where I found him standing, having his hat in his hand. Not addressing me

1.   Le Mémorial de Sainte-Hélène. Le Comte de Las Cases. Garnier Frères. Paris 1895.

*when I came in, but apparently waiting for me to speak him, I broke silence by saying, "I am come, Sir, to present my respects to you.' **'You speak French, Sir, I perceive; but you also speak Italian. You once commanded a regiment of Corsicans' (Je suis venu, Monsieur, pour vous présenter mes devoirs.' Vous parlez Français, Monsieur, je vois, mais vous parlez aussi Italien. Vous avez commandé un régiment de Corses'.)***

*I replied, the language was alike to me. **'We will speak, then, in Italian'**, he said; and immediately commenced in that language a conversation which lasted about half an hour, the purpot of which was principally as follows: He first asked me where I had served –how I liked the Corsicans– **'They carry the stiletto: are they not a bad people?' ('Portano stiletto: non sono cattivi?')** looking at me very significantly for an answer.*

My reply was, 'They do not carry the stiletto, having abandoned that custom in our service; they have always conducted themselves with propriety. I was very well satisfied with them' ('Non portano stiletto; hanno perduto quella usanza del nostro servizio: si conducevano sempre molto bene. Era molto contento di loro.').

*He asked me if I had not been in Egypt with them; and, on my replying on the affirmative, entered into a long discussion respecting that country. **'Menou was a weak man. If Kleber had been there, you would have been all made prisoners.'***

He then passed in review all our operations in that country, with which he seemed as well acquainted as if he had himself been there; blamed Abercromby for landing sooner, or, if could not land sooner, not proceeding to another point; Moore, with his 6000 men, should have all been destroyed; they had shown themselves good generals, however, and merited success from their boldness and valour.

He asked me if I knew Hutchinson –whether it was the same who had been arrested at Paris. To which a reply was, of course, given in the negative. His question on this point, betrayed great interest. The subject of Egypt was again resumed. It was the most important geographical point in the world, and had always been considered so.

*He had reconnoitred the line of canal across the Isthmus of Suez; he had calculated the expense of it at ten or twelve millions of livres- **'Half a million sterling, (Mezza milione di lire sterline)'** he said, to make me understand more clearly the probable cost of it: that a powerful* colony being established there, it would have been impossible for us to have preserved our empire in India.

He then fell again to railing at Menou; and concluded with the following remark, which he pronounced in a very serious manner: **'In war, the game is always with him who commits the fewest faults'** (**'Dans le métier de la guerre, le jeu est toujours à celui qui fait le moins de fautes').** It struck me as if he was reproaching himself with some great error.

'He then asked me some further questions regarding myself -whether I was not married? -if I had not become so shortly before my leaving England' -how I liked Saint Helena? I replied, I had not been sufficient time here to form a judgement upon it. **'Ah! You have your wife; you are well off!** (**'Ah! Avete la vostra moglie; state bene!').** After a short pause he asked how many years I had been in the service. 'Twenty-eight,' I replied. **'I am, therefore, an older soldier than you'**, (**'Je suis donc plus vieux soldat que vous')** he said. 'Of which history will make mention in a very different manner' ('Dont l'histoire le fera connaître d'une bien autre manière') I answered.

He smiled, but said nothing. I proceeded immediately afterward to take my leave, asking permission to present to him two officers of my suite, Lieutenant-Colonel Sir Thomas Reade and major Gorrequer, who had accompanied me, to which he assented. He spoke little to them, but, as we were going away, turned to me and said, **'You are settling your affairs with the Catholics. I see; it is well done. The Pope has made concessions, and smoothed the way for you.'** Thus the interview terminated'.[1]

---

1. History of the Captivity of Napoleon at Saint Helena. From the letters and journals of the late Lieut. Gen. Sir Hudson Lowe and official documents not before made public by William Forsyth, MA. Harper Brothers. 1853, New York.

THE BRITISH CHRONICLERS

Dr. O'Meara

The Irish Dr. Barry Edward O'Meara (1786-1836), studied medicine in Dublin before entering the Army in 1804 as assistant surgeon. He served in Sicily, Egypt and Italy with bravery, even though he would be court-martialed for acting as a second in an illegal duel at Messina, and thus discharged from the army. He would then join the Navy serving in the West Indies and the Mediterranean.

Barry would meet Napoleon for the first time aboard the Bellerophon. This young Irish doctor

(KGM. ©Andrea Press).

would be attached to Napoleon after his French surgeon Maingault declined the 'honor' of travelling with him to Saint Helena (see page 31). O'Meara being able to speak some Italian, would soon get close to the Emperor; who seemed to have professed true affection towards his new doctor and even encouraged him to write a detailed account of the exile that, eventually, would play a significant role in shaping the legend of Saint Helena.

Once on the island, and during the first phase under the rule of Cockburn and Malcolm[1], Napoleon and O'Meara were allowed to entertain a pleasant relationship and enjoyed a relative degree of freedom, but things would change with the arrival of Hudson Lowe...

The new governor, suspicious of everything and everybody, immediately exerted a tight control over all O'Meara's movements and

---

1. *Admiral Sir Pulteney Malcolm (1768-1838). Commander-in-chief on Saint Helena in 1816-1817 to enforce a rigid blockade and keep Napoleon under a close watching eye.*

even pushed him to spy on Napoleon, taking advantage of his closeness to the great man. Upon the constant refusals of O'Meara and after a series of quibbles, they reached a turning point in August 1817 with a bitter argument concerning newspapers being delivered by the doctor to Longwood, in open departure from Lowe's orders. O'Meara still managed to stay there another year, but he would be obliged to leave the island a year later because of his persistent reluctance to be a spy.

O'Meara constantly tried to appease Lowe by assuring him that Napoleon was not trying to escape, but at the same time insisted that he was in poor health and should be located in some other place; quite different from Saint Helena. In fact O'Meara took a lot of trouble to spread the idea that the Emperor was agonizing at Saint Helena because of the poor climatic conditions and –not the least– the 'insane' Hudson Lowe's ruling. He obviously failed, as ministers at London uniformly sided with Lowe: O'Meara would be estranged from the naval career and consequently deprived of his pension. Our doctor began practicing as a dentist in London and profited from his closeness to the Emperor by displaying in his office window one of his wisdom tooth that he had extracted during his stay at island. Clearly a sagacious businessman, he is said to have even developed a best selling toothpaste... (see page 240)

Just after Napoleon's death in 1821, O'Meara published his 'Napoleon in Exile, or a Voice from Saint Helena' blaming Lowe for his treatment of Napoleon. The book was an immediate success and went through five editions in a few months. Lowe took a libel action against the doctor that failed to meet any success on the grounds of legal technicalities after quite a long time. At this point, Lowe resolved to write his own, vindictive, version of the facts. O'Meara´s memoirs were effective in boosting the Napoleonic legend outside and inside Britain if only because of the fact that he was British, and thus not liable to produce a biased version on the side of Napoleon. There is no general agreement on O'Meara's account, as it might be regarded as a bit too 'passionate' and wanting of accurate documentary support. In any case, and dramatically speaking, there is no doubt O'Meara did a great work shaping Lowe's figure as the despicable villain... that most probably he never was.

Barry's finances were certainly not thriving in 1823, but his luck would change when he married lady Theodosia Beauchamp Leigh (a 66 year old rich heiress of intriguing past and two previous marriages). When poor Lady Leigh departed from this world in 1830 Barry still would enjoy six years of pleasant life before dying from a deadly chill at his home in London in June 1836.

Gorrequer

Major Gideon Gorrequer (1781-1841) was a professional soldier who entered the army at the age of sixteen. He served for thirty years in the 18th or 'Royal Irish Regiment of Foot' and later in the 4th or 'King's own regiment of Foot'. He accepted Lowe's offering to serve as his aide-de-camp and secretary and sailed with him for Saint Helena staying there all during the exile and finally returning to Britain in July1821, shortly after Napoleon's death. He would spend the rest of his life enjoying a peaceful living in London till his death in 1841.

(KGM. ©Andrea Press).

Gorrequer was the man keeping the closest contact with Hudson Lowe during his governorship at Saint Helena, dealing with all kind of administrative matters and, in such capacity, meeting most of the significant personalities living on the island at that time. He was a learned man who could speak French and Italian fluently and with a keen eye for any event, rumour or gossip at Saint Helena; which he would consign on a daily basis in a personal diary full of sarcastic remarks and an endless series of ding-dong details only useful to illustrate the oppressive, extremely boring atmosphere reigning all over the island. At the beginning of the first chapter –for example– the reader is confronted with a Kafkaesque depiction of an overwhelmed Hudson Lowe because of the trivial difficulties and inconveniences involved in finding suitable lodgings for his cynical secretary at the governor's residence; Plantation House...

Gorrequer uses a series of mocking nicknames to designate the different characters appearing in his diary; which makes a funny point as, in all probability, he never thought this diary would be published. As a matter of fact it remained unpublished until 125 years after his death[1]. These pseudonymous should be better attributed to the

---

1. *Saint Helena during Napoleon's Exile. Gorrequer's Diary. James Kemble. William Heinemann Ltd. London 1969.*

sardonic Gorrequer's personality that seemed to engulf in spilling ironical and depreciative remarks on practically everybody around and –very especially– on Hudson Lowe to whom he dedicated this –somewhat abstruse– last entry of the diary:

'*Mach* (Hudson Lowe. Presumably an abbreviation for Machiavelli) *is but a machine- he is just what his nature and circumstances have made him. He slogs the machine which he cannot control. If he is corrupt, it is because he has been corrupted. If he is unamiable it is because he has been marked and spitefully treated. Give him a different education, place him in other circumstances, and treat him with as much gratefulness and generosity as he has experienced of harness, and he would be altogether a different nature. A man who would be anxious to be loved rather than feared; and instead of having the accusation of being a man who was satisfied to spread around him anguish and despair, one who has an instinct for kindness. To some his motives were ambiguous. It is dangerous particularly when we have an anxious and inexperienced mind and do nothing to improve a fault; and live in a great (? illusion) in the opinion of others, especially those we respect. While thought incapable of error, it is difficult (if you) fall into one; but if warned, particularly in a case which questions your capacity (?), you have already a means of escape.'[1]*

Betsy Balcombe

When Napoleon finally arrived to Saint Helena on October 17th 1815, he spent his first night on the isle in the humble Porteous pension in Jamestown. Next morning –anxious for some exercise after the long months aboard the Northumberland– he rode to Longwood House in the company of Bertrand and Ali. This lodging, located on the highlands, and perhaps out of comparison with the seedy accommodation

(*KGM. ©Andrea Press*).

1.   *Saint Helena during Napoleon's Exile. Gorrequer's Diary. James Kemble. William Heinemann Ltd. London 1969.*

of the night before, apparently didn't displease him. However, on descending back to Jamestown they happened to reach a very pleasant setting called the Briars; home of William Balcombe, an East India Company functionary that came to the island in 1807 accompanied by his wife and his two daughters Jane and Betsy.

The Balcombes lived comfortably in the Briars, which Betsy would depict as *'a perfect little paradise- an Eden blooming in the midst of desolation'*[1].

Napoleon liked the place so much that he would be delighted in setting up his 'headquarters' in a little pavilion next to the main house that, initially conceived just as a summerhouse, was furnished in a cozy Regency style, had a single room of around 100 sq ft (9 m^2) and a smaller attic above. He soon became very fond of the Balcombe family, who had very politely offered him the main house; which he –very politely too– had refused. In fact he was already speculating about the possibility of relaxing there and possibly writing his memoirs. Soon two accessory sheds or huts were erected by the British; one intended for dining and the other serving as a study for the Emperor, who in no time commenced to dictate the memoirs of his early campaigns to Las Cases.

Betsy, whose original full name was Lucia Elizabeth Balcombe lived between 1802 and 1871, was educated in England and could speak French. She was only 14 years old when she first met Napoleon and would leave us an interesting little book of memoirs. Her recollection of her relationship with Napoleon is quite different from any other perhaps because of her age and the fact that Napoleon seemed to have developed a real liking for this girl. He allowed her liberties unknown to those in his closer circle and Betsy, who initially had very negative feelings towards the Emperor, would change her mind shortly after meeting him. For more details about this rather peculiar relationship see the chapter 'The Briars' (see page 127).

Betsy and her family would leave Saint Helena in March 1818 and returned to England, after Hudson Lowe suspected them of smuggling secret messages out of Longwood House. She would marry Edward Abell, have a daughter and spend some years in Australia with her family before returning to London where her life finally ended. She always kept a warm remembrance of the fallen Emperor and maintained a close contact with his family.

1.   *To Befriend an Emperor. Betsy Balcombe's Memoirs of Napoleon on Saint Helena. (Originally published in 1844). Ravenhall Books.*

Betsy's memoirs were originally published in 1844 as 'Recollections of the Emperor Napoleon during the First Three Years of his Captivity on the Island of Saint Helena' as authored by Mrs. Abell (her married name).[1]

Lady Malcolm

Lady Clementina Malcolm was the eldest daughter of the Hon. William Fullerton Elphinstone, third son of the 10th Lord Elphinstone, and eldest brother of Admiral Lord Keith. She married Sir Pulteney Malcolm (1768-1838) while he was still a captain, in 1809. Being Rear-Admiral in 1813, Pulteney would be appointed third in command of the fleet engaged in the war with America and in 1815 he commanded the squadron co-operating with Wellington's army during the Waterloo campaign.

In 1816 the Admiral was appointed commander in chief of Saint Helena, and it was during the period of June 1816-July 1817, that Lady Malcolm purportedly wrote the memoir known as the 'Lady Malcolm's Diary', despite the fact that the oldest copy which has been preserved is in Sir Pulteney's handwriting, and though the entries referring to interviews at which his wife was also present may be taken as her own recollections, the greater number describe occasions when he went alone to Longwood, and it is quite clear that these were written from his dictation.

The couple was reported to have visited Longwood about twenty times and they were much liked by the Emperor, who was always ready to welcome them there enjoying some chatting, drinking tea or strolling across the small garden. Not surprisingly, the Admiral kept their discussions to non-contentious subjects like Napoleon's memories of his adventurous past and always tried to avoid any conversation connected with his present grievances, while also rendering interesting and objective reports of well known passages of the captivity as the one which happened on August 18th 1816 of the occasion of Hudson Lowe's last interview with the Emperor, that is included here for sake of comparison with the well known French accounts of the incident[2]:

'*August 18th*

The Admiral met Sir Hudson at Hutt's Gate, from whence they proceed to Longwood. On their arrival they saw Bonaparte walking at the front of the house with Madame de Montholon and Count Las

---

1.   *To Befriend an Emperor. Betsy Balcombe´s Memoirs of Napoleon on St. Helena. (Originally published in 1844). Ravenhall Books.*

2.   *See Lowe´s own report of this last interview in page 209.*

Cases; he endeavoured (sic) to avoid them. Count Montholon came to
them. Sir Hudson desired him to say to Bonaparte that he wished to
speak to him. He returned to say that the Emperor waited for us.

On joining, Bonaparte took little notice of Sir Hudson, but received
the Admiral in his usual manner, and conversed with him for a few
minutes on common subjects. Sir Hudson then addresses him nearly as
follows: 'I am sorry to importune you on any disagreeable subject, but
the very improper conduct of Count Bertrand renders it indispensable.
Having received instructions to limit the expenses at Longwood, I
mentioned the subject to Counts Bertrand and Montholon; the latter
fully met my wishes, but I was desirous to converse with yourself,
that I might be enabled to make such arrangements as would be most
agreeable to you. I came here for that purpose, but was told that you
were in the bath, and that you requested that I would communicate
with Count Bertrand. In compliance with this request I waited on the
Count, who received me in a very extraordinary manner; nevertheless
I told him my business and put the necessary papers into his hands. He
took them and said he would show them to the Emperor. I proposed to
explain, when abruptly he replied: 'The less communication you and I
have either verbally or in writing the better'.

I replied the wish was reciprocal, and left him. Now I think the
conduct of Count Bertrand towards me, as Governor of this island,
highly improper, and particularly so as I called on him in compliance
with a request of the person he acknowledges as his sovereign.

There was a silence for several minutes; they continued to walk
to and fro, Bonaparte, apparently, meditating an answer. At length,
addressing himself to the Admiral, he began: '**Count Bertrand is a man
well known, and esteemed in Europe; he has been distinguished,
and has commanded armies. 'He'** –nodding at Sir Hudson– '**treats
him like a corporal. Madame Bertrand is a lady well born, who
has been accustomed to the first place in society; he does not
treat her with the regard that is her due; he stops her letters,
and prevents her seeing those that wish to visit her, except under
restrictions.'** Then, turning to Sir Hudson, he continued: '**Since
your arrival we have experienced nothing but vexations. Your
instructions are the same as Sir George Cockburn's** –he told me
so– **but you execute them with fifty times more rigour. He never
vexed us with trifles. I had reason to be displeased with some
of his proceedings, but we never conversed that we were not
satisfied with each other; but there is no talking to you- you are
quite untractable** (sic). **You are a Lieut. General, but you do your**

duty line **un consigne** *(sic), you never commanded any men but Corsican deserters; you vex us hourly, by your little ways; you do not know how to conduct towards men of honour, your soul is too low. Why do you not treat us like prisoners of war? You treat us like Botany Bay convicts.'*

Here he stopped. Sir Hudson with much coolness replied: 'I have every desire to render your situation as agreeable as it is in my power, but you prevent me. General Bertrand has written to me that I render your situation dreadful (affreuse); he accuses me, as you do now, of abuse of power and injustice. I am the subject of a free government; I hold every species of tyranny and despotism in execration, and I will repel every attack upon my character on this point, as a calumny against a man who cannot be attacked with the arms of truth.'

Bonaparte said: **'Il y a des gens qu'on honneur et qu'on déshonneur.'** *Sir Hudson replied; 'je connais bien cette tactique, pour chercher se flétrir lorsque on ne peut pas se servir des autres armes.'*

The Admiral said he knew that Sir Hudson was very desirous to show him (Bonaparte) every attention in his power, but they did not understand each other; he was certain there was much misrepresentation, by communications coming through a third person.

Bonaparte turned to the Admiral, and said: **'Do you know he has had the meanness to keep from me a book, because on its cover I was designated Emperor, and he has boasted of having done so.'** *'I boast?' said Sir Hudson.* **'Yes,'** *added Bonaparte;* **'colonel Keating, late Governor of Bourbon, told me so.'**

Sir Hudson replied that he knew the author of that book, and was certain he would approve of its not being delivered. 'Permit me,' –said the Admiral– 'to explain to you the story of the book. Sir Hudson showed it to me, and told me the author had desired him to give it, or not, as he thought proper. The book itself was of little consequence, but Sir Hudson is forbidden to give you the title of Emperor. I think he could not with propriety have sent it you, with the inscription that is on it.'

Bonaparte replied: **'He has sent letters addressed Emperor'.** *'Yes,' –said Sir Hudson– 'but they came through the Secretary of State's office, and from your own relations, not Englishmen.' Bonaparte continued:* **'He has also had the meanness to speak of the contents of our letters that came open to him. My old mother, although I forbade her to write to me, wrote to say that she would come to**

Saint Helena and die with me. This was told round the island.' 'Not by me,' said Sir Hudson. *'Yes, by you,'* rejoined Bonaparte; *'Mr. Balcombe mentioned it.'*

The Admiral said he had never heard about the circumstance, and he knew that Sir Hudson held sacred the contents of all letters that came open to him. Bonaparte mentioned other grievance, particularly not being permitted to write notes of civility to the people of the island, except through the Governor: *'for example, suppose I wished to invite Lady Malcolm to dinner, and I put a piece of gallantry into my note, could a gentle man send this open to another for his inspection? –impossible. If I meet an officer of the 53rd regiment and am desirous to ask him to dinner, I cannot without obtaining his (Sir Hudson's) permission, for which there is not probably time.'*

Sir Hudson interrupted him, by saying that he had refused to see officers of the 66th regiment. *'Yes,'*–said Bonaparte– *'because their Colonel had not called on Marshal Bertrand to make the request.'* Sir Hudson said he had written to the Count to say he wished to introduce them. Bonaparte replied with warmth: *'I am an emperor in my own circle, and will be so as long as I live; you may make my body prisoner, but my soul is free. Europe will hereafter judge my treatment, and the shame of it will fall on the English nation; even the poor sentinels of the 53rd regiment weep at my unworthy treatment.'*

He continued: *'you ask me for money to pay for my living; I have none; but I have plenty of friends, who would send me whatever sum I required if I could write to them. Put me on rations if you please. I can dine with the officers of the 53rd regiment, and if not with them, with the soldiers.'* Sir Hudson said he had not sought the situation he now held, it was offered to him, and he would do his duty, and execute his instructions. Bonaparte replied: *'I you were ordered to assassinate me, would you do so?'* 'No,'–answered Sir Hudson, – 'I would not. My countrymen do not assassinate.' Bonaparte went on: *'I see by your arrangements that you are afraid I should escape; you take useless precautions. Why do you not tie me hand and foot? And then you will be tranquil. You are not a general, you are only a scribe of office. Tomorrow you will receive a letter from me, which I hope may be known in all Europe.'* Sir Hudson answered, that he should not have any objections, if all his proceedings were published in England and in every other country.

Bonaparte recommenced his invectives; he said Sir G. Cockburn had permitted them to correspond with people on the island on points of civility. The Admiral said he believed the change had been made, or at least intended, by Sir George, improper use having been made of the indulgence. Bonaparte exclaimed: **'The governor tells you so, but it is false.'** *Bonaparte then abused the English Government and spoke of the blind hatred of Lord Bathurst towards him.* **'It has insulted me in sending a man like you to guard me; you are no Englishman.'** *Sir Hudson replied, 'that makes me laugh.'* **'what, laugh, sir!'** *said Bonaparte, turning to Sir Hudson with a look of surprise. 'Yes, sir,' –answered Sir Hudson– 'I say what I think; I say it not only makes me laugh, but it excites my pity, to see how misinformed you are with respect to my character, and for the rudeness of your manners. I wish you good morning.' Sir Hudson then quitted him abruptly without further ceremony.*

Bonaparte stopped his walk, apparently much surprised by this sudden retreat. The Admiral said, 'I must also wish you good morning.' Bonaparte returned his bow, and desired his compliments to Lady Malcolm. During this conversation Sir Hudson never for a moment lost his temper; Bonaparte frequently, particularly when he addressed Sir Hudson. They walked to and fro in the garden, and could not fail to be overheard by Count Las Cases, madame Montholon, and Major Gorrequer, who continued walking at a little distance.[1]

William Warden

Naval surgeon William Warden (1777–1849) was appointed in 1815 to the Northumberland, ordered to convey Napoleon to Saint Helena, which enabled him to compile a memoir collected during and after the voyage published under the title of *'Letters written on board His Majesty's ship the Northumberland, and at Saint Helena: in which the conduct and conversations of*

(KGM. ©Andrea Press).

---

1. *A Diary of Saint Helena. The Journal of Lady Malcom. (1816-1817). Edited by Sir Arthur Wilson, K.CJ.E.*

Napoleon Buonaparte, and his suite, during the voyage, and the first months of his residence in that island, are faithfully described and related (...)'.

These 'letters' contain a vivid and poignant depiction of the Emperor and his entourage even though they could be not entirely reliable, due to Warden's limited knowledge of French that made necessary the intervention of Las Cases, whose translation might have been biased at least to some extent.

Warden's book, published in 1816 with notorious success, rapidly ran through five successive editions, surely thanks to the scarcity of news about Napoleon's exile at this early time of his captivity. The Emperor, here mostly favorably represented, is said to have commented on these memoirs: **'Le fonds est vrai, mais il y a cento coglione e cento bugie'**[1] *(The basis is true, but there are lots of bullshit and mistakes).* The British government and his supporters on their side disliked and criticized the book stating that Warden's account had been intentionally distorted by Las Cases' translations.

Warden´s letters read well and, even assuming some distortion by Las Cases' in the narrative, there are interesting depictions of Napoleon as seen through Warden's always inquisitive eyes; such as this of Napoleon on the very moment of his arrival to the ominous island:
'The sensation aroused in the remote Colony of Saint Helena, on the arrival of this extraordinary Guest, may be more easily imagined than described. Curiosity, astonishment, and interest combined to rouse the inhabitants from their habitual tranquility, into a state of busy activity and inquisitive solicitude.

Napoleon did not leave his cabin for a full hour after the ship had anchored in the bay; however, when the deck became clear, he made his appearance, and ascended the poop ladder, from which he could examine every gun that bristles at the mouth of James Valley, on the centre of which the town of that name, and the only one in the Island, is situated. While he stood there, I watched his countenance with the most observant attention, and it betrayed no particular sensation: He looked as any other man would look at a place which he beheld for the first time. I shall also take this opportunity to mention that, during the whole voyage, from the moment the Northumberland set sail from England, to its arrival at Saint Helena, I never saw any change in the placid countenance and unassuming manners of our distinguished shipmate; nor did I hear of a discontented look, or a peevish expression, being remarked by any other person in the ship. The Ladies, indeed,

1.   *Sainte-Hélène. Île de Mémoire. Fayard.*

experienced some distress on the first view of their rocky cage; but their general conduct on the occasion, displayed a degree of self-possession which was not expected of them.'[1]

James Roche Verling

Being appointed artillery surgeon to Saint Helena, James Roche Verling (1787-1858) would sail aboard the Northumberland all across the long journey to the island and managed to entertain an amiable relationship with the French. Especially with Montholon and Bertrand whose respective families he attended during his stay on the island. Notwithstanding, the Emperor would eventually refuse him as his personal doctor after O'Meara's parting in July 1818, as Verling had been unilaterally designated for the post by Hudson Lowe. In fact Verling was never able to meet the Emperor and had to resign himself to accompany Dr. John

(KGM. ©Andrea Press).

Stokoe –the one finally appointed as Napoleon's surgeon– in his regular visits to Longwood.

It is not surprise that Verling, being mostly relegated to the role of Sir Lowes' informer and unable to get personal or professional contact with Napoleon, finally took part against the French party and even came to state that Napoleon was feigning his illness before leaving the island in 1820.

Even though Napoleon's figure is absent in this journal, there is still some interesting material concerning the peculiarities of life and intrigues around Longwood and Plantation House.

---

1. *Letters written on board His Majesty Ship the Northumberland and at Saint Helena in which the conduct and conversations of Napoleon Buonaparte and his suite during the voyage and the first months of his residence in the island are faithfully described and related. William Warden. Ackerman. London 1816.*

The original manuscript remained unpublished in the Verling family until being presented to Napoleon III. In 1915 a copy of the original work was made and deposited at Oxford University. It was only in 2005 that the Verling memories were made accessible to the general public.[1]

John Stokoe

J'aurais vécu jusqu'a quatre-vingts ans, s'ils ne m'avaient pas amené dans cette île maudite! (I would have lived till 80 had they not brought me to this damned island!)

Such are the words allegedly pronounced by the Emperor to Dr. John Stokoe as consigned in the book the latter wrote under the title of 'With Napoleon at Saint Helena: being the memoirs of Dr. John Stokoe, Naval surgeon.'[2]

(KGM. ©Andrea Press).

Stokoe was born in 1775 in Britain and, being twenty years old, he entered the Royal Navy as Surgeon's Mate. In this capacity he would participate in the long fight entertained by Great Britain against Napoleon. He saw considerable action before departing for Saint Helena early in 1817.

Stoke was certainly not a skilful writer. His memories on Saint Helena are but one in a set of five volumes discovered by Paul Frémeaux[2] in the possession of one of Stokoe's great-grand-nieces. He was at Saint Helena just from June 1817 to September 1819 and –quite naturally– was only able to relate the events he could witness during this time. Despite its poor composition and rather boring reading, there are some fresh depictions of remarkable passages. In all, the real significance of the doctor's account should be laid in the fact that Stokoe –being an Englishman– sympathized with the Emperor much against the will of

---

1. *Napoleon and Doctor Verling on St Helena. J. David Markham. Pen & Sword, 2005.*
2. *With Napoleon at Saint Helena: being the memoirs of Dr. John Stokoe, Naval surgeon. Jonh Lane the Bodley Head. London and New York, 1902.*

Hudson Lowe, who despised and hated the young doctor. When he finally abandoned Saint Helena he would be sent back to the island upon his arrival to London, to be court martialed and discharged. Stokoe certainly had to pay a high price for contradicting the official attitude towards Napoleon imposed by the British government and so scrupulously watched over by Lowe at Saint Helena. Finally back in Britain again, he would be compensated by Napoleon's family before sailing to the United States in 1820, where he would spend two years beside Joseph: the elder brother of Napoleon.

In his memories Stokoe tell us about his second visit to Longwood on October, 10th 1817 at which he finally could not only see the Emperor but spoke to him too:

O'Meara and I had been walking for some time about the grounds at a considerable distance from the house, when we saw Napoleon come out of the billiard-room, accompanied by Count and Madame de Montholon. After taking a few turns before the house, he seated himself on the steps, with Madame de Montholon beside him, and with his back towards us. We approached to the distance of fifty yards and stopped for a minute or two, then turned to walk away. The Count came to O'Meara and asked who I was; he returned to Napoleon, and came back immediately, saying the Emperor would be glad to see me.

I was delighted, and yet I felt a dread in approaching the man whose fame as a warrior had reached the remotest corners of the earth. I followed the Count who, on coming near, took off his hat, and presented me. I did the same and made my best bow, remaining, as the Count did, with my hat off, when Napoleon, after slightly touching his, addressed me in the following words:

- Surgeon Conqueror, man-of- war. Fine ship.

Upon this O'Meara informed him I spoke Italian. On looking behind me I saw that O'Meara had his hat on, and I supposed that I should have followed his example, but it was then too late. I could not have put it on without being guilty of rudeness; therefore I remained uncovered to the end of the interview.

The first question asked in Italian was what part of Italy I had been in. I answered that Gaeta was the only place on the Continent that I had landed at, but that I had been about three years in the Mediterranean, and the greater part of that time in Sicily:

- Ah! A beautiful island, a little better than this one! Are you senior to O'Meara?

- Yes, sir, by ten years.

- Then you can command him? What service have you seen?
*- I was surgeon of a 74 in the battle of Trafalgar, and in the passage of the Dardanelles. - **What countryman are you?***
- From the north of England.
*- **That is a mountainous country, is it not?***
- It is.
*- **Are you married?***

To this question I stupidly replied 'non ancora,' when I observed a smile on Madame de Montholon´s face, and I thought there was a faint reflection of it on Napoleon's countenance, which I was puzzled to account for. O'Meara explained afterwards by telling me that I only confirmed the common report on the island that I was paying my addresses to the eldest Miss Balcombe (Jane Balcombe. Betsy Balcombe's elder sister).[1]

A couple of pages later Stokoe consigns his first impression cast on him by Napoleon:

During the short time I was in the presence of Napoleon, my opinion of his character underwent a complete change. I had formed in my own imagination the man I expected to see, but I found him so totally the reverse that I had not been two minutes in conversation with him before I felt myself as much at my ease as if talking to an equal. I am not ashamed to confess that this sudden change was accompanied with such a friendly feeling towards him, that I could have been at that moment his ambassador to Sir Hudson, to plead for a rescinding of those orders that caused him to convert his miserable retreat into a voluntary prison.[1]

Captain Nicholls

George Nicholls (1776-1857) was a captain of the 66th Regiment based at Saint Helena and one of the British officers eventually attached to Longwood commissioned to watch Napoleon at close quarters. He served from September 1818 to February 1820 and left a journal[2] covering a period in which Napoleon had no doctor; many of his most significant companions in exile had abandoned the island, and he began to be really ill. Nicholls's memoirs are boring and repetitive,

---

1. *With Napoleon at Saint Helena: being the memoirs of Dr. John Stokoe, Naval surgeon translated from the French by Paul Frémeaux. John Lane the Bodley Head. London and New York, 1902.*
2. *Journaux de Sainte-Hélène. Docteur Verling & Capitaine Nicholls. Librairie Historique F. Teissedre. Paris.*

with this pitiable officer struggling day after day around Longwood trying to check via some window that the Emperor was still there, in compliance with the orders of his feared master Hudson Lowe. Nicholls's account´s only interest resides in the scarcity of available testimonies for that crucial period of Napoleon's stay on the island.

In the last months of 1818, Napoleon used to take as many as three hot baths a day and refused to leave his inner apartments precisely to spare the humiliation of being watched by British officers on a daily basis. Such was indeed the embarrassing duty of Captain Nicholls, who on October 10th of that year reported to Hudson Lowe that he had caught sight of General Bonaparte and 'his countenance appeared excessively cadaverous and ghastly'[1]. Whatever the case, even if Nicholls was able to 'catch sight' of the illustrious prisoner sometimes, he would never meet Napoleon in person; in desperation, Hudson Lowe would even order Nicholls to enter 'General Bonaparte's' apartment, if necessary by force, to check every day that he was still there. The Emperor on his side was determined to defend his intimacy with his life, refusing the entrance of any unwelcome visitor to his private rooms; which in turn moved Lowe to relinquish his claim...

Lieutenant Basil Jackson

Jackson (1795-1889) served as Hudson Lowe's aide-de-camp in 1814 and was also present at Waterloo before being brought with the new governor to Saint Helena, where he remained until 1819. An assiduous guest at Plantation House, he was in charge of Longwood's maintenance, which considerably upset him because of the frequent repairs demanded by its French occupants; obviously not at all happy with their forced accommodation.

(KGM. ©Andrea Press).

1.   *The Drama of Saint Helena. Paul Frémeaux. New York. D. Appleton and Company, 1910.*

Jackson, never a sympathizer of Napoleon and his retinue, mostly regarded these complaints unjustified, accusing the prisoners of being exacting, always discontent, and heartily picturing 'Bonaparte' as a conceited schemer; a liar always ready to discredit his British opponents by any means.

He left a series of recollections on his stay at Saint Helena that exemplifies quite well the tone of the anti-bonapartist accounts of this history mostly promoted by the British government. Jackson's reminiscences and sincere judgments are interesting as representative of the British point of view on Napoleon and his stay on the island as can be deduced from he following fragments:

– On watching Napoleon for the first time:

'Notwithstanding my daily presence at Longwood, and often strolling round the house and in the garden, I saw nothing of our great captive for several months, all my watchings for a glimpse of him proving vain. At length, when riding one day close to the house, on turning a corner, I came upon three figures advancing, the centre person wearing his small cocked-hat square to the front, the others, one walking on each side of Napoleon, bareheaded. Turning a little aside to get out of the way, I took off my hat and made a low bow, which was returned by Napoleon raising his. He was dressed just as we see him in his portraits, viz., with a green cut-away military coat, white waistcoat, breeches, and silk stockings; of course he bore the tri-coloured cockade, and the star of the Legion of Honour.

Occasionally, but very rarely, I have seen him strolling in the garden, when, of course, I took care to avoid , if possible, his seeing me. Keeping himself, as he did, much secluded, in fact seldom leaving the house for weeks together, the orderly captain on duty, whose business it was to ascertain one way or another that the captive was safe, had an arduous and unsatisfactory task to perform.'

– Meeting Napoleon in person. Jackson being a subaltern officer could scarcely dream of it... but somehow he did it:

'When chatting one day with Count Bertrand, I expressed regret that, as a mere subaltern, I had little chance of being presented to Napoleon. To my great surprise, he said that possibly it might be managed, and he would think of it. Not long afterwards, recurring to the subject, he said that Napoleon was not indisposed to receive me, and if I would bring Major Emmett, he thought he could contrive to have us both

presented. Now Emmet (our Commanding Royal Engineer) was known to entertain very liberal sentiments in politics, and hence was in some favour at Longwood; doubtless, the idea of receiving me arose from a desire of Bonaparte to have a talk with him. On telling Emmett what Bertrand had mentioned, he was much pleased, and agreed to accompany me to Longwood.

We went thither accordingly, and, on calling at Count Bertrand's house, were told by the countess that her husband was with Napoleon; after waiting as long as politeness allowed, in expectation of the count's appearing, we took our leave, and were about to go away re infectâ *when we encountered Mr. O'Meara, and, on telling him our object, he said he thought he could assist us. He went at once to Napoleon's apartments, and returned in a few minutes to say that Napoleon would see us presently; Bertrand then came out, and desired us to follow him.*

On entering the drawing-room, we found Napoleon standing at the fireplace, leaning on the mantelshelf, with cocked-hat in hand, evidently a studied position. When we were announced he advanced towards us, and, addressing, my companion, the following dialogue took place. (I shall give Bonaparte's questions in French verbatim, *as I noted them down on the same evening.)*
Combien avez-vous de service?
Nine years.

Où avez-vous servi?
In Spain. Portugal, France, and America.

Vous avez fait des sièges?
Yes, those of Ciudad Rodrigo and Badajoz.

Vous avez manqué la brèche à Badajoz, un peu brusqué la chose?
We were obliged to risk an assault, and had it failed, we must have raised the siege. It would then have been doubtful whether, with our scanty means, the place could have been taken.

Eh! Cependant les places se prennent. Vous aviez du canon à Elvas-de combien est Elvas éloigné de Badajoz ?
Three leagues.

Ah! Trois lieues; ce seraient donc les projectiles et le transport qui auraient causé de difficultés; main la Guadiana est

navigable, n'est-ce pas ? Non, ah! Que faisiez-vous donc de votre argent? Quand il n'y a pas d'autres moyens de se rendre maître d'une place, il faute ouvrir la bourse et fermer les yeux. Napoleon then spoke of Burgos, when Emmett said that a hornwork there had created a difficulty, upon which Napoleon, with animation, said that he had ordered its construction.

Est-ce qu'il fut emporté?
Yes, on the first night.

D'assaut?
Yes, by assault.

Il n'était donc pas défendu?
It was defended, but entered by the gorge.

Est-ce que la gorge n'était pas palissadée?
The palisades were cut down.

Napoleon then referred to the celebrated lines of Torres Vedras, seeming to think that Masséna ought to have attacked them.

Lastly, Napoleon, alluding to two or three block-houses then in course of erection at the island, asked whether Emmet expected to attack them, **est-ce les rats et les souris?** We were then dismissed. During the interview, I was standing very close to the great man, observing him narrowly. I estimated his height at something under five feet seven. His make thick about the shoulders, with very short neck; eyes grey, which at times appeared devoid of expression. He was habited as I have already described him.'

- The fact that Basil met the Emperor only one time was no impediment to analyze his personality through a series of remarks as follows:
'He could not tolerate persons who were independent of him: therefore he disliked the wealthy, whilst he revered la noblesse.

It was a necessity in him to say unpleasant things to people around, and to disparage merit.

Mistrustful and on his guard with all who approached him —apt to talk too much, and then to recourir après, or seek to undo what he had said.

Ignorant on many subjects, but readily acquiring knowledge of anything worth treasuring.

Of a good disposition naturally –had much feeling– desiring affection, though doing his best to defeat such object.

Timid by nature –hence his want of ease when in company.

Constantly seeking to entrap persons, but deceiving nobody by his dissimulation.

Could bear no obstacle to his will, or contradiction, but ready to welcome truth if well motivée.

Flattery failed towards him; probity and diligence succeeded, because they served his interests; whereas flattery only touched his passions, and those he sacrificed to his interests.

Immorality le froissait *–the memoirs of Madame d'Epinay were distasteful to him.*

An organised system of espionnage *existed in his household, and he ever sought to set its members at variance, in which he was only too successful.*

Wanted good manners, from not seeing good society in early life. Often used coarse and vulgar expressions, as calling people f-------, bêtes, *etc*

Thought much of his personal appearance –anxious to learn what people said of his physique.

*Fond of teasing (*taquinerie*).*

Absence of dignity in his deportment and manner. 'Il lui manquait d'être né sur le trône'.

Thought with precision, but was diffuse in expressing his thoughts, having a poor command of words, though fancying himself master of the French language, which was not the case.

Could not have friends, for he loved no one, and frequently inflicted mortal wounds on the amour propre *of others.*

For his ministers he often selected mediocrity rather than talent, lest his projects should be penetrated.

With his servants at times too familiar —at others capricious and violent, administering coups de poing.

He had no religion —was a materialist.

Talking with a lady of rank and wit, whose father had been a fermier général *of the revenue; he asked if she remembered what Mezeray says about* fermiers généraux? *'Yes,' she replied, 'and I also remember what he says of* parvenus.' *We may feel sure that, if true, it occurred before he wore the imperial purple.*

As to his daily habits at the island, there is little to be said. He rose late, partook of a slight breakfast; often passed hours on end in a tepid bath, read after his manner, which was to glance over a page avec la pouce, *thus getting through two or three volumes in less than as many hours; dined early, usually alone, and very abstemiously, drinking a little claret and water; had a horrid habit of spitting, and when lying in bed would indulge it without regard as to where the* crachat *might fall, whether on bed-curtains or carpet. All stood in his presence, and when on his deathbed, poor Antommarchi (his doctor) was kept standing until ready to faint; slept badly, and, as we have seen, would have Montholon often roused out of bed for dictation. That Napoleon had moral courage in the highest degree is certain, but it is equally certain that he had not the kind of courage which prompted Gustavus Adolphus to rush into the midst of the fight at Lützen, or like the hero of Trafalgar, to make himself a mark for the foe by appearing in the battle decorated with* stars *and* orders. *Most assuredly, it is seldom the duty of a commander-in-chief to expose himself in the van, but occasions will arise when personal danger should not be considered. For his fame, Napoleon ought to have headed the Imperial Guard in the last onset at Waterloo; but he forgot what he told his army when about to cross the frontier —that the time arrives when very brave Frenchmen should conquer or die!'*[1]

Following this colourful portrait of Napoleon —that Jackson admittedly had to compose mostly relying on accounts from Napoleon's retinue whose company he frequented— he ended his memories engulfing himself in a long, rather dithyrambic vindication of his much admired Hudson Lowe.

---

1. *Notes and reminiscences of a Staff Officer, chiefly relating to the Waterloo Campaign and Saint Helena matters (London, Harrison &Sons, 1877. Lieutenant-Colonel Basil Jackson).*

Admiral Cockburn

Sir George Cockburn (1772-1853) was appointed by the English government to take Napoleon to Saint Helena aboard the Northumberland. He was also governor of the isle from October 1815 until April 1816. Although always polite and correct with Napoleon he didn't fail to follow orders, moving the French party to Longwood and imposing the first set of restrictive measures. Notwithstanding, and unlike his successor Sir Hudson Lowe, Cockburn managed to avoid direct confrontation with the Emperor, whose respect he enjoyed at least to some extent. Whatever the case he left Saint Helena without being received by Napoleon in the course of his last visit to Longwood when he had intended to present the new governor to him. Apparently due to a mistake in the stiff –and rather preposterous– etiquette of the Emperor's 'court'.[1]

(KGM. ©Andrea Press).

Cockburn's memoir published under the title 'Napoleon's Last Voyage'[2] narrates the crossing to Saint Helena aboard the Northumberland and contains some interesting scenes of life on board together with some candid Cockburn's remarks on Napoleon. (see page 35).

1. *'The Emperor had been in the drawing room for ten minutes chatting with the grand marshal when he was told of the governor and the admiral's presence in the parlor. At this point there was an unfortunate misunderstanding: Noverraz was on duty at the door to the drawing room. When the Emperor was receiving people, the practice was to allow only the person requested into the room where he was.' The grand marshal opened the door slightly and said to Noverraz: 'Have the governor come in.' The admiral was at the other side of the room, talking with his back turned; he did not see Sir Hudson Lowe enter, and when he presented himself, Noverraz did not dare open the door again, saying to him that only the governor had been requested. The admiral, offended, went out to the saddle horses, where the grooms were watching, took his horse, and went back to town'. Marchand Memoirs. Proctor Jones's first English edition.*
2. *Napoleon's Last Voyage. Extract from a Diary of Rear-Admiral Sir George Cockburn. Simpkin, Marshall & Co. 1888.*

Antommarchi

The Emperor suffered chronic hepatitis for a long time after O'Meara and Stoke had left the island, when the French doctor he had been insistently demanding finally arrived to Saint Helena in September 1819. This was the Corsican Francesco Antommarchi (1780-1838). This physician, selected by Cardinal Fesch was indeed not a good choice as he lacked professional experience and was probably preferred to others, more proficient

(KGM. ©Andrea Press).

doctors, in order to cut the expense. Notwithstanding Antommarchi managed to give the impression that he was a good doctor, prescribed some light remedies that alleviated Napoleon at least to some extent, and –most of all– succeeded in persuading the Emperor to do some gardening as a measure to combat his inactivity. In all Antommarchi failed to give Napoleon the attention his poor health demanded perhaps influenced by Hudson Lowe and the main officers on the island that sustained the idea that the Emperor was feigning his illness.

A skirt chaser and always an air head, Antommarchi was frequently absent from Longwood seeking diversion at Jamestown and also probably to escape the extremely boring and stifling atmosphere prevailing at Longwood. This of course aroused the displeasure of the Emperor who, enraged, dismissed Antommarchi three times even forbidding him to enter his bedroom. The last time Napoleon stated that he would not see him again and Antommarchi, very disappointed, took steps to leave Saint Helena the next morning. In fact he would be present at the moment of Napoleon's death only because he was still awaiting his permission to leave.

Antommarchi's good eye for business couldn't miss the occasion to make his stay at the island profitable. Surely inspired by the success of Las Cases' Memoire, he would publish his *'Les Derniers Moments de Napolèon'*[1] with no more than a mild success. This work, interspersed with inaccuracies and mystifications, is generally considered a second rater. Notwithstanding it contains some interesting information regarding Napoleon's autopsy and the famous –and controversial– death mask allegedly taken by Antommarchi from the corpse of the Emperor. Both subjects are dealt with in later chapters (see pages 273 and 286 respectively).

After leaving Saint Helena our doctor had a rather hazardous life in Poland, the USA and Mexico before settling in Cuba, where he finally died.

THE CHURCH

Amongst Napoleon's retinue´s many needs, spiritual relief was certainly not a priority. Sons of the French Revolution, most of them would probably be agnostics or just simple materialists in practice. In fact only Madame de Montholon is recorded as demanding the assistance of a catholic priest that could take good care of the captives' souls[2]. Being Saint Helena a British domain the Anglican Church was the prevailing religion there. So new born children delivered on the island by Montholon´s and Bertrand's ladies had to be baptized by the Anglican reverend Vernon and, when the Emperor's mysterious alter ego Cipriani died (in mysterious circumstances too), it was also Vernon who celebrated his funeral; naturally in Anglican fashion.

It was precisely upon Cipriani's death that he (Napoleon) asked his uncle Cardinal Fesch for a catholic chaplain to be sent to Saint Helena. Perhaps he was already thinking about his own death and, while not really being a man of faith, it is pretty obvious that, extremely foresighted as he was, the completion of his legend couldn't miss the presence of at least a qualified representative of the Church under which he had been crowned.

Napoleon had requested a learned, broad-minded priest able to entertain cultivated conversations, the kind he so desperately missed amidst the suffocating atmosphere reigning at Longwood and the constant quibbles –and eventual rages– of his tormented

---

1.   *The last days of the Emperor Napoleon. Doctor F. Antommarchi. London 1825.*
2.   *Sainte-Hélène. Île de Mémoire. Fayard.*

companions. Instead, Fesch just as he did with Antommarchi, failed to meet Napoleon's expectations by sending to Saint Helena a couple of Corsican priests who could only speak Corsican and Italian, not matching at all Napoleon's requirements.

One was a gouty, 67 year old deaf man: the abbé Antonio Buonavita. A missionary in Mexico in old times, he had been Madame Mère's chaplain too. He was affected by a number of illnesses that didn't improve under Saint Helena's climate and had to leave the island on March 1821. His rather non significant role in this drama practically consisted in celebrating Sunday's masses. Buonavita would disembark in Europe to find that the Emperor had already died. After some bitter disagreement with Madame Mère about his pension he returned to his old missionary life until his death in 1833.

The other was a more colorful, younger priest intended to be an assistant to Buonavita: the abbé Ange Paul Vignali, another rough Corsican who was hot off the seminary and, like Buonavita, quite deficient in manners and education; even though it seemed he had some medical knowledge... At least he was more active than his elder, to whom he assisted in marrying Saint-Denis and Mary Hall, besides baptizing a couple of newborns or teaching Bertrand's children Latin. In all, a prominent feature of Vignali's personality was probably a daring sense of humour, as shown by the practical joke he played in July 1820, when dressed like Napoleon galloped in front of the astonished English garrison[1]. (See page 263).

But doubtless the most significant service rendered by Vignali at Longwood was being Napoleon's last chaplain who administered his last sacraments and performed his funeral.

Back in his birthplace Vignali remained there until his death in June 1836. Involved in a family vendetta he was shot by an unknown murderer...

The priest Ange Paul Vignali. (KGM. ©Andrea Press).

---

1.   *Sainte-Hélène. Île de Mémoire. Fayard.*

THE DOMESTIC STAFF

Most of Napoleon's servants at Saint Helena had also been in the Emperor's service before the captivity. A majority of them also set an unparalleled example of loyalty under difficult circumstances. They never failed either in keeping the stiff etiquette judged by Napoleon as inalienable from his imperial status. Accordingly, all his retainers wore at Saint Helena the same livery they sported at the Tuileries: a green frock embroidered in gold or silver; fine wool white waistcoats; black silk breeches; white silk stockings and black buckled shoes. Clad in these anything but comfortable outfits, they performed their duties to perfection until the end...

Noverraz

At Longwood, those ingratiated by the Emperor with an audience would face at the threshold of the room in which Napoleon was about to receive them a gigantic man of imposing appearance, clad in the resplendent imperial livery: Noverraz.

(*KGM.*
©*Andrea Press*).

The Swiss Jean Abram Noverraz (1790-1849) was a surly man of about 190 cm. (6 feet 2.8 inches) in height. He had entered the Emperor's service as a footman in 1809 proving to be a fully loyal and dependable butler, ready at anytime to risk his life to protect his beloved Emperor. Such was the case at the time of Napoleon's first abdication in 1814, when the Emperor was crossing Provence on the way to Elba and Noverraz kept him holding his sword against the enraged, menacing populace that surrounded them when reaching Orgon in April of that year. Napoleon by his side was very fond of Noverraz whom he nicknamed the '*Ours d'Helvétie*' (Swiss Bear), bequeathed a considerable sum in his testament and even appointed him depositary of some precious hunting items that were to be delivered to his son when he turned sixteen years old.

Once at Saint Helena Noverraz would marry Joséphine Brulé; Madame de Montholon´s chambermaid whom he would divorce in 1828. Back in France Noverraz would still leave his pleasant villa of *La Violette* to join the 'Return of the Ashes' expedition; sailing to Saint Helena for the last time to recover the remains of the Emperor in 1840. Long after his death a book titled '*Souvenir de l'empereur Napoléon 1er. Journal des cendres*' was published in 1941. Apparently written or dictated by Noverraz, its authenticity is still matter of some debate.

Noverraz's bibliographical references include an interesting interview published in the '*Le Magasin Pittoresque*' in 1840 in which he stated that:

> '*Marchand and I took shifts for watching the Emperor every night; he loved this attention and repeated to us how sensitive he was. He didn't speak but he liked being spoken to. He was absolutely not so overweight as has been told; he has been represented in caricature and not as he really was; his complexion had been only altered by the illness but his size remained basically the same.*
>
> *He has been commonly depicted as irascible and violent; he was indeed a family man, and he told us often that he couldn't live if we were pushed aside from him; when somebody disappointed him, he just showed a cold silence. Those that thought they could win him by flattering or deference normally failed. He was especially fond of Caulaincourt; he appreciated his frankness and firmness. He didn't like always being told that he was right. I have an excellent memory, he didn't ignore that: when discussing with his Marshalls upon a matter known to me, he immediately called me and made me recall the thing as it really happened; he mostly resorted to me, because he knew I would tell the truth regardless of anyone, including himself; I have hundreds of times sustained statements he denied, and denied those he confirmed. Far from being irritated or disappointed I could see that this independence didn't displease him.*
>
> *Regarding his so often reproached ambition, I heard him many times saying that:*
>
> **'The French have not understood me. They have accused me of personal ambition, and I strove only for them. I wanted France to be what it should be, what its geographical position demanded it to be in Europe."**

Cipriani

Cipriani Franceschi –or rather Jean Baptiste Cipriani– was in all probability the most mysterious character around Napoleon in Saint Helena. Even his birth date, which was either 1773 or 1780 in the little Corsican village of Guano, is open to debate. Born out of wedlock, his entire life seemed to have been shrouded in mystery and tragedy even from his early childhood; when his mother was reportedly found strangled in her bed...

(KGM. ©Andrea Press).

Family ties between Cipriani's mother and the Bonapartes would explain how he was brought up in close relationship with the future Emperor and his brothers. It has even been suggested that Cipriani's mother could have been the lover of Napoleon's father; who would have even considered marrying the unfortunate woman. Whatever the case, the fact is that Napoleon and Cipriani were very close during their childhood.

In 1793 Cipriani would have accompanied Saliceti at the siege of Toulon in time to witness the striking success of the young Bonaparte. Much later, in 1806, Cipriani was in the court of the new King of Naples (Napoleon's elder brother Joseph) serving in the minister Saliceti's household. The Corsican *Antoniu Cristufaru Saliceti* is also interesting to this story as a significant revolutionary politician who, among other things, backed Napoleon's promotion to General after the siege and... was thought to be Cipriani's real father too.

Cipriani was a cold, intelligent man whose lack of formal education was no obstacle to performing excellent service as a spy or secret agent dealing with delicate and obscure matters. An early and notable example was his intervention in the political intrigue resulting in the capitulation of the isle of Capri when –amazing coincidence– the commander in chief of the garrison was Hudson Lowe... Both men's paths would cross again many years later at Saint Helena, where the two shadowy characters could employ themselves in what probably was their shared main interest: intrigue.

After Saliceti's death in 1809, Cipriani –probably financed by the Fesch family[1]– become a successful businessman in Genoa, running a fleet of merchant ships. At the time of the Emperor's first abdication in 1814 –and quite strangely– Cipriani left his lucrative business to join Napoleon in Elba. The grounds on which Cipriani made such a critical decision are only open to speculation; including the possibility that he was already serving the English as a spy very close to Napoleon who, in any case, had Cipriani arranging some obscure affairs on the continent at that time...

Besides any possible surreptitious activity, Cipriani's official role at Elba was that of *Maître d'Hotel*, a position he would maintain during the Hundred Days and also at Saint Helena, where he would follow the Emperor, remaining at his service till the end of his life which happened on February, 27th 1818, when he died in mysterious circumstances too. According with Georges Retif[2] and later Bruno Roy-Henry[3] Cipriani served as a spy on Napoleon directly reporting to Hudson Lowe. His secrecy and dubious movements soon raised suspicions among Napoleon's retinue –especially Gourgaud. The Emperor, who initially disregarded any questioning on Cipriani's loyalty, finally surrendered to the evidence entirely withdrawing his confidence in his old servant and –at least to some extent– confidant, who repented and ashamed would have put an end to his life with arsenic. Cipriani was doubtless a fascinating character in this drama whose intervention goes beyond his death as we will see in a later chapter (see page 292).

While Cipriani's only known portrait is a sketchy caricature by Ibbetson[4], most knowledge about him should be extracted from the memories and accounts such as the following excerpt from Marchand's:
    'To this pitiful departure (Gourgaud) followed fifteen days later a moving and regrettable death for the entire colony. Cipriani had just died, overtaken by death in only two days; he succumbed to acute intestinal pains which appeared all of a sudden. The Emperor truly missed him, telling me that he would have accompanied him in his grave, had it been within the enclosure. A large number of dignitaries and garrison officers joined the whole French colony to the Plantation

---

1.   *A noble family from Basel influential in European affairs from mid 16th century. Cardinal Joseph Fesch was the uncle of Napoleon and as such a member of the imperial family during Napoleon's rule.*
2.   *'Anglais, rendez-nous Napoléon'. Georges Retif. Jérôme Martineau, éditeur. (1969).*
3.   *'Napoléon. L'énigme de l'exhumé de Sainte-Hélène'. Bruno Roy-Henry. L'Archipel. (2001).*
4.   *Known for his sketches of Napoleon, Denzil Ibbetson (1788-1857) sailed to Saint Helena on the Northumberland with Napoleon, and was one of only four English officers to remain there for the duration of the captivity.*

House. I was the only one beside the Emperor that sad day. General Gourgaud, who had not yet left the island, asked to join the cortege but was not allowed.

I had known Cipriani very well on the isle of Elba; he had then a charming young woman and two children that he had brought with him; I had known his joys and pains, and our friendship from the isle of Elba would only grow at Saint Helena. Cipriani was Corsican and he has been practically raised in Napoleon's home. He thought his mother had a mysterious death and told how she had been found strangled in her bed. Grown into a young man, he found a protector in M. Salicetti, then in Italy. He became superintendent of his household and, in view of his rare intelligence, commissioned with sensitive missions which he successfully accomplished. In no time he would be involved in secret police affairs and, had his protector not died, he would have gained a high position.

Having acquired a considerable amount of money, he became a ship owner and ran a sailing business. When 1815 took him by surprise whilst in this situation, he decided to enter Napoleon's service as a butler and followed him to Elba. Cipriani was very fond of the Emperor, he was a very tempered man with a good heart and a sensitive soul. He died of an inflammation of the lower abdomen showing the most alarming symptoms that became critical in no time. The Emperor, very worried, sent me at every moment for news. On the first day, he could yet tell me about his wife and his children whom he commended to the Emperor.

In the night of the 25th to the 26th the Emperor had Dr. O'Meara come and asked him if his presence could have a 'healthy effect on Cipriani'; the doctor advised on the contrary saying that he was still conscious enough and that the emotional arousal caused by his love and devotion for him could hasten his death. The next morning Cipriani had ceased to exist. Cipriani was a self-made man, he had seen plenty and learned much, which made his conversation interesting and amusing. He was a dependable man, his feelings were republican and he admired the Girondists, of whom he had known and befriended some. May these memories still inside me grace him.'[1]

---

1.   *Mémoires de Marchand. Libraire Plon. Paris 1952.*

Pierron

Jean-Baptiste Alexandre Pierron (1790-1876) lived a long life mostly dedicated to his beloved Emperor. *'Officier de Bouche'*[1] in the service of Napoleon he excelled on the making of pastries and candies that sweetened the lives of the French retinue – children especially– at Saint Helena, in a similar way as he had previously done at the Tuileries and Elba. Just like Marchand or Ali, Pierron set an extraordinary example of love and loyalty to Napoleon until the end of his life and took part in the *'Retour des Cendres'* sailing one last time to Saint Helena to recover Napoleon's corpse.

(KGM. ©Andrea Press).

Besides his culinary capabilities Pierron was a veritable factotum to the Emperor, who trusted and commissioned him with confidential affairs taking advantage of the relative freedom of movements he enjoyed on the island as, being in charge of Longwood's pantry, he was allowed to go to Jamestown frequently to purchase the many provisions needed and... served as a secret courier for the French party.

Back in France after Napoleon's death, Pierron married a young woman and carried a quiet life before dying of old age in Paris.

The Archambault Brothers

Achille (1792-1858) and his younger brother, Joseph (1796-1874) were born out of wedlock and when their mother died, they went into the hospice. It is not clear how they entered the imperial stables but at any rate they were serving Napoleon during the Empire and were with him at Elba, during the Hundred Days and Waterloo; where Achille

---

1. *An old term designating the master of fine dining for French royalty.*

was one of those left in charge of the Emperor's carriage. As recounted by Saint-Denis, Achille was unable to save the carriage, but managed to rescue some belongings:

'The Emperor's couch was seized during the evening. The postilion Horn, who drove it, unable to pass trough the mess of carts and other vehicles obstructing the road, seeing the Prussian cavalry on the point of cutting him off, and also seeing cannon balls and bullets falling around him, unhitched the horses, while the first foot butler, Archambault, took the portfolio and toilet case out of the carriage. The coach was almost immediately taken by the Prussians, who plundered it, as they did with Marchand's, which contained the Emperor's clothes.'[1]

Once at Saint Helena Achille would become head groom seconded by Joseph. Achille's role at the island obviously being of no foremost relevance, there are just a handful of anecdotes illustrating his character. The next one by Betsy Balcombe that happened sometime during Napoleon's stay at the Briars is one of them:

Achille Archambault. (KGM. ©Andrea Press).

'One day, Archambault, his groom, was breaking in a beautiful young Arab, which had been bought for the Emperor to ride. The colt was plunging and rearing in the most frightful manner, and could not be induced to pass a white cloth which had been purposely spread on the lawn to break him from shying. I told Napoleon it was impossible that he could ever ride that horse, it was so vicious. He smiled, and beckoning to Archambault, desired him to dismount; and then, to my great terror, he himself got on the animal, and soon succeeded in making him not only pass the cloth, but put his feet upon it; and then rode him over and over it several times. Archambault, it seemed to me, hardly knew whether to laugh or cry.'

---

1.   *Souvenirs du Mameluck Ali sur L'Empereur Napoléon. Payot, Paris 1926.*

He was delighted with his Emperor's prowess, but mortified at his managing a horse so easily which he had been trying in vain to subdue.[1]

Betsy also throws some light on Achilles's character as being very skilled and daring with horses, but somehow missed portraying his fondness for spirited drinks and his bravado, as reflected by the English surgeon Dr. Walter Henry reporting an incident which happened in September 1817 in the course of a horse racing:

'A certain half-mad and drunken 'piqueur' of Napoleon, named Archambault, took it into his head to gallop within the ropes when the course was cleared and the horses coming up. For this transgression he was pursued by one of the stewards, and horse-whipped outside the forbidden limits. This gentleman knew not that the offender belonged to the Longwood establishment, or he would, no doubt, have spared his whip; particularly as Napoleon was sitting on a bench outside his residence watching the crowd through a glass; and we were apprehensive that he might interpret the accidental chastisement his servant received as a premeditated insult to the master. But we did Napoleon injustice by this supposition. Dr. O'Meara told me the next day that he had distinctly witnessed everything and had been very angry when he saw Archambault galloping alone along the course, and was pleased to see him chastised, and that he had called him to his presence, and expended on him a few 'f-bêtes!' and sacrés cochons!'[2]

Like some other young men in Napoleon's entourage Achilles was naturally interested in women and eventually would fall madly in love with a mulatto girl called Mary Ann Foss; much to the disappointment of the Emperor who forbade the marriage. Achilles would remain on Saint Helena until the very end besides his beloved Emperor. Once back in France he married and raised a family and would even be back to the Tuileries as an usher after the revolution of 1830. Ten years later he was ready to return to Saint Helena to retrieve Napoleon's remains. It would be only during the reign of Napoleon III that Achilles would finally obtain the funds bequeathed to him by Napoleon together with the Legion of Honour.

Like his fellow servants Santini and Rousseau, Joseph Archambault had to leave Saint Helena in October 1816 as part of Hudson Lowe's measures to reduce Longwood's household expenses. After disembarking in Europe he would sail to the United States where he met Joseph Bonaparte at the beginning of a new adventurous life in

---

1.   *To Befriend an Emperor. Betsy Balcombe´s Memoirs of Napoleon on St. Helena. (Originally published in 1844). Ravenhall Books.*

2.   *The Drama of Saint Helena. Paul Frémeaux. New York. D. Appleton and Company, 1910.*

America. There he married, fathered five children and made his living performing various different occupations, such as dentist, shopkeeper or hotelier. He sailed to France in 1856 to meet his brother Achille one last time, before returning to the USA to join the union cavalry and fight in the American Civil War. Being promoted to the rank of major and the fact that he was then 65 years old give us an idea of the kind of man he was. He died in Philadelphia at the age of 77.

Santini

Jean Noël Santini (1790-1862), like the majority of Napoleon's French servants at Saint Helena, was also in the Emperor's service before the captivity. He was a Corsican that served as a drummer in his childhood before entering the Emperor's service. He would later serve him too in Elba and Saint Helena as an usher; at least officially, as in fact Santini was a kind of handyman that repaired Napoleon's clothes, dressed his hair and –being a remarkable shooter– was also able to supply the Longwood's pantry with partridges and doves.

(KGM. ©Andrea Press).

Santini was a noble and temperamental, mercurial man that regretted Napoleon's miseries on the island very deeply. At a given point he was even determined to kill Hudson Lowe and he could be only stopped by Napoleon in person after Cipriani had informed the Emperor on Santini's intentions.

According to Marchand:
'Santini's anger against the Governor became more dangerous every day. His fellow countryman Cipriani was forced to restrain him from committing a crime. He had shared with him his plan to wait for the Governor in the woods and free the Emperor from this wretch with a shot of his musket. Cipriani being unable to cool off the man he so well knew let the Emperor know, so that he could reason with him about his outburst.

*The Emperor called immediately for Santini and told him: **'What, you rascal, you want to kill the Governor? Don't you see that I would be blamed for giving the order! Oh fie! Commiting an assasination! I forbid you from now on to think like that! If you put your mind to it again, I will oblige you to leave the island.'** All these words from the Emperor were said in Corsican. Santini answered in the same language that it was revenge and not an assassination: **'very well,** the Emperor said to him getting up from the sofa bed on which he was seated, **if this is revenge, I forbid you to carry it out.'** Santini left promising not to dwell on the matter anymore. However the Emperor told me to advice Cipriani to convince him in order to prevent such a crime being committed. Santini had served in the Corsican Legion commanded by colonel Ornano. He had left this post to become a staff courier. He kept on serving in the same position at Fontainebleau when the Emperor abdicated in 1814. Introduced to the great Marshall count Bertrand by general Ornano, he was allowed to go to Elba and was appointed keeper of the portfolio (gardien de portefeuille). He kept this post during the Hundred Days, and as such came to Saint Helena. His duties became insignificant; he waited the table and spent the mornings hunting. Smart, he managed to create a coat for the Emperor, flannel vests and even shoes, cut the Emperor's hair and fixed his chapeau liners when necessary. All these chores were not enough to keep him fully occupied. He often partook with Cipriani his desire to return to Europe to inform the world, he said, about the bad treatment given to the Emperor.*

The Emperor didn't ignore Santini's feelings and –trusting his discretion– the moment arrived to put it to the test. He summoned him, instructed him at length on what he should say to his family, and delivered to him a copy written on satin of the protest dictated on August 18th to the count of Montholon, to make it known once he had returned to Europe providing he could escape being searched by Hudson Lowe's agents. The Emperor dismissed him with the assurance that his family would take care of him."[1]

When in October 1816 Lowe judged Napoleon's household expenses unbearable he ordered the departure of a number of people, including Santini. He was forced to leave the island –much to the regret of the Emperor– but would pass Napoleon's objection alluded by Marchand sewn into his coat lining revealing it to the public immediately upon his arrival to London. Shortly after, Santini would be back to his beloved Corsica where he spent the rest of his days...

---

1. *Mémoires de Marchand. Libraire Plon. Paris 1952.*

Coursot

Jacques Coursot (1786-1856) arrived on Saint Helena on September 21st 1819 in the company of the priests Buonavita and Vignali and Napoleon's last cook Chandelier. The four men had been longingly awaited by the captives as they were supposed to be a relief –both material and psychological– after the long years of captivity and privations on the claustrophobic island. While the priests largely failed to meet Napoleon's expectations, this is not the case of Coursot or Chandelier, whose services at Longwood were highly appreciated.

Coursot had been *maître 'd'hôtel* of *Madame Mère'* (Napoleon's mother) and performed as such during the nineteen months he stayed on the island. By enrolling as a General Gourgaud's servant, he managed to return to Saint Helena for the recovery of Napoleon's remains despite the fact that he was in principle not included among the participants on the expedition. The Emperor left him 25,000 francs that served Coursot to spend his last years peacefully in his natal town of Vitteaux, amidst the appreciation and respect of his fellow citizens.

Joséphine Brulé

In the early 19th century, on a small, isolated island in the middle of nowhere where everything but a terrible boredom was lacking, men –specially the young men in Napoleon's company– anxiously longed and looked for ... pretty women.

The alluring eyes of Joséphine Brulé –Countess of Montholon´s chambermaid– drove Noverraz and Ali crazy and led them to fight for her favour. Finally the first would win marrying the girl that, upon leaving her mistress, would join the Longwood household as laundry supervisor and possibly donning a much needed feminine touch during the oppressive, sad end of this drama at the time of Napoleon's illness and death.

Considering that Josephine divorced Noverraz once back in Europe in 1828, it is not clear if she married him out of love or perhaps just to evade following Madame Montholon when she left the island. In any case she had a business eye and collected a considerable amount of lingerie embroidered with a letter N which still appears in specialized auctions nowadays...

Catherine Sablon

According to Marchand:

'Having known that his cook[1] was ill, the Emperor requested news from Dr. O'Meara; who replied that, although young, he is a worn- out man with not many years left and that he must be replaced for some days. The Governor being informed about this circumstance, offered a Belgian girl serving him that spoke French and knew how to cook. Despite the Emperor's repugnance to accept anyone coming from Hudson Lowe, he allowed Cipriani, his maître d'hôtel, to use her. Her cooking was not bad: she had a soup recipe much liked by the Emperor: it consisted on two yolks with a bit of flour forming a light paste that she threw over the broth at the moment of maximum boiling. She stayed at Longwood all through Lepage's illness and, when he entered his convalescence, the Emperor decided to retain her. Some months later she married the cook giving later birth to a girl, but then her formerly sound health became poor and, that of her husband no better; both had to abandon the island returning to France where Lepage died a year later. He was substituted by an Englishman; son of a French and a mediocre cook that would keep the post until the arrival of Chandelier, sent by princess Pauline.'[2]

This 'Belgian Girl' alluded by Marchand was Marie Catherine Sablon, born in Belgium in 1784. As with many newborns in that pre-contraceptive era, Catherine was conceived out of wedlock, in a humble environment. She is known to have been working as a cook in Brussels in 1809, giving birth there to a daughter –natural too– in 1810.

It has been speculated that she could have been in Hudson Lowe's service in Belgium in 1815, but, in principle, Lowe's rank at the time (Colonel) wouldn't be high enough to support a private cook. Why, how and when Catherine arrived to Saint Helena is not precisely known. Probably she was in the service of some English official or military officer. Perhaps Colonel Mark Wilks, the new governor who arrived on the island in 1813; as she is known to have been in the Plantation house's service that year.

In June 1816 Catherine Sablon (also named Jeannette or Finnette in some accounts) arrived at Longwood for the pleasure of Napoleon,

---

1. *NOTE FROM THE ORIGINAL TEXT: Michel Lepage –formerly Joseph Bonaparte's cook– became Napoleon's cook rather accidentally, when his predecessor Joseph Rousseau refused to go to Saint Helena. Then the Emperor's brother gallantly gave him up. Eventually Napoleon –mostly a simple-food eater– would not really care much for the elaborated 'cuisine' of his brother's cook.*
2. *Mémoires de Marchand. Libraire Plon. Paris 1952.*

who seems to have enjoyed her cooking. Lepage on his side would have been even happier –even if it was for different reasons– as they would be very soon living together. As a result, Catherine would give birth to another girl in mid 1817; typically born out of wedlock.

Lepage's family left Saint Helena in June 1818 only arriving in Paris in early 1819, after a pretty hazardous long voyage during which they were accosted by English and French authorities always suspicious of the couple because of their proximity to the Emperor. However –and most probably– Lepage and Catherine had no political implication or closeness of any kind with the great man as they were merely kitchen servants.

Although, according with Marchand, Lepage died in 1819, there seems to be no documentary evidence supporting that date nor, on the other hand, any further notice about him. Catherine's fate is not much different: a two-time widow, she remarried in 1831 and 1836. After that her memory vanished into the dust of History...

Mary Hall

Let's once again refer to Marchand´s account of Mary Hall:

Saint-Denis, whom the Emperor appreciated, had married a charming young English girl who was as sweet as kind and beautiful; she had been sent from London to educate Miss Hortense Bertrand, today Mrs. Thayer. The Emperor had opposed this marriage out of affection for Saint-Denis; without any benefit, and which would deprive Countess Bertrand of her daughter's governess. He demands waiting six months before

(KGM. ©Andrea Press)

the wedding, thinking that time would change Saint-Denis' mind. But that time passed and feelings remained the same. Priest Bonavita blessed the marriage, but was sharply reprimanded by the Emperor for having celebrated it without letting him know in advance. When all was over, the Emperor said nothing more; Saint Denis had in Miss Hall a charming wife and his children an excellent mother.[1]

Bernard Heymann and his wife had been serving the Bertrand family for years and loyally followed them to Saint Helena. Once on the isle Bernard, perhaps out of the unbearable boredom reigning all over the place, became excessively fond of spirited beverages and, at a given point, Bertrand decided to send the Heymann couple and their child back to Europe.

New servants were then recruited in Europe including Mary Hall. She was a charming English girl sent to Saint Helena by countess Bertrand's aunt, lady Jerningham in June 1818[2]. So Mary entered the Longwood scene: a blonde, pretty girl immediately wooed by the young men around, always desperately in need of female companions. One of them was Saint-Denis who didn't waste time and married her in October 1819. Though initially the Emperor opposed the marriage (as stated above by Marchand) he would relent after some months and, when Mary gave birth to her first child, a girl, he would present the baby with a beautiful gift. It seems Mary and her husband were very close to each other all during their lives. Back in France she became naturalized French and had other two daughters. She died in 1841.

Esther Vesey

If white women on Saint Helena were certainly a small number, the situation at Longwood was much worse; especially for the young single men in the French party. Under these circumstances, finding a suitable wife was certainly not easy and women like Joséphine Brulé, Catherine Sablon or Mary Hall would be practically wooed and coupled upon arrival. So, there being not enough women for everybody, the racist feeling so common in the 19th century relaxed and men resorted to entertain coloured females.

Half breeds seem to have been second preferred choices. Such

1. *Mémoires de Marchand. Libraire Plon. Paris 1952.*
2. *Souvenirs du Mameluck Ali (Louis-Étienne Saint-Denis) Sur L'Empereur Napoléon. Payot, Paris 1926.*

was the case of Esther Vesey, a maid in the service of the countess of Montholon. She had been fathered by an English garrison soldier and was reportedly a fine looking girl, not passing unnoticed by the restless eyes of Longwood's males including the Emperor...

Finally it would be Marchand the fortunate in winning Esther's favors, who soon became his mistress and pregnant. When Napoleon ordered her to leave Longwood for unclear reasons, she would still discreetly visit Marchand there on Sundays (his free time). Marchand must have been very fond of this woman, as he recognized her son Jimmy Vasey as his. She gave birth to a second child in 1821 of unknown father.

When Marchand left, Esther would remain there until her death in Jamestown in 1838.[1]

---

1. *Sainte-Hélène. Île de Mémoire. Fayard.*

The Briars Pavilion.

THE BRIARS

'C'est le diable qui a chie cette île en volant d'un monde à l'autre'[1]

ailing round the isle from the south to take advantage of favourable winds, the Northumberland entered Jamestown dock from the west immediately before mooring at Saint Helena on the morning of October 15th 1815.

First to go ashore were Cockburn and Colonel Bingham, the new commander of the garrison[2] to pay the obligatory visit to the Governor Colonel Wilks, during which the government instructions regarding Napoleon were carefully examined. The three of them would be back on the Northumberland by noon. Wilks, somewhat relegated to a secondary position after Cockburn was invested as the top authority on the island, probably relaxed enough to make a favourable impression on Napoleon, with whom he even entertained a conversation about India[3].

At the Jamestown roadstead one can imagine the anchored Northumberland and its constrained French passengers; their anxiety, low spirits and uncertainty after the long months of seclusion incarcerated in the claustrophobic cabins, continually being watched by curious and even hostile eyes...

Next day Cockburn disembarked again, this time to ride all around the island in search of a convenient lodgement for his prisoners. Exhausted, he was back to the ship in the early evening happy enough to announce to the French that he had found a proper place on the

---

1. *'That's the devil who shat this island when flying from one world to the other'. A spontaneous comment from one of the French dames upon her first sight of Saint Helena. La Vie quotidienne à Sainte-Hélène au temps de Napoléon. Gilbert Martineau. Tallandier.*

2. *Sir George Ridout Bingham (1877-1833) was the new commander of the 53rd foot regiment based on the island. He has been usually reported as being a gentleman and appreciated by the Emperor, even though he wrote in his diary the following remark as quoted by J.R. Rose in his Life of Napoleon I: 'You have no idea of the petty intrigues of himself (Napoleon) and his retinue: if Sir H. Lowe has firmness enough not to give way to them, he will in a short time treat him in the same manner. For myself, it is said I am a favourite (of Napoleon), though I do not understand the claim I have to such'.*

3. *Wilks´ conversations with Napoleon would be published in 1901 by the Monthy Magazine under the title 'Colonel Wilks and Napoleon' referred in 'La Vie quotidienne à Sainte-Hélène au temps de Napoléon'. Gilbert Martineau. Tallandier.*

Longwood plateau: the summer residence of the lieutenant governor colonel Skelton. The bad news –to the dismay of the French– was that enlargement and refurnishing works would take at least four months before occupying the house. In the meantime –the admiral added– a temporary lodging had been found in Jamestown, just beside the Castle[1]. This was a relatively modest building called Porteous House[2]. The French should have received this news with considerable relief, as anything would be better than living four more months aboard the inhospitable ship.

However, Porteous House's facilities could scarcely meet the minimum requirements expected by Napoleon. It was a two story building not large enough to host the entire French party, with no garden and which opened directly to the main street, so exposing the illustrious captive to nosey passers-by. In addition Napoleon's room was too small and offered no privacy. As a matter of fact he would stay at Porteous House just one night; between the 17th and 18th October 1815, after finally disembarking at 21:00 hours at dusk, probably trying to avoid or minimize the great expectation caused by his arrival on the island, as by then most people in Saint Helena were aware of Napoleon's arrival and there were already people poking around eager to catch a glimpse of the great man. Let's have eyewitness Betsy Balcombe picturing the scene:

> *'We were so eager to see the illustrious exile that we determined to go in the evening to the valley to witness his disembarkation. It was nearly dark when we arrived at the landing place, and shortly after, a boat from the Northumberland approached, and we saw a figure step from it onto the shore[3], which we were told was the Emperor, but it was too dark to distinguish his features. He walked up the lines between the Admiral and General Bertrand, and enveloped as he was in his surtout, I could see little, but the occasional gleam of a diamond star, which he*

---

1. *Former Governors' residence placed at the entrance to Jamestown, just beside the port. It became an administrative building –including the governor's office– once Plantation House was built.*

2. *Porteous House was sold in 1937 and demolished to allow the building of a garage. By amazing coincidence, Napoleon's room at the house had been occupied 10 years earlier by Sir Arthur Wellesley, later duke of Wellington. (Sainte-Hélène. Île de Mémoire. Fayard.)*

3. *Eventual visitors to the island might find it interesting that the stairs at the dock usually depicted as those stepped by the Emperor on his arrival are not such, as Jamestown's present configuration differs from that of 1815. At that time there were three stairs running from east to west, the middle one being the oldest that is today used by fishermen and was the real one taken by Napoleon. The Emperor didn't walk along the way used today. In 1815 the path leading to the town passed the wall into the fortified enclosure by a spot east of the porch running all along the inside on one level with the crenels facing to the sea and leading to a drawbridge still visible today besides the swimming pool built on the moat. (La Vie quotidienne à Sainte-Hélène au temps de Napoléon. Gilbert Martineau. Tallandier.)*

wore on his heart. The whole population of Saint Helena had crowded to behold him, and one could hardly have believed that it contained so many inhabitants. The pressure became so great that it was only with difficulty that a way could be made for him, and the sentries were at last ordered to stand with fixed bayonets at the entrance from the lines to the town, to prevent the multitude from pouring in. Napoleon was excessively provoked at the eagerness of the crowd to get a peep at him, more particularly as he was received in silence though with respect. I heard him afterwards say how much he had been annoyed at being followed and stared at like a wild animal.

We returned to the Briars that night to talk and dream of Napoleon.'[1]

Despite Marchand's efforts to fix Napoleon's room properly 'his majesty' found it extremely uncomfortable and spent most of his first night at Saint Helena awake until the wee hours, speculating about Longwood in the belief that by no means could it be worse than Porteous House. Cockburn arrived at 6:30 and, having to wait on horseback at the entrance for the Emperor, visibly disappointed, pronounced some crude words that should have confirmed to Napoleon his true position on this his first morning at Saint Helena: that of a defenceless prisoner. Given the circumstances all that he can say is groaning that **'Monsieur l'amiral est un grossier personnage'[2]**

Finally the Emperor, escorted by Cockburn, Bertrand and Ali started riding up the steep and winding road (about 6 miles) to Longwood, where colonel Skelton and his wife –who was very impressed by the presence of the Emperor there– managed to do their very best to welcome Napoleon with a splendid breakfast. Notwithstanding Mrs. Skelton's culinary skills couldn't have favorably influenced Napoleon's judgement as, according with Marchand:

'The Emperor, on arrival to Longwood, was not very enthusiastic about the house that was without shade or water and exposed to the ever present south-east wind that was blowing strongly at that time. He immediately overviewed the pending works before occupying the place and paid little attention to all that the admiral told him about the building and embellishments works'[3]

---

1. *To Befriend an Emperor. Betsy Balcombe´s Memoirs of Napoleon on St. Helena. (Originally published in 1844). Ravenhall Books.*

2. *'The admiral is a coarse character'. Général baron Gourgaud. Journal de Sainte-Hélène 1815-1818.*

3. *Mémoires de Marchand d'après le manuscrit original par Jean Bourguignon. Plon, Paris 1952.*

In a similar way that the decision of taking Napoleon to Saint Helena keeps sparking pro Napoleon historians and sympathizers, hosting him in Porteous House and the choice of Longwood as his permanent residence, has been traditionally accounted as a decision aimed to degrade Napoleon's status, intended more as a punishment than just out of security reasons. However, all this lodging business put into perspective, the truth is that the only place on Saint Helena matching Napoleon's 'requirements' was Plantation House that, being the Governor's residence, couldn't at any rate have been given to Napoleon but, even if he had been allowed to occupy Plantation House that –quite probably– would have not stopped the incessant flow of complaints produced by the French party all along their stay on the island.

It was probably Wilks who made this rather improvised decision about Longwood, just attending to availability and security reasons, but also setting the stage for the final act in Napoleon's amazing life. On his side, the Emperor would eventually develop a special relation with Longwood. He never missed an opportunity to remark how inhabitable this house was while, at the same time, showing no interest at all for the new prefabricated building specially designed in a hurry by the British that supposedly should gain his content (Longwood New House) and which would be ready only shortly after his death...

In any case, the perspective of being secluded at Porteous House for months waiting for Longwood to be ready should have tortured Napoleon's mind during his first visit to Longwood, and perhaps he was still immersed in these thoughts when, on the way back to Jamestown he remembered a small house in a charming place that he had noticed shortly after leaving Jamestown earlier that day: The Briars[1]. On approaching the place again he asked Cockburn about visiting it[2].

This is how Betsy Balcombe would remember his entrance to the Briars many years later:
    'At four o'clock in the evening, the same horsemen whom we had seen in the morning, again appeared on their return from Longwood. As soon as they reached the head of the narrow pass which led down to the Briars, they halted, and, after apparently a short deliberation, with terror I saw them begin to descend the mountain and approach our

---

1.   *Briar: a Mediterranean shrub or small tree (Erica Arborea) in the heather family, whose woody roots are used to make tobacco pipes.*
2.   *That's according to Marchand. A British version (J.H. Rose) differs: 'As he disliked the publicity of the house in Jamestown, Cockburn suggested on their return that he should reside at a pretty little bungalow, not far from the town, named The Briars'.*

cottage. I recollect feeling so dreadfully frightened, that I wished to run and hide myself until they were gone; but mamma desired me to stay, and to remember and speak French as well as I could. I had learned that language during a visit my father had paid to England some years before, and as we had a French servant, I had not lost what I had then acquired.

The party arrived at the gate, and there being no carriage-road, they all dismounted except the Emperor, who was now fully visible. He retained his seat and rode up the avenue, his horse's feet cutting up the turf on our pretty lawn. Sir George Cockburn walked on one side of his horse and General Bertrand on the other. How vividly I recollect my feelings of dread mingled with admiration, as I now first looked upon him whom I had learned to fear so much. His appearance on horseback was noble and imposing. The animal he rode was a superb one, his colour jet black, and as he proudly stepped up the avenue, arching his neck and chomping his bit, I thought he looked worthy to be the bearer of him who was once the ruler of nearly the whole European world!

Napoleon's position on horseback, by adding height to his figure, supplied all that was wanting to make me think him the most majestic person I had ever seen. He was dressed in green, and covered with orders, and his saddle and housings were of crimson velvet richly embroidered with gold. He alighted at our house, and we all moved to the entrance to receive him. Sir George Cockburn introduced us to him.

On closer approach Napoleon, contrasting, as his shorter figure did, with the noble height and aristocratic bearing of Sir George Cockburn, lost something of the dignity which had so much struck me on first seeing him. He was deadly pale, and I thought his features, though cold and immovable, and somewhat stern, were exceedingly beautiful. He seated himself on one of our cottage chairs, and after scanning our little apartment with his eagle glance, he complimented mamma on the pretty situation of the Briars. When once he began to speak, his fascinating smile and kind manner removed every vestige of the fear with which I had hither to regarded him.[1]

Approximately 1.5 miles from Jamestown, the Briars cottage was placed on an exuberant green elevation in the middle of a deep hollow surrounded by harsh, rocky heights with just one aperture facing Jamestown and the sea. Around the house and a small pavilion flourished all kind of colourful and fragrant trees and vegetation,

---

1.   *To Befriend an Emperor. Betsy Balcombe's Memoirs of Napoleon on St. Helena. (Originally published in 1844). Ravenhall Books.*

while the cooing of turtle doves excited by the many fruits completed an Eden-like picture leaving nobody indifferent. In addition, behind the pavilion extended a huge orchard planted with vines, lemon and orange trees, guavas and mangoes and further back, a waterfall falling from a cleft 200 foot high that vaporized before reaching the ground...

The exuberant vegetation around Briars Pavilion.

Immediately upon arrival Napoleon expressed his desire to occupy the pavilion near the main house. A petition the owner, Mr. Balcombe, wholeheartedly accepted, even offering his house as being more appropriate to Napoleon's status. A kind proposition the Emperor kindly declined, as he wouldn't like at any rate to disturb the family's quiet living there. The sudden apparition of this hidden 'oasis' in contrast with the roughness of Saint Helena's highlands, should have given him considerable relief after the long crossing aboard the Northumberland and the idea of being lodged in the much inappropriate Porteous House. In fact, the next seven weeks that Napoleon spent at the Briars could be defined as a kind of hiatus since his departure from the Malmaison early in the summer of that same year.

He would stay there accompanied by Las Cases and his son and assisted by the loyal butlers Marchand and Ali, while the other servants went back and forth between Jamestown and the Briars. Bertrand, Montholon and their respective families would remain at Jamestown too. Only Gourgaud would be later authorized to join the Emperor.

The pavilion comprised just a ground floor with a small hall and a relatively spacious room with four windows reserved for the Emperor. Two other small rooms under the roof accessible by a narrow staircase served as living quarters for Las Cases and his son. Marchand and Ali, in their turn, had to get along with two simple mattresses; probably the same they had been assigned aboard the Northumberland[1].

In no time –and in full accordance with Napoleon's 'traditional style'– he set a daily work routine consisting in dictating his memories, taking care of keeping everybody occupied around him. So, Las Cases would be responsible for the Italian campaigns; Bertrand for those of Egypt; Gourgaud for the Consulate, the retirement to Elba and the subsequent Hundred Days. Montholon wouldn't be idle either, being in charge of the Empire. Marchand and Ali were involved too; being responsible for copying and correcting the dictations[2].

The Briars. Napoleon at work dictating the Egyptian campaign to Bertrand. (Bombled. ©Andrea Press).

1. *Souvenirs du Mameluck Ali sur L'Empereur Napoléon. Payot, Paris 1926.*
2. *Mémoires de Marchand d'après le manuscrit original par Jean Bourguignon. Plon, Paris 1952.*

Mr. Balcombe was a kind man that, like his wife and two daughters[1], didn't spare any effort to make Napoleon's life at the Briars as comfortable as possible, given the circumstances. Special mention deserves Betsy, the younger girl that, being 14 at the time, entertained a peculiar and intriguing relationship with our man through which Napoleon, the 'human being', emerges from the somewhat stiff political personage he embodied until the very end.

A blonde, quite pretty teenager, Betsy was able to speak some French, which eventually would facilitate a direct communication with the Emperor, whom she had feared and hated until the first time she saw him in person when, almost all of a sudden, hatred converted into admiration and, eventually, even into tenderness... But all the above said, with the perspective that time gives, she mostly would be a naughty, impertinent girl bordering on the unbearable, as proved by the next episode which occurred at the Briars as narrated by Betsy herself:

'Napoleon then produced from a richly embossed case, the most magnificent sword I ever beheld. The sheath was composed of an entire piece of most splendidly marked tortoise-shell, thickly studded with golden bees. The handle, not unlike a fleur-de-lys *in shape, was of exquisitely wrought gold. It was indeed the most costly and elegant weapon I had ever seen.*

I requested Napoleon to allow me to examine it more closely; and then a circumstance which had occurred in the morning, in which I had been much piqued at the Emperor's conduct, flashed across me. The temptation was irresistible, and I determined to punish him for what he had done. I drew the blade out quickly from the scabbard, and began to flourish it over his head, making passes at him, the Emperor retreating, until at last I fairly pinned him in the corner; I kept telling him all the time that he had better say his prayers, for I was going to kill him. My exulting cries at last brought my sister to Napoleon's assistance. She scolded me violently, and said she would inform my father if I did not instantly desist; but I only laughed at her, and maintained my post, keeping the Emperor at bay until my arm dropped from sheer exhaustion.

I can fancy I see the figure of the grand chamberlain now, with his spare form and parchment visage, glowing with fear for the Emperor's

---

1.   *William Balcombe was a minor official of the East India Company, handling provisions for ships putting in at Saint Helena. He had fathered Betsy and her 15 year-old sister Jane and two younger brothers, ages five and seven.*

safety, and indignation at the insult I was offering him. He looked as if he could have annihilated me on the spot, but he had felt the weight of my hand before on his ears, and prudence dictated him to let me alone.

When I resigned my sword, Napoleon took my ear which had been pierced only the day before, and pinched it, giving me great pain. I called out, and then took hold of my nose, which he pulled heartily, but quite in fun; his good humour never left him during the whole scene'[1].

British soldiers watching Napoleon's movements at The Briars. (Bombled. ©Andrea Press).

1. *To Befriend an Emperor. Betsy Balcombe´s Memoirs of Napoleon on St. Helena. (Originally published in 1844). Ravenhall Books. (Bombled. ©Andrea Press).*

On returning to the Briars from a promenade along the road to Jamestown, the Emperor meets Mrs. Balcombe and another young lady called Stuart. When they come across some black slaves heavily loaded Mrs Balcombe orders them to move away in a rather crude fashion. Then Napoleon surprises the ladies by exclaiming **'Respect au fardeau, Madame!'** *(Respect the burden, madam!)* (Le Memorial de Sainte-Hélène. Le Comte de Las Cases.) *(Bombled.* ©*Andrea Press).*

Why Napoleon allowed Miss Betsy to go so far has always puzzled both detractors and exegetes. Some even dared to suggest the existence of a love affair, of which there is certainly no basis at all. Perhaps she was mainly an outlet for the strong psychological pressure Napoleon bore in all the months elapsed since his abdication till the arrival to the Briars where, for the first time he could at last relax his demeanour, relatively free from being watched and scrutinised by both sympathizers and foes around. By entertaining the Balcombe girls –and even their younger brothers– he didn't jeopardise the forbearance or the authority associated with his imperial persona allowing him a relaxing freedom in speech and behaviour not excluding the possibility of releasing his emotive impulses until then practically restricted to the 'funny' pranks and ear pinches he liked so much to exert on his closest assistants and servants like Gourgaud or Marchand.

That is not to say anyway that he enjoyed total freedom of action at the Briars as there were of course British watchers around[1], but compared with what was awaiting for him at Longwood House, or even with the close guard imposed on those still living in Jamestown, it was paradise.

Days went by peacefully while the Emperor worked enthusiastically on his memoirs usually in the morning, strolled with Las Cases in the garden or killed some time entertaining/suffering Betsy and her siblings. Even though he was always courteously invited to the balls and dinners Cockburn often celebrated, he also courteously refused to assist. Aware as he was of the great curiosity and expectation his figure awakened on everybody on the island; very especially the socialites, he rightly chose not to expose himself to indiscretion.

By virtue of the regulation imposed on Napoleon during his captivity, he was obliged to have a British 'escort' when riding about the island. He considered this contrary to his dignity and, consequently gradually gave up his habit of riding which, in due course would contribute significantly to the progressive decline of this health. The first in a series of conflicts concerning his riding happened at the Briars and was accounted by Marchand as follows:

'Since the Emperor had been at the Briars, he had not attempted to stroll beyond what he named his favourite walk. One day he felt like riding across some area of the island; horses were soon sent from the town; M. de Las Cases and Saint-Denis prepared themselves to go with him; but just as he was about to saddle up, the Emperor learned that the guard officer, that had allowed him to ride alone the day before in case he disliked being escorted by him, had just been ordered to stick to his instructions. The Emperor being disappointed ordered Saint-Denis to send the horses back: he would not be going out.

After dinner he went out into the garden as usual. Ambling around he discovered a small path that was only used by slaves. He started walking down the path towards the little valley visible from the windows of his pavilion.

---

1. *There was an artillery captain named M. Greatly together with a sergeant and a handful of soldiers posted at the Briars though later Admiral Cockburn gallantly acceded to leave there just the captain and dressed in civilian clothes. Mémoires de Marchand. Libraire Plon. Paris 1952.*

Even though walking this path was dangerous, the Emperor, M. de Las Cases and his son walked through it and arrived safely to major Hodson's home[1], target of his foray. It was night when the Emperor left the major; they couldn't return by the same path and accepted the horses they were offered before. They arrived at the Briars quite late, which made us wonder where the Emperor could have been, as he couldn't be found either in the garden or in Balcombe's place.

Next morning the Emperor was delighted with his excursion of the day before, he speaks in very honourable terms of major Hodson and the good treatment he had been given. There is something deeper in this pleasure: that of having cheated his guardians, who couldn't imagine that the Emperor and the count Las Cases dared to take such a dangerous path.[2]

Napoleon's rejoicing however wouldn't last much longer. Even though admiral Cockburn took considerable care dealing with the Emperor and his retinue, the fact that they all were prisoners could be hardly ignored in view of the regulations and guarding imposed onto them, very especially for those living at Jamestown. The scarcely two months spent at the Briars were elapsing fast and the works at Longwood were near completion. It was a rather short break in which Napoleon could give free rein to his most tender feelings and good moods amidst a peaceful environment: a picture that have always pleased his panegyrists. That could be the case with his relationship with Betsy Balcombe and the affability shown to her parents and siblings or some other passages illustrating Napoleon's 'human nature' which happened at the Briars, like that of the slave Tobie that the Emperor tried –unsuccessfully– to liberate.

Since boarding the Bellerophon Napoleon had been wearing his legendary uniform of colonel de *chasseur à cheval de la garde* but, curiously enough, on November 28th he changed to a new outfit composed of a green frock only decorated with his plaque de *Grand-Aigle de la Légion D'Honneur* and the sash of the *Legion D'Honneur* almost unnoticeable

---

1. *Major Charles Robert George Hodson was a giant that the Emperor surnamed 'Hercule'. Major of an infantry regiment, he was judge-advocate and acted as town mayor in Jamestown. His property visited by the Emperor on November 20 was called Maldivia. He would be present at Napoleon´s burial and at the exhumation ceremonies in 1840.*
    Mrs. Hodson was the daughter of Sir W. Doveton, member of the island council, who owned Mount Pleasant in Sandy Bay, a nice house by the sea, three leagues and a half south of Longwood. The Emperor paid a visit to Sir Webber Doveton on January 3rd 1816 and would also visit him in his last excursion outside the limits on October 4th 1820; accompanied by Generals Bertrand and Montholon, Napoleon accepted having lunch with his host in the garden. Mémoires de Marchand. Libraire Plon. Paris 1952.
2. *Mémoires de Marchand. Libraire Plon. Paris 1952.*

The Briars. Napoleon's typical and compulsive inspection of a bundle of books immediately upon arrival. (Bombled. ©Andrea Press).

under the frock, that he wore always buttoned. White trousers, silk stockings, buckled shoes and his trademark hat completed the look that he would be donning at Longwood where he would finally go on December 10th after waiting for some days till the odour of the fresh paint –that he couldn't bear– dissipated. After presenting Mr. Balcombe with a gold box sporting his coat of arms, and expressing his desire to receive him and his family in his new residence, he parted from the Briars towards his final abode: Longwood House...[1].

1.   *Mémoires de Marchand. Libraire Plon. Paris 1952.*

*With the British guard presenting arms, Napoleon's horse -a nervous and jumpy animal-
would only enter the enclosure spurred to full gallop. (Bombled. ©Andrea Press).*

LONGWOOD

THE HOUSE

ongwood house is a pivotal element in the history of Napoleon's seclusion at Saint Helena. In a similar way that the entire island has been frequently presented as a suitable or disgraceful choice depending on authors' tendencies, Longwood's appraisals varied from that of a pleasant little cottage to that of an unliveable shack planted in a most unhealthy environment, infested by rats and constantly battered by unpleasant, strong winds... The British historian J. H. Rose renders a short depiction of the place that epitomizes the positive version:

'The new abode contained five rooms for Napoleon's use, three for the Montholons, two for the Las Cases, and one for Gourgaud: it was situated on a plateau 1,730 feet above the sea: the air there was bracing, and on the farther side of the plain dotted with gum trees stretched the race-course, a mile and a half of excellent turf. The only obvious drawbacks were the occasional mists, and the barren precipitous ravines that flank the plateau on all sides. Seeing, however, that Napoleon disliked the publicity of Jamestown, the isolation of Longwood could hardly be alleged as a serious grievance. The Bertrands occupied Hutt's gate, a small villa about a mile distant.

The limits within which Napoleon might take exercise unaccompanied by a British officer formed a roughly triangular space having a circumference of about twelve miles. Outside of those bounds he must be so accompanied; and if a strange ship came in sight, he was to return within bounds. The letters of the whole party must be supervised by the acting Governor. This is the gist of the official instructions. Napoleon's dislike of being accompanied by a British officer led him nearly always to restrict himself to the limits and generally to the ground of Longwood.

And where, we may ask, could a less unpleasant place of detention have been found? In Europe he must inevitably have submitted to far closer confinement. For what safeguards could there have been proof against a subtle intellect and a personality whose charm fired thousands of braves in both hemispheres with the longing to start him once more on his adventures? The Tower of London, the eyrie of Dumbarton Castle, even Fort William itself, were named as possible places of detention.

Were they suited to this child of the Mediterranean? He needed sun; he needed exercise; he needed society. All these he could have on the plateau of Longwood, in a singularly equable climate, where the heat of the tropics is assuaged by the south-east trade wind, and plants of the sub-tropical and temperature zones alike flourish.[1]

Longwood House.

Representative of the opposite view is Michel Dancoisne-Martineau's authoritative version[2] which denies that Longwood was the best possible option at the time of Napoleon's arrival and even suggests quite a few other residences as exceedingly better, particularly regarding the climate[3]. Thanks to the successive and extraordinary efforts of Gilbert Martineau[4] and Michel Dancoisne-Martineau Longwood house has been painstakingly and amazingly restored through many years of dedicated work until getting the house back to how it was at the time of Napoleon's stay. No detail has been spared, including authentic furniture or even the garden; closely recreated according to period drawings and reports.

Immediately upon arriving at Saint Helena on the afternoon of July 15th 2007, I started to walk the stepped and long 6 miles way between Jamestown and Longwood house. I was mesmerized by the surrounding

1. *The Life of Napoleon I. John Holland Rose, M.A. George Bell and Sons 1902.*
2. *Michel Dancoisne-Martineau. Honorary consul, and curator of the French properties on St Helena since 1987.*
3. *Sainte-Hélène. Île de Mémoire. Fayard.*
4. *Gilbert Martineau (1918–1995). Honorary consul, and curator of the French properties on St Helena, 1956-1987.*

silence, the solitude and the rare beauty of the landscape. Wrapped in my thoughts, I barely noticed that I was completely alone and a little exhausted following the endless slope, when an approaching car driven by a most kindly young Saint Helenian gave me a lift covering the last two or three miles to the plateau. All of a sudden there it was: Longwood house in the twilight. Nobody on sight, a gentle wind, the sun slowly hiding inside the deep blue sea...

As a quintessential element in the phenomenal drama developed by Napoleon at Saint Helena, his persona seemed to have 'transubstantiated' into Longwood house, as if he lived there forever. Perhaps for this reason there shouldn't be much sense in evaluating if Longwood was a proper residence for the illustrious prisoner; or even if there could have been a better 'setting' for what would follow from Napoleon's arrival to Longwood until the end...

The new –and last– residence of the fallen Emperor was placed on a high table land at the East of Saint Helena, frequently lashed by the south-east winds. In former times a thick forest of gum trees, Longwood would be eventually deforested by greedy inhabitants, always ready to get free firewood, until governor Byfield had all the Longwood-Deadwood area fenced in 1723.

In 1743 a farm was built there. In 1752 the place would be used as a summer residence for the first time by lieutenant governor Adamson and the first known depiction of the original Longwood House is rendered in 1776 by an official called Daniel Corneille as having a visiting room and three small rooms[1]. Shortly after, during 1777 and 1778, governor Skottowe spared no means to replant the lost forest enclosing the entire area within a stone wall 30 km long but, unfortunately, this forest, which had protected the place from inclement weather, had practically disappeared by Napoleon's time exposing Longwood House to fogs, gusts and torrential rains. In addition, there would be some subsequent improvements before his arrival, including those carried out during his stay at the Briars.

When Napoleon finally set foot in Longwood House it was a T-shaped building with a usable area of approximately 2,368 sq ft (220 m²) and walls 10.5 feet (3,20 meters high): certainly not a spacious residence for a man that had occupied some of the most luxurious palaces in the world. Back of the T cross bar there were a courtyard and some additional spare rooms for servants and staff besides the kitchen, laundry and store rooms...

---

1.   *Sainte-Hélène. Île de Mémoire. Fayard.*

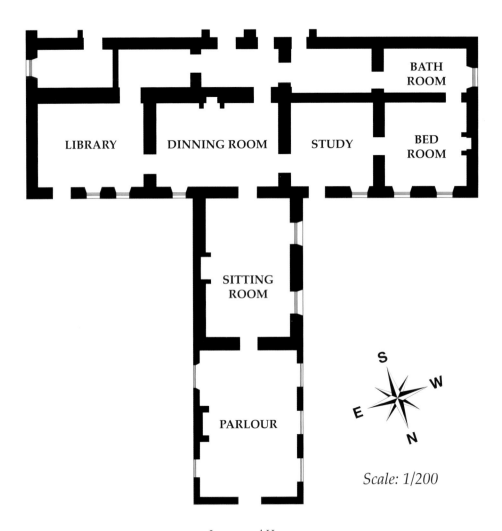

Loongwood House.

A view of the left T-cross of the building showing the library door to the garden

A view of the right T-cross showing the door and windows to the Emperor´s study and bed room

The Parlour

The Emperor and his companions entered Longwood House on 10th December 1815 by climbing the steps leading into the wooden lattice veranda; the same from which he would in later years watch through his spyglass the horse races celebrated twice a year on the plain of Deadwood. The first room they saw was the parlour, a huge chamber of around 463 sq ft (43 m²) that had been hastily built by the sailors of the Northumberland to enlarge the prisoner's accommodation. This was the largest and probably most pleasant room in the house, well ventilated and illumined by five windows even though, being entirely of wood, it became too hot in the afternoon under the strong tropical sun. Napoleon –always a curious man– would like to pace this parlour up and down, again holding his spy glass, snooping at the exterior now and then through the scooped out window shutters.

The walls were painted green and decorated with a black fret in the Regency style so fashionable in Britain at the time. There were also an impracticable fireplace painted black and a cracked mirror above, which Napoleon would give to Mme. Bertrand in 1819. The first use given to this parlour was that of a dinning room but in July 1816, upon the arrival of a billiard table shipped from London, the room was converted into a sort of topographical study. The Emperor, being not really fond of billiards, would dictate his memoirs there taking advantage of the large table for

Scooped out shutters through which Napoleon snooped the exterior.

spreading the maps and books he referred to in his dictations. In fact he would only rarely play billiards there, contenting himself with idly holding the ivory balls and clashing them into each other. In time, when he became aware that his servants played billiards when he was out, the Emperor give them the huge table, that would be removed to a back service room. Once it was gone, the parlour remains just being a spacious waiting room where Napoleon could stretch his legs. This was also the room in which his autopsy would be eventually performed...

The Parlour.

The furniture consisted of five chairs of different models, two settees and three armchairs. A carpet was added in October 1817 and there were seven tables of assorted styles, most of them in mahogany; either octagonal tea or Pembroke card tables[1]. Two earth and celestial globes on tripods stood at the corners[2] and two large –and similar– sideboards were placed both sides of the door leading to the sitting room.

All this furniture was provided by the British Government. Some pieces directly requisitioned from the homes of notable Saint Helenians and the rest as part of the materials and furniture which arrived to the isle in May 1816 intended to be used in the building of the new 'mansion' for the Emperor that would be ready shortly before his death and that he never used: New Longwood House...

---

1. *Sainte-Hélène. Île de Mémoire. Fayard.*
2. *Souvenirs du Mameluck Ali sur L'Empereur Napoléon. Payot, Paris 1926. According to Ali he missed the globes in later times, possibly because Napoleon gave them to Mmes. Montholon or Bertrand to help with their children's education.*

The Sitting Room

Immediately beyond the parlour was a sitting room of about 366 sq ft (34 m²) with two windows facing west. It was here where the Emperor and his retinue liked to retire after dinner. When Napoleon arrived at the house this chamber looked pretty much as it had when used by Lt. Col. Skelton and his family during Saint Helena's hot summers. A few chairs and armchairs, a sofa, a carpet and white curtains decorated with some coloured drapery completed a rather sparing setting only enhanced by a nice black marble fireplace. Included in this 'early decoration' was a sort of yellow wall paper that

A corner of the sitting room facing north.

would be substituted in 1819 by a new one in ivory colour with blue stars; a replica of which can be admired nowadays in the stunning reconstruction alluded before.

Just a few days after Napoleon's arrival to the house a new piece of furniture was added to the sitting room: a pianoforte. That should help to lift the spirits of the French party to some extent, especially in the case of Mme. de Montholon, apparently known to be a skilled player of the instrument.

A small ceiling lamp and a mirror above the fireplace completed the ensemble until July 1816, when an accidental fire destroyed most of the furniture and it was replaced with pieces from the shipment destined for the New Longwood House commented above. This new decoration would basically remain the same until the very end, and comprised two large mahogany sofas decorated with ebony inlays placed both sides of the fireplace and a set of about a dozen Regency chairs and armchairs made from beech wood, finished in black ebony, decorated with leather inlays and gilt details and upholstered in velvet green with yellow piping. In addition there were also two fine marble plant stands, a couple of side tables (one octagonal and the other Pembroke style) and a library table with a stool.

Between the windows –dressed with lace curtains topped with velvet valances– protruded Napoleon's marble bust of his beloved son the King of Rome standing on a green marble console, above which hung a portrait of the boy in the Tuileries garden. The bust arrived to the island in 1817 and was immediately placed in the sitting room. The painting was sent to Saint Helena by Mme. Mère and the Cardinal Fesch with the priest Buonavita and Vignali, who arrived to the island in September 1819.

Possibly thanks to the large mirror hanging above the chimney, the huge carpet entirely covering the floor and specially the 'sumptuous' ceiling chandelier, this would be the nearest to a stately room in Longwood. But beyond all prior remarks, the most prominent feature of this room in connection with the drama of Saint Helena is the fact that it was here where the Emperor drew his last breath on Saturday 5th May 1821 at 17 h 49 m...

The sitting room as it was at the time of Napoleon´s death recreated.

On April 28th 1821 Napoleon, until then reluctant to abandon his bedroom, finally gave up and had himself installed in the more spacious and comfortable sitting room. This was rearranged for the last time in Napoleon's life. Marchand, who among other capabilities was a remarkable artist, rendered an atmospheric and highly detailed drawing of the room shrouded in a hazy, disturbing light and exactly capturing how it looked at that moment. The Emperor's two campaign beds were then moved there: one between the two windows, just in the same spot where his son's bust stood before. The other one was next to the opposite wall, close to the door to the parlour. As clearly shown in Marchland's drawing, a night stand beside the bed and a folding screen concealing the door to the dinning room were installed too. The last use given to his chamber was that of a mortuary chapel where Napoleon's body was reverentially exposed surrounded by many personal items like his uniforms, toiletries, or weapons... already invested with a strong symbolic meaning, as relics from the phenomenal Napoleonic epic.

The Dinning Room

Next coming from to the sitting room is the dining room. Third largest chamber in the house slightly above 323 sq ft (30 m²), it was indeed a sombre, rather inhospitable place. A sort of hall only obtaining natural light through a French-window facing north-east that opened to the garden and four doors: that of the sitting room; a second to the left leading to the library, a third on the right communicating with the Emperor's apartments and a last one leading to the kitchen.

At the beginning Napoleon had this room doubling as a topographical study and library but, upon the arrival of the billiard table on July 1816 mentioned above, it converted into a dining room composed by a simple six-guest table, a dozen mahogany chairs, one console, a carpet and two screens. On Sundays and special occasions this rather humble ensemble would be decorated with all the regalia and splendour of the Tuileries: servants donning the imperial livery, splendid Sèvres china and striking cutlery and glassware in full assertion of the inalienable royal status of the great Corsican, who always sat with his back to the fireplace above which was a large mirror flanked by gilt columns reflecting the dim light coming through the opposite French-window.

Picture yourself there... All this pomp and circumstance inside a damp, small house that was supposed to function like a palace. Wouldn't it have been easier –and nobler– skipping all these demonstrations for a more modest, sober existence? There always was a kind of duplicity in Napoleon's personality: Bonaparte and Napoleon; the young revolutionary of the Enlightenment and the absolutist monarch... Even in his physical dimension there is a sharp contrast between the emaciated general of the Battle of the Pyramids and the stout Emperor of Waterloo. In all probability the two of

The fireplace in the dinning room facing south.

them would be still coexisting inside that man sat with his back to the fire place. How he managed to harmonize such explosive contradictions –very especially in the harsh conditions of his long captivity– one can only guess but, at Saint Helena the 'Emperor personae' should prevail regardless of the tremendous psychological cost Napoleon should have suffered. When sat in this damp, gloomy dinning room, surrounded by his diminutive court and this rather parodic re-enactment of the bygone pageantry, wouldn't he sometimes stare at the only window in front of him, dreaming of the past?...

The Emperor having been consecrated by the Catholic rite, and being this religion not represented so far at Saint Helena, he joyfully welcomed Vignali and Buonavita's arrival (see page 110) as they could at last provide an essential element to any self-respecting European court then and now: a chapel rendering regular religious services.

The first mass at Longwood was celebrated on Sunday 3rd October 1819 in the sitting room. But Napoleon would soon after express his desire for a movable chapel to be displayed on Sundays and festivities in the dining room. Everybody seemed to receive the idea very enthusiastically, and contributed their very best to have the detachable chapel ready in about a week. The ceiling was wallpapered in white and the walls dark red with golden flowers. Many other makeshift gadgets and details were wittily produced till the chapel was completed, as accounted by Ali:

> The two Sundays after the priest's arrival, the Emperor attended mass in the sitting room where the altar had been set, but he would like mass celebrated in the dining room in future; as it suited him and the priests better. Consequently he ordered to procure anything necessary to getting this room worthy of the divine service. The dining room was then converted into a chapel, Sundays and festivities, at mass time.

> The priest had brought the sacred vases, the altar stone[1], their vestments and ornaments, but all the rest was missing. First the room is rearranged. White paper is pasted all over the ceiling and a red Chinese paper decorated with golden flowers and borders covered the walls. A large amount of white satin is purchased for covering the back and the two sides of the area around the altar, with green satin for the decoration or drapery border. All this ensemble could be removed at will by mean of hooks fixed to the wall and rings sewn to the cloths. Two gilt, wooden curtain rods joined end-to-end and decorated with a silk, striped green-yellow border and bells, divided the bottom of the room in two. At both ends of the rod hung two curtains made from the same fabric as the border. They were lifted by mean of two silk cords tied to gilt bronze pegs. These borders, curtains and rods came from the sitting room windows.

> There still remained two similar curtains to those already taken whose ornaments and trimmings would be used on the front of the altar and the carpet later placed there. A new carpet covered the floor entirely. From the beautiful dessert table an altar was made. The altar front was in white satin framed with a green velvet edge; on the lower angles were fixed crowned N's and, in the centre, a cross of gold braid. The altar was covered by two table cloths of percale batiste decorated with lace. A small tabernacle, in the shape of an ancient temple, was produced with cardboard by Pierron; four candelabras with candles and vases filled with flowers completed the decoration on top of the altar. The Emperor having known that the Grand-Maréchal had a painting representing the head of Jesus Christ (Ecce homo), real size, asked for it and had it placed above the tabernacle. The two consoles from the sitting room

---

1.   A stone containing relics that served as a essential part of a Catholic altar for the celebration of mass at the time.

were placed left and right of the altar adding a silver girandole with five arms on top of each. A large velvet carpet covered the altar steps; it was embroidered with a yellow silk cord and trim; on front, at the middle, was a large crowned N and, on the two corners, two crowns, all in braid. Two large screens six feet high[1] with six panels –one covered with a crimson cloth with intertwined roses and green foliage and the other with a red paper resembling the room's wall paper– concealed the doors to the corridor, the bedroom and the sitting room. These screens were made by Noverraz. All the hangings were Joséphine's work.

The Emperor's armchair was four or five feet from the steps of the altar, a chair ahead of him. The chairs of the grand Maréchal, Mme. Bertrand and M. de Montholon, were located at the Emperor's sides and a little to rear. The house staff stood near the screens. Priest Buonavita celebrated the mass; priest Vignaly, in small rochet or small surplice, and Napoleon Bertrand fulfilling the functions of the altar boys. It was Vignaly who offered the Gospel for kissing.

The chapel was only lighted with candles from the candelabra and candle sticks, as the glass door to the garden was screened by the hangings.

Mass was officiated every Sunday. The Emperor assisted, providing that he was not ill or indisposed in bed; but, in this case, his bedroom remained open and the screens folded so that the priest's words could reach him. Once mass was over, Napoleon went into the garden or the sitting room. The chapel was then reconverted into the dining room; all returning to its prior condition.

*One of the first Sundays, the Emperor, when leaving the mass, said smiling at his companions: **'I hope that the Holy Father will reproach us nothing; we have become again Christians. Had he seen our chapel, he would have granted indulgences to us...'** and later insisted: **'If any of you have his conscience overloaded with sins; Buonavita is here to collect all of them and provide absolution.'**[2]*

---

1. *French 'pieds'. Aproximately 33cm.*
2. *Souvenirs du Mameluck Ali sur L'Empereur Napoléon. Payot, Paris 1926.*

The Library

Even though Napoleon couldn't really be defined as a bibliophile, books played a prominent role all during his life. His inquisitive mind and insatiable thirst for knowledge made of books an indispensable means to an end. Classical and modern literature, geography, history, law, science... practically any possible topic intrigued him. So he was a voracious and fast reader gifted with an amazing memory. He never stopped reading even in the most adverse situations and, once he reached the power as first Consul and Emperor, gave free rein to this longing for more and more books which filled extensive libraries in his palaces totalling about 60,000 volumes...

At Saint Helena the situation was of course quite different as even his reading was subjected to British control. But, even in such unfavourable circumstances, he managed to gather a considerable collection of books and never ceased reading all along those oppressive final years.

Aligned with the dinning room on the left side of the crossbar of the T was the library. A comparatively spacious room of about 291 sq ft (27 m²), it was accessible to the visitor entering through a door on the left side of the dinning room. By entering via this door there were in succession two windows and a door opening to the front garden on the left. An interior door on the opposite wall led the to the service area.

A view of the library facing east.

The windows and the garden door facing east provided good lighting and a pleasant atmosphere, only spoiled by the ever present humidity caused by the strong winds and rains.

Upon arrival at Longwood House the room that would be converted into a library holding about 3,000 books was originally assigned to Bertrand and family but, when they found better lodgings facing Hutt's Gate, the Emperor –visibly disappointed– gave the room to Montholon who, together with his wife and child lived there until July 1816, when they moved to a new abode. Napoleon then had this room serve as a library till the very end of his life.

Initially there were just three cabinets with two cases each: the upper one with chicken wired doors and green curtains concealing the books; the lower one with blinded doors. Eventually, as more and more books arrived, a fourth cabinet and two smaller cases were added. A large white table covered by a green tablecloth and usually with some maps laid on top was placed in the middle of the room beside a couple of side tables and two armchairs.

Ali who, among his many other occupations at Longwood, was in charge of this library has rendered an interesting account of Napoleon's reading habits:

> The Emperor holding in his hands a book arousing his interest, wouldn't stop until he had obtained a full knowledge of the content. 'He read word by word' (Il lisait avec le pouce), as the Abbé de Pradt[1] has said and, however, he didn't miss any of the content, assimilating it so well that, long after, he could deliver a detailed analysis and even remember almost literally those fragments that had moved him in a special way. On hearing about topics that were unfamiliar or unknown to him, he would have any related book from his library brought on the spot. He wouldn't be satisfied with any superficial approach, going as deep as possible into the matter. That was how he cleared his mind and furnished the spirit.

> When book boxes arrived, the Emperor had them immediately opened. Books were then given to him one after another. He hastily leafed through them, leaving on a table those he suspected might contain something. The others were heaped aside for further checking. The ones he had picked out were carried to his study and placed on the gueridon beside his canapé.

---

1.   The abbé Dominique G. F. de Rion de Prolhiac Dufour de Pradt was a French clergyman and ambassador that became Napoleon's secretary in 1804 and Bishop of Poitiers in 1805.

Reading news helped him to allow some mornings to pass pleasantly. When he received newspapers, he would never leave them without checking anything he judged interesting. At such times he entirely changed. His bearing, expression and voice; all announced that fire was running through his veins. His imagination soared in such a way that he became a supernatural man. He seemed to still be the master of Europe. This vigorous and lively mood lasted a few hours, after which the Emperor resumed his usual pace and quite routine.

Sometimes, when he read the British newspapers, I stayed by his side with an English-French dictionary and, when he found a word he didn't understand, I searched it. He continued so reading until being again stopped by another word.[1]

The Emperor's Apartments

If Longwood House overall couldn't really qualify as a sumptuous dwelling, Napoleon's private chambers were certainly not better. They were located on the west half of the cross-bar in the Longwood T configuration. The Emperor would spent there most of his mornings carelessly dressed in his white redingote by way of dressing-gown and full length, close flitting wool trousers, red or green leather slippers and wearing the madras bandana he used at night.

Interestingly, and regarding with the two main rooms in this section –the study and the bedroom– there is some confusion in the memoirs due to the fact that Napoleon had beds installed in both rooms. As an example, while Marchand simply would refer to these two chambers as 'the bedrooms', Ali reversed the terms referring to the 'bedroom' as the 'study' and vice versa.

Access to these rooms –coming from the entrance– was via the dining room through a door on the right. There were three rooms adding up to about 538 sq ft (50 m^2) as follows:

The Study

The study or '*cabinet de travail*', of almost 215 sq ft (20 m^2) was Napoleon's first private room. Contiguous to the dining room it

---

1. *Souvenirs du Mameluck Ali (Louis-Étienne Saint-Denis) Sur L'Empereur Napoléon.* *Payot, Paris 1926.*

had one sash window[1] and three doors: one to the dining room, one leading to the front garden and a last one opening to the bed room. There was no fireplace and the Emperor is reported to have disliked the room immediately upon going there for the first time. What follows is an excerpt from Dr. O'Meara's memoirs (see page 86) that serves quite well to illustrate Napoleon's demagogic use of Longwood House in sustaining his unwaiverable cause as the ever humiliated prisoner, in the hands of his terrible British gaolers. In this interesting piece he goes so far as to compare his own position with that of the war prisoners jailed in the hideous pontoons...

'September, 1817.

Napoleon complained about rheumatic pains and a slight headache that he attributed, rightly, to the dampness and temperature of the house. **'Every evening'**, *he said,* **'on leaving my little room where there is a fireplace, when I go into my bedroom[2], I feel like entering a damp cave. Were it not for the well lighted room built with dry wood Cockburn ordered to be made, where I stroll and exercise, I would be buried long ago. That is, I believe, what your oligarchy demands. Its behaviour in my view may be compared with the treatment given to prisoners aboard pontoons: the most impolitic and cruelest act ever practised. Your ministers had never made anything comparable to their pontoon system, and which incensed the French and other nations. Even if not considering humaneness, they should treat prisoners well for political reasons. It will be not without difficulty that an accurate idea is made regarding the effect good treatment given in France to war prisoners has had on other nations, and particularly on the Germans and the Russians. That has frequently resulted in great advantages. Thousands of soldiers that would have desperately fought surrendered their weapons saying: we want to go to drinking the good wine of Bourgogne.'**[3].*

In time for Napoleon's arrival Cockburn had the study and the contiguous bedroom walls dressed with a sort of ochre nankeen fabric decorated with a green edging. But not much more could –or wanted to– be done and the decoration of these chambers would be certainly spare; at least in the first years. Books and papers

1.   *According with Ali there were originally two windows; one of them later converted into a glass paneled door, opening to the front garden following Napoleon's orders to get a direct access to the garden.*
2.   *NOTE FROM THE ORIGINAL TEXT: Napoleon had changed his bedroom sometime before.*
3.   *Napoléon en Exil à Sainte-Hélène. Barry E. O'Meara. Plancher. Paris, 1822.*

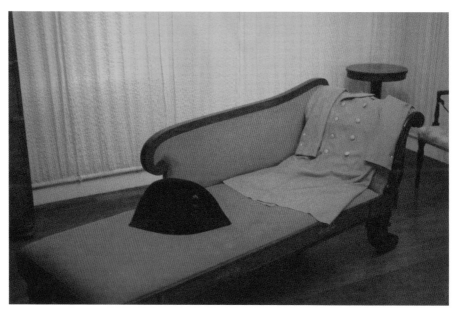

A detail of the study facing south.

would rest on makeshift stands arranged with crude boards and trestles placed beside the window, while a cupboard used as library and a working table mostly completed the ensemble. This was the table at which Las Cases and his son would spend long hours writing down the Emperor's fluent dictations.

One of Napoleon's two camp beds was also placed in the study, facing the window and the door to the garden. Like many other objects and garments related to him these camp beds would eventually become an icon of the Napoleonic legend. He surely was a forerunner of modernity in many aspects, but his understanding of the tremendous importance of images and symbols in the political handling and control of the masses is simply astonishing. The best example of this would probably be that of him clad in his legendary redingote and hat: an image instantly recognizable all across the world nearly two centuries after his death. From this point of view, the fact that he chose to sleep in these –presumably uncomfortable– camp beds[1] all during his captivity at Saint Helena cannot be overlooked. Accepting –or demanding– a larger, more convenient bed, would have diminished the powerful image he stubbornly struggled to cast at Saint Helena: that of the military, sober, unshakeable

1.   *These camp beds were used by Napoleon throughout all his campaigns and were made by Desouches, 'Serrurier du Garde-Meuble de S.M. l'Empereur et Roi'. They could be folded and packed in a leather case for easy transportation and were mounted on wheels. The mattress was fixed by mean of hooks set in the frame.*

Emperor. He was –as always– on campaign. And on campaign he would die... in one of his camp beds. He would use the bed in the study to take some rest during the day and sometimes alternated this with the other one –the 'proper' bedroom– during the long nights. There were white calico curtains in the windows and a rather poor carpet on the floor.

The improvements implemented in the dining room after the arrival of the priests encouraged the Emperor to keep going on with the reforms as recounted by Marchand. Note that he refers to the study as another bedroom, due to the fact that the Emperor eventually slept in this chamber too.[1]

'The arrangement of the chapel being so easy, the idea occurred to the Emperor to change the nankeen wall hangings of his two bed rooms that were dirty and rotten because of the humidity. Count Montholon suggested using white muslin and have some spares in order to have the hangings always clean. The Emperor preferred silk but I pointed out that getting the small quantity required for the back of the chapel was not easy and that it wouldn't be feasible to get all the material needed to cover all the walls of his room. On the contrary, a muslin from India –striped or not– could be easily purchased. The Emperor was in a cheerful mood and told me: 'Well, I see that you don't want any silk. Give me the height and the perimeter of the chamber so that I can calculate the expense.' I gave him the measurements; he made approximative calculations and gave me carte blanche *to arrange his two rooms one after the other.'*

He felt extreme repugnance for the English coming into his house to clean the furniture and the walls, so I told him that we all together, helped by a Chinese, needed nobody else. Using a pocket knife the Emperor had cut a large slash in the hangings to check the state of the walls, which were very dirty and in bad shape. The next day everybody did his best: the nankeen covering on the frame was removed and white paper pasted all over the walls of the bed room. The Chinese whitewashed the ceiling while others cleaned and waxed the furniture outside. After measurements were taken, a quantity of striped muslin had been purchased. Noverraz's wife, helped by a woman from the camp, cut and assembled the lengths of fabric together. Then she sewed top and bottom tucks on all the hangings and, as the length of these hangings was much longer than the walls, they were pleated in rolls by mean of tightening cords passing up and down the hangings, so achieving a

---

1. *In fact, the function of these quite similar rooms was never precisely defined. Interestingly, Ali reverses the terms in his memoirs calling 'bedroom' to the 'study' and vice versa...*

more graceful appearance than if they had been laid just flat. A small, eight inch gathered drapery from the same fabric, concealed the top hem while the bottom one rested on the baseboard. Count de Montholon had a rug brought from town to replace the one that had not been changed for the past four years.

I had some green silk bought in town to make new curtains for the Emperor's two small iron beds, and substituted the brass balls topping the bedposts with crowned eagles from the broken silverware. They fitted perfectly and produced a great effect. The portraits of the Empress and the King of Rome were put back to place. Eight days had been enough to complete the metamorphosis we had planned. The grand marshal wanted to contribute by sending a small gilt-brass clock and a small bust of the King of Rome as a child, and these objects were placed on the mantelpiece. Our plans would have been disrupted had everything not been put back in place on the same day as it was mandatory that the Emperor took possession of his chamber in the evening and slept there. Count the Montholon understood the intentions I explained to him and was in charge of keeping the Emperor in the drawing room a few hours longer than usual.

No matter how hard we worked all during the day we only finished at seven o'clock in the evening. The Emperor was so kind as to come back into his room just at that time. Two tablets of Houbigant[1] were burning in the incense burner; as he had been content for a long time just with sugar or vinegar, his sense of smell was pleasantly surprised and he thought it was aloe wood; but I told him that these were two tablets coming from two boxes which had arrived in town. Pierron, knowing that I had long been looking for these whenever a new ship arrived from Europe, has brought them. The room so freshly decorated, scented and well illuminated by the screen lamp, made the Emperor smile and say: **'This is no longer a bedroom; it is the boudoir of a young mistress!'** He had not yet noticed his bed; when he saw the eagles replacing the brass balls, he turned to me and pinching my ear and smiling, with that smile so revealing of the feeling of his soul: **'This'**, he said, **'is the complement; the idea looks even better now that it is done, what do you say of this Montholon?'**

The coolness of this chamber contrasted significantly with the preceding one. The Emperor had at Saint Helena two small camp beds; during the night he went from one to the other, passing back and forth between the two contiguous rooms. He had often told me that in case

---

1. *Houbigant was the name of a Parisian perfume manufacturer established in 1775 made famous for serving the major European courts; from Napoleon to Queen Victoria.*

he fell ill, these beds were too narrow. Count de Montholon had one in gilt brass that he had purchased in town and suggested placing it in the second bedroom. Doing that without the approval of the Emperor –who didn't really liked changes– was certainly risky, as it was the possibility of losing the precious reward we all hoped from him: an expression of satisfaction. Green curtains were purchased for this bed. I had an assortment of laces in the Emperor's toiletries; including one from Alençon. I had the quilt and the pillowcase trimmed with it. This bed was in fact to be nothing but a catafalque. There wasn't mirror in that room and when I couldn't find anyone in the town Mr. Darling, who was in charge for the furniture of the new house, upon learning about this, sent one measuring four feet high by three-and-a half feet wide that was intended for the new house. We placed it on top of the commode as there was no fireplace in this room. I had also received two small bookcases that were used to furnish this room.

*Once all was finished the Emperor came in apparently as satisfied as he had been before. Only when he was getting into bed he said to me: '**I don't want to deprive Montholon of his bed, we'll have to give it back to him.**' It was replaced by the second camp bed, as the Emperor had tried it finding that it was pretty uncomfortable. '**All this braiding**' he said to me the next morning, '**is good for Mme. the marshal's wife**'. As these two rooms were more or less the same size, I had a third set of wall coverings made, which allowed a change every two months in one of the two rooms, what was easily performed in two hours.[1]*

Also in this room were two large and identical screens placed either side of the bed and decorated with gold and silver Chinese motives, on a black lacquered background. One of these screens was used to conceal a stack table[2] and a chair on which Napoleon's garments were laid, along with '*two indispensable pieces of furniture*' (*deux petits meubles indispensables*) mentioned by Ali[3]; probably chamber pots used by the great man to answer nature's call... The other screen hid another small, mahogany table holding a carafe with water, two glasses, a teaspoon, a sugar bowl, a plate and some bottles of orange blossom syrup and Klein Constantia, the South African wine greatly favoured by the Emperor.

1. *Mémoires de Marchand. Libraire Plon. Paris 1952.*
2. *One of a set of four small tables of graduated size that can be stacked together, each fitting within the one immediately larger.*
3. *Souvenirs du Mameluck Ali (Louis-Étienne Saint-Denis) Sur L'Empereur Napoléon. Payot, Paris 1926.*

'Chaise longue' used by the servants in the small room next to the bath room.

Completing the furniture were another chair; a large armchair of mahogany and ebony, upholstered with red silk fabric decorated with flowers and leaves (that Napoleon would mainly use during the last phase of his illness); and –somewhat offsetting the humidity of the room– a generous, thick carpet and a bedside rug.

Culminating all that, and quite naturally, there were some spectacular pieces reminiscent of a past from which Napoleon would never part. The imposing washstand that had left the Balcombes open-mouthed at the Briars would now follow him in his rather whimsical 'forays' from one room to the other, while two beautiful green ice compartments fixed with silver gilt handles rested on top of the commode, flanking the rather effeminate mantle clock decorated with cupids and a pendulum with two hearts pierced by an arrow gifted by Mme. Bertrand...

The Bedroom

The most intimate chamber in Napoleon's private 'apartments' was scarcely 205 sq ft (19 m^2). It was rather a prolongation of the study; both rooms being separated by a partition wall and a communicating door. A second door on the bottom left coming from the study opened to the Emperor's bathroom and two sash windows on the right faced the front garden. The main and quite significant difference from the study was the fire place at the end of the room, which helped a lot in making this chamber more comfortable in the never ending battle against dampness[1].

As seen before, the same muslin used for the study in 1819 was also used to cover the walls of this bedroom. The most prominent piece of furniture here was one of Napoleon's camp beds. It seems that the Emperor vacillated around this 'bed business' before arriving at a final decision. By the summer of 1816 he was still complaining about his beds being too narrow which –incidentally– would be a peculiar remark; if only considering that he should have tested these beds sufficiently all along his campaigning experience. Whatever the case, his insistence on this point was strong enough as to have Mme. Bertrand suggesting that coupling the two beds would solve the matter. A couple of weeks later, the Emperor changed his mind and the beds reverted to their prior location, apparently because the bed dressings didn't fit this rather strange contrivance.

The bedroom facing west.

1. *According to Ali this fire place 'was of mahogany, decorated with gilt bronzes. This fireplace was a replacement of a prior one that, like the usual English fireplaces, had, as a mantel, just a painted wooden flat board.' However, the mantel mounted today at Longwood in this room is in black marble as fitting the depiction given by Bernard Chevallier in the book 'Sainte Hélène, Île de Mémoire'.*

The bedroom facing south.

In addition, and before returning for good to his 'cherished' camp beds, there would still be a last episode: Upon arrival to the house he had found a cumbersome canopy bed supplied by the English in his bedroom; clearly intended to serve as his bed. He ordered Marchand to substitute this immediately by his old camp bed. Notwithstanding, in November 1816, certainly tired by so many months sleeping in these –obviously– uncomfortable beds, he asked for the old canopy bed to be installed in his bedroom again. That was a cumbersome, huge piece of furniture, whose legs had to be sawn off to enter in the modest abode of the fallen Emperor. Once assembled, it made Napoleon exclaim: *'Avez-vous jamais vu une façon de lit plus plaisante? C'est un château branlant où l'on atteint qu'avec une échelle, un piège à rats dont le goût anglais pouvait seul accoucher'[1].* Disillusioned, he resumed using his camp beds... once and for all.

Seating comprised a large white canapé (where the Emperor liked to stretch out and rest); a light rattan cane armchair that has survived to the present and appears in a couple of period illustrations and a couple of mahogany chairs –equally of rattan cane– furnished with cushions. The Emperor used to place his Austerlitz sword on one of them.

1.   *'Have you ever seen a more ridiculous bed? This is a shaky castle only accessible by a ladder: a rat trap that only the English taste could produce'. Commented by Bernard Chevallier in the book 'Sainte Hélène, Île de Mémoire'.*

Concealing the door to the bathroom was a large screen upholstered with a sky blue silk fabric decorated with large roses and leaves. Hung on one of the panels was a portrait of his son in the arms of Marie Louise.

At the beginning, by way of a desk, there was an inconspicuous table covered by a green drapery and a wobbly gueridon serving Napoleon at breakfast time. These pieces would be substituted later in 1816 by another gueridon and a proper desk topped by a watch usually surrounded by papers and books... There was a screen protector facing the fireplace topped by a mirror coming from Mme. de Montholon´s cheval glass, on both sides of which hung another two small portraits of the King of Rome.

In the autumn of 1817, the bedroom was enriched by the addition of another stack table, a huge carpet and two small hearth-rugs. This chamber would be the one in which the Emperor would spent the longest time at Saint Helena. Marchand, surely for that reason, took a lot of effort to convert it into a sort of sanctuary by displaying portraits of his mother, wives and –very specially– his beloved son the King of Rome; as well as some tokens of past glory, like the Frederick the Great's alarm clock and an array of Napoleon's toiletries and personal objects...

The Bathroom

The Emperor's bathroom at Longwood was but a kind of tight corridor of 124 sq ft (11.5 m^2) hastily arranged by the Northumberland's carpenters. This might possibly be the most important room in the house for Napoleon, who could be depicted as a 'bath addict', as it was his custom to spend immersed in his bath tub filled with extremely hot water between one and two hours everyday. There he could have breakfast, read dispatches, books and papers; dictate letters on important and lesser business; receive people and –one can only guess– relax... sometimes.

Marchand described how joyfully he took his first bath at Longwood on 10th December 1815 after leaving the Malmaison on 29th June, which is 164 days deprived of his beloved baths. Now, once finally settled at Longwood, he could at last resume his bathing and hygienic habits with the help of Marchand of course and –nonetheless– the indispensable bathtub provided by the English. In fact there were three successive pieces. The first was a crude wooden specimen worked by the seamen that, being of an excessive capacity, hindered the always problematic water supply. The second, a lead one, was contributed by O'Meara and it is still serving as a pond in the Longwood's garden.

The last one –made of copper– was installed in November 1816. It also has stood the passing of time and could even be retrieved to be displayed as originally in the course of the reconstruction effectuated by the Martineaus. It was a large, deep vessel measuring 6 feet (185 cm.) length, 2 feet (61 cm.) width and a 'frightening' depth of 2.3 feet (71 cm.); which makes one wonder whether the Emperor used some kind of 'underwater' seat or perhaps was fond of taking a spontaneous dive in the course of his long bathing sessions... Whatever might it be, he would take these baths on an almost daily basis and even when the supply of fresh water failed, the tub could be filled with brine. Significantly, bathing served his English guardians well too; as they could easily check everything was in order by simply watching the considerable and evident work needed to heat such a big quantity of water...

Napoleon's washstand. Note the basins are missing.

Bathtub in the bathroom facing east.

The always diligent Marchand, who occupied a contiguous room of similar proportions, had a made-to-purpose mahogany tray that, once hooked onto the bathtub, served Napoleon to perform the many activities he liked to carry out during his eternal baths. A white marble stand holding two basins, a small side table and chair completed the furniture of this rather gloomy and small room that was only poorly lit through a window facing west.

When entering this bathroom as it is today there's a sort of disturbing feeling floating around. A kind of silent, brooding presence projected by the image of the fallen man immersed in his huge, steaming tub...

A view from Longwood House.

A DAY IN NAPOLEON'S LIFE

This Longwood House occupied by Napoleon extended backwards with a series of complementary, service buildings hosting the staff and servants, whose number would progressively decrease as years went by. From the arrival on 10th December 1815 to his death on 5th May 1821, he spent there 1974 days in a permanent struggle against the overwhelming boredom of Saint Helena and the ever increasing oppression exerted by the pernickety and short-sighted executioner of the orders issued by the British government: Hudson Lowe.

The life of the French party all along those awkward years would be always subjected to the court etiquette. A suffocating imposition derived from Napoleon's obsession with posterity and his stern determination for the survival of his dynasty, then personified in his son the King of Rome. At the beginning there would be frequent outings on horseback and carriage and visitors came to the house eager to meet this man of legend but soon, and coincidental with the arrival of Hudson Lowe, the general situation deteriorated. The Emperor would opt to stay alone in his private rooms more and more each day as the atmosphere at Longwood House rarefied. Jealousy, ridiculous quibbles and disaffection grew all around him until the end...

Immediately upon arrival to Longwood Napoleon proceeded to regulate the daily life of its occupants in order to prevent idleness and enforce order, as was his custom. It was certainly no different from his own routine, that began at around 6:30 everyday, when he awaked requesting that windows and louvers were opened (when he was in good mood) exclaiming *'Laisse entrer l'air que le bon Dieu fait'* (*Let the air that the good Lord has made come in*). Clad in informal attire, it was only after he had drunk his coffee that the elaborated process of his personal toilette –performed in a quite ritual fashion– began. He shaved himself while his valet –normally Marchand or Ali– held a mirror in front of him. It has been said that he adopted this practice to prevent assassination attempts after the Consulate but, most probably he simply enjoyed doing it himself as, in all probability, his confidence in his first valet at Saint Helena was unquestionable.

Normally he wouldn't take a bath in the morning, but just performed some ablutions and washed himself using his magnificent wash stand. He took a lot of care of his teeth, brushing them vigorously before having the valet rub his torso with *eau de cologne* vigorously too. Napoleon was very fond of these morning rubbings; always demanding his assistant to rub harder and harder while telling anybody around how healthy it was. All these processes were sprinkled with continuous pranks, advocative remarks or trivial questions. It was as if he faced those mornings with a positive, even cheerful mood perhaps because, deep inside, he still hoped something could change his pitiful condition. Perhaps because he was still wondering about a possible deliverance during those long, sleeplessness nights lying in one of his narrow camp beds or walking from one to another...

The toilette accomplished, it was the turn for the doctor on duty. Napoleon had scarce or null faith in the medical profession and –at least judging by the series of physicians that attended him at Saint Helena– he may have been correct. Among them all, O'Meara (see page 86) would be the one he most sympathized with: a reciprocal feeling that enabled the Emperor to indulge in one of his favourite pastimes: gossiping. He would pester O'Meara every morning with a barrage of banal questions about Lowe and other significant Saint Helenians, or just check the current opinion about him, while the young doctor struggled to perform the examination.

When the time for a hair cut came, it was Santini (see page 119) who rendered this service that –according to some surviving sketches taken from life showing Napoleon with an unruly lock of hair– was certainly not top-of-the line. Perhaps Napoleon´s frequently quoted remark to Santini, made during the course of hair cut sessions and pronounced in Corsican: **'Eh brigante! Mi voi tagliare une orecchia'** *(Hey rascal! You're going to cut my ear)*, was not just a joke after all...

At this point, and depending on the weather (and his mood), he would consider going outside for a walk or a ride or just stay inside, still informally dressed, remaining in the study or the parlour, usually dictating his memoirs or just killing time... If, on the contrary, he opted for an outing he would don a hunting frock with engraved silver buttons, white vest and trousers and riding boots. When simply strolling on foot he wore gold buckled black shoes and white stockings. In both cases he would always donned the Cross and Grand Eagle of the Legion de Honour. In regard to Napoleon's wardrobe at Saint Helena it should be noted that he favoured simple and comfortable garments. Surviving iconography shows him clad in the typical attire commonly associated with his personage, mostly patterned after his legendary green uniform of colonel of *'Chasseurs de la Garde Impériale'* on which even the hunting frock mentioned above was inspired. More casual wear departing from his 'official' appearance like the one worn after awakening or the white nankeen outfit topped with a broad brim straw hat that he used when directing ongoing works in Longwood's gardens, were duly noted and captured for posterity by surrounding onlookers, so offering a contrasting, more intimate image that would be immediately incorporated to the Saint Helenian iconography.

Napoleon was also rather sober in regard to the complements he usually carried on him: a pocket watch, a small spy glass, a handkerchief, a liquorice box and a fashionable snuff box. When back from a morning ramble around 10 AM, he undressed reverting to his more comfortable dressing gown to have a rather ceremonial breakfast presented by Marchand. When being in good humour he had one or several staff members joining him; the better his humour was, the more guests he had. Weather permitting; breakfast would be staged outside beneath the pergola or under a shady tree. Inside the house he used to have breakfast in his apartments. Service was then laid in the bathroom, from whence Marchand would take the dishes to be presented to his majesty...

A dethroned Emperor clad in shabby clothes with breakfast served from his bathroom. That is, at least seen with today's eyes, a pretty laughable scene but, the fact that nobody there is reported to have even smiled, certainly makes a point in measuring and understanding the deeper nature of Napoleon Bonaparte. What was the inner force of this man that could prevail and even imposed himself on foes and sympathizers alike? He was deprived of any factual power and amidst the most unfavourable circumstances, but he kept projecting his figure in a constant, steady way. No matter if it was Austerlitz, Waterloo... or Saint Helena.

Cook Lepage and his later successor Chandelier struggled in the poorly conditioned kitchen to produce the elaborated delicacies expected to please royalty, but the Emperor, loyal to his humbler background and long life on the field, would rather eat a simple soup. Like the one called *'soupe de soldat'* (soldier's soup): a broth stuffed with lots of bread and beans that he always took very hot. Chicken and mutton were his best choice regarding meat, and beans and lentils for greens. He showed no significant inclination for alcoholic beverages either, contenting himself with a glass of Chambertin diluted with water. His inveterate habit of spending not much more than ten minutes for meals would be kept at Saint Helena too.

A typical lunch at Napoleon's home in Saint Helena would normally start with some kind of soup, followed by a well grilled, bread coated, mutton breast and washed down with claret wine and a roasted chicken –or a couple of mutton chops– with a side dish of legumes. Lunch finished by drinking the indispensable and duly hot cup of coffee, the Emperor raised and either moved into his private rooms for a nap or proceed directly towards the parlour for a working session in the company of his 'general staff', clearly presided by Las Cases until his abrupt departure in late 1816 and by Montholon in the later years; once Bertrand opted for a more private living outside Longwood and after Gourgaud's snubbing departure in 1818.

Napoleon's steps reverberating in the spacious room as he walks up and down, hands behind his back and delivering a torrential speech to his abnegated officers in full style dress, quill pens and ink ready to not miss a single word... Outside, the stark plateau lost in the immensity of the South Pacific Ocean; a silence only broken by the whistling wind, a dog barking or the distant voice of some English soldier from the surrounding garrison. Occasionally, with a blank stare, he stops and spins the earth globe representing the world he had once at his feet...

The Emperor's best time at Longwood usually arrived just after these working sessions in the parlour were over. The by-no-means simple proceedings to provide him with his beloved bath had begun long before he abandoned the parlour and involved the work of several Chinese men under Marchland's orders and no little ingenuity. They used a heating coil fitted around a fire box that burned for hours to supply the enormous quantity of hot water needed to keep Napoleon satisfied inside his deep tub. There he could spend hours before getting in formal dress helped by Marchand and going into the sitting room where the ladies and gentlemen of his diminutive court were already in waiting. During the first two years living at Longwood House there were frequent visitors. Mostly Saint Helena's English socialites and significant voyagers sailing to or from the Far East; all of them naturally excited –and eager– to meet the man of the century and providing in exchange an anxiously needed element of relief from the overwhelming boredom.

Needless to say visitors would be presented with a flourished display of Longwood's etiquette. Santini or Noverraz would wait for them in the garden sporting livery outfits (see page 111) and leading the way into the parlour, where the newcomer was formally welcomed in the name of the Emperor by one or several officers according to rank. Then appears Bertrand in full Grand Marshal's regalia, standing at the door to the sitting room, and invites the stunned visitor to come in. There finally is the mythical man that would invariably stage the same performance: standing by the fireplace, hat under his arm and ready to entertain a profuse conversation. Or rather a monologue sprinkled with many successive questions that his guest would nervously answer the best he could.

The duration of these visits varied mainly depending on the Emperor's mood. When he was not pleased or interested he retired in short time to his 'interior' until about four in the afternoon, when the time for his promenade –that he favoured mostly in the first years– arrived. Normally he liked to be accompanied by his 'full retinue', including Madams Bertrand and Montholon, that used to sit by his side in the carriage back while Bertrand and Cases seated at front and the flamboyant Gourgaud prancing around on horseback. It was he who was in charge of the stables and supervised the Archambault brothers (see page 116) to have the six-horse- drawn carriage ready. They rode wildly, as if trying to escape from their ineluctable fate across the plateau, around the meagre wood or towards the Betrands' home... inside the permitted area. Some other times he just contented himself with extenuating strolls on foot across the garden, in endless conversation, until twilight.

At sunset, marked by a cannon shot from the English garrison, the group returned to the house and, while the Emperor rested for a while in his private rooms, the others probably tried to relax a little before getting in formal evening dress to meet again the talkative Emperor in the sitting room, entertaining new conversations or just playing chess. Incidentally a game at which Napoleon didn't really excel. Much on the contrary he played poorly and even took pride in cheating openly as –revealingly– accounted by Mme. de Montholon: '*Sometimes he ruled 'fallen piece, piece played', but it only applied to his opponent as it was all different for him and he had always a good reason why it didn't matter and if somebody pointed it out, he laughed.*'[1]

Dinner time at Longwood varied over the years, depending on circumstances, from 7 to 9 in the evening. The Emperor and his guests are gathered in the sitting room when the door to the dining room is opened by Santini exactly on schedule. He is also wearing the imperial livery and pompously announces: '*Le dîner de Votre Majesté est servi*' (The dinner of His Majesty is served). Then the Emperor led the entourage into the dining room, where everybody takes their pre-arranged seats. Napoleon is at the middle of the table with Albine de Montholon at his left and Las Cases at his right facing Montholon, Gourgaud and Las Cases' young boy. When Bertrand and his wife assisted, Albine would cede her post beside the Emperor to Mme. Bertrand; a gesture only reluctantly performed, as jealousy would be a permanent driving force among the French group. English guests are not uncommon in the beginning, but they would dwindle with the passing of time because, among other reasons, they tended to be shocked at the magnificence and abundance displayed at General Bonaparte's table, which is not surprising considering the sharp contrast among the 'plentiful' pantry of the French and the scarcity the islanders were used to.

---

1. *As referred by Gilbert Martineau in his book 'La Vie Quotidienne à Sainte-Hélène au Temps de Napoléon'. Tallandier.*

Diners talked in a low voice while eating in this dining room lighted by an excessive number of candles that created a suffocating atmosphere and reflected in the outstanding silverware and glass. This was the most copious meal, usually comprising the customary soup, two or three starters, a roast and two desserts. As the saying goes, 'Gluttony kills more than the sword' and, even though Napoleon's sobriety appears to be sufficiently documented, the fact that he reached 90 kg shortly before dying, as well as some contemporary remarks hinting at his majesty's liking for chocolate and wine, could be some factors to be considered in connection with his premature death.

As dinner rarely lasted above half an hour, the house residents still had time to kill before going to bed. They would return to the sitting room after dinner and have coffee served there, in the amazing Sevres china called the '*Cabaret Egyptian*' that was exquisitely decorated with Egyptian landscapes. To entertain these late hours the French party resourced to board games like Reversi or Piquet; listened to Mme. de Montholon singing and playing the piano or –worst of all– bore the Emperor reading out some newspaper or declaiming a fragment from some book of choice: mostly classical or French literature and drama. The best account of these weird soirees can be found in Gourgaud's gritty memoirs[1] from which the following fragments are taken:

January 19th 1816, Friday.
'After dinner, reading of Delphine until midnight,
Everybody is bored.'

January 26th 1816, Friday.
'Sad dinner, followed by chess.'

February 1st 1816, Thursday.
'Sad dinner, boredom, bed time at 10.'

February 7th 1816, Wednesday.
'The dinner is sad, nobody spoke. The English press is read.
His majesty is sad, worried. He plays mechanically with the chips
during the reading. He suffers.'

March 28th 1816, Sunday.
'His Majesty is with Bertrand and says nothing to me. We have a
carriage ride. The dinner is sad, the soiree mournful.'

---

1.   *Général baron Gourgaud. Journal de Sainte-Hélène 1815-1818.*

June 8ᵗʰ 1816, Sunday.
'After dinner, reading of the Gospels, Mme. de Montholon declares that she will end being devout and adds that I will be too.'

January 8ᵗʰ 1817, Wednesday.
'After dinner, reading of the Death of Caesar, Spartacus, Philoctetes ...Sadly and fighting sleepiness, awaiting midnight.'

January 11ᵗʰ 1817, Saturday.
'The Emperor demands Zaïre at 10 and reads until midnight. All of us fight the sleep and boredom.'

Things are not so bad when Napoleon just let his memories flow in candid conversation, or some interesting subject arises. Chatting may then stretch well into the wee hours... But, more often than not, he retires no later than midnight. As he doesn't sleep well, he may request some of his aides to keep on with reading until falling asleep. Then Marchand extinguished the candles and another day is over... or nearly, as frequently our man awakes in the night and wanders up and down stoically awaiting the next dawn...

THE YEARS

1815

DECEMBER 1815

When Napoleon and his party finally arrived at Longwood the year 1815 was nearly over; just short of 21 days. The whole site had been hastily arranged and much improvised. The French would try to improve it in the forthcoming years. Las Cases, Gourgaud, the servants, O'Meara, and the British duty officer assigned to Longwood were hosted in the service building next to the main house, while Bertrand managed to settle stay in a 1.25 mi. (2 km.) distant private house at Hutt's Gate. Consequently, the only people from Napoleon's inner circle living under the same roof were Montholon and his family, who would occupy the room that would eventually be converted into the library.

In these first weeks of acclimatisation to his new –and last– abode there still should be novelties, even surprises that didn't foretell the routinary tedium, the overwhelming boredom and the attrition lying ahead...

His first bath and some intimacy after five long months, or even the unexpected arrival of the picturesque and intriguing Captain Piontkowski who disembarked from the store ship Cormorant on 29th December and went immediately to Longwood offering himself at the service of the Emperor[1] surely added some colour to the situation. Perhaps he had the first clear indication of what was coming when he was aware of the fact that going beyond the established limits around the house was strictly forbidden unless he was 'accompanied' by a British officer...

Napoleon's first outing on horseback at Longwood. (Bombled. ©Andrea Press).

1.   *A Polish Exile with Napoleon. G. L. DE ST. M. Watson. Harper & Brothers, 1912.*

Saturday 30th, December 1815. Coming across a field being ploughed, the Emperor dismounts and, taking the plough from the hands of a greatly surprised peasant, draws a long furrow by himself very fast and pronouncing no other words than ordering Las Cases to give one napoleon to the peasant (Le Memorial de Sainte-Hélène. Le Comte de Las Cases. Garnier Frères. Paris 1895). *(Bombled. ©Andrea Press).*

1816

JANUARY 1816

At the beginning of 1816 most of the exiles felt that their situation wouldn't last much longer and were confident that Napoleon would find a prompt solution. The Emperor has regular outings on horseback, exploring the surroundings. The discovery of the beautiful Sandy Bay in the course of a ride accompanied by admiral Cockburn cheered him up. His mood is good and he enjoyed the frequent visits to Longwood of English officers and personalities, what perhaps even encouraged him to keep taking Las Cases' lessons in the English language. On the other hand, work on his memoires progressed steadily... All seems to be rather quiet at Longwood.

Sailors from the Northumberland stalk behind the trees to catch a glimpse of the great man. (Bombled. ©Andrea Press).

Thursday 11th January 1816. Admiral Taylor arrives unexpectedly to Longwood heading a considerable cavalcade in the hope of being allowed to present his respects to the Emperor during a layover of two days at the island on his way to Europe. He wasn't. (Bombled. ©Andrea Press).

Tuesday 30th January 1816. Napoleon takes a break in the course of a ride at Longwood. (Bombled. ©Andrea Press).

FEBRUARY 1816

February comes bringing unpleasant hot weather that the French fight with difficulty, though probably still thinking their awkward situation couldn't last much longer. Then they learn that two English sentinels, on Cockburn's orders, have been detached around the house to keep a close night watch. That was instantly perceived as a bad omen causing a general depressive feeling that Napoleon tried to fight by couching all of them in moral strength. It was a psychological trick to which he would resource all along the seclusion and, in due time, another factor leading to his own moral –and physical– weariness.

March 1816

March elapsed with not very significant events; just the first horse races at Deadwood camp, the visits to Longwood of a series of British naval officers on their way back to Britain, the sad news of Ney's execution and some denouncing letters reporting the captives' conditions that they managed to smuggle to Britain.

April 1816

April could be tagged as Lowe's month, as the new governor arrived at Saint Helena on the 14th so inaugurating a new crucial phase in this story. Napoleon's appraisal of the personage took place on the spot of their first, tense meeting (see page 83) and, if any, only changed for worse with the passing of the years. Lowe would be converted in his nemesis; a dumb, evil figure without which the legend of Saint Helena would have been very different, or even perhaps never existed. Showing an extraordinary lack of tact, Lowe's first measures did nothing to improve the conditions at Longwood but, much to the contrary, enraged them by exerting closer controls and enforcing strict obedience to the rules. There was a second meeting on the 30th that lasted just ½ hour[1]. They conversed alone this time but Napoleon referred the encounter to Las Cases:

> *Tuesday 30th.*
>
> *About half past eight we are on the way back to Longwood; it was very dark. Weather has changed to a driving rain, hitting like hail; which makes our riding very dangerous and pitiful. We could fall down the cliffs at anytime, as we galloped blind and aimlessly. We were soaking wet on arrival.*
>
> *The Emperor had given orders for me to go into his room when I came back. He was well, but has stayed at home all day and had received nobody else. He was waiting for me –he said– and had many things to tell.*

---

1.   *Général baron Gourgaud. Journal de Sainte-Hélène 1815-1818.*

On knowing that the governor had arrived, he admitted him into his room, even though he was not dressed and was lying on his canapé. He had gone over all that came naturally to his mind, vis-á-vis with him, in a perfect calm –he told me. He had talked of protesting the treason of the 2nd of August, when the allied monarchs declared him banned and prisoner. He demanded what was these sovereigns' right to decide about him without his consent. He: who was their equal and had been one time their master.

Had he wished to retire in Russia –he told him– , Alexander, who called himself his friend, with whom he had just political quarrels; if he had not kept him as a king, at least would have treated him as such. The governor did not disagree.

Had he wished –he continued– to take refuge in Austria, the Emperor Francois, at risk of stigmatization and immorality, couldn't have banned from him not only his empire, but even his home, his family, of which he, Napoleon, was a member. The governor agreed again.

'Finally, if taking into account my personal interests,' –he said to him– 'had I been determined to defend them by taking up arms in France, there is no doubt that the allies would have granted me many concessions; perhaps even a territory.' The governor, who had resided for a long time in those places, agreed in that he could have easily gotten a great sovereign domain.

'I did not want it' –followed the Emperor– 'I was decided to retire, outraged by watching the fatherland betrayed by its agitators, or clumsily misjudge its most dear interests, outraged at seeing that the mass of representatives could, rather than dying, compromise on the sacred independence that, not less than the honour, is also a steep and shoreless island. At this state of affairs, what was my decision? Which party did I take? I sought asylum in a country thought to have powerful laws, the land of a people of which for twenty years I had been its bigger enemy. You people, what have you done? History won't honour your acts! And there is however a vindictive providence; sooner or later you will be punished! It won't be long before your prosperity, your laws expiate this affront! Your ministers, through their instructions have sufficiently proved that they wanted to get rid of me! Why the kings that have banned me did not dare to openly order my death! One and the other would have been equally lawful! A prompt end would have shown more vigour than the slow death I have

been sentenced to. The Calabrians have been far more humane, more generous than the sovereigns or your ministers! I will not commit suicide. I think that would be cowardice. It is noble and brave to overcome misfortune! Everyone down here must meet his destiny! But if I must stay here, you owe me that as a good deed, because my staying here is dying each day! The island is too small for me that have ridden ten, fifteen, twenty leagues daily on horseback. The climate is not like ours, these are neither our sun nor our seasons. Everything here breathes a deadly boredom! The location is unpleasant, unhealthy; there is no water at all; this part of the island is deserted, it has rejected its inhabitants!'

The governor replied then that his instructions ordered a reduction of the limits and an English officer to follow him at any time. *'If these instructions should be followed literally, I will never leave my room; and if your people cannot enlarge the limits, there is nothing you can make for us henceforth. Besides, I don't demand nor want anything. Transmit my feelings to your government.'*

The governor let slip out the following remark: 'That's what happens when instructions are given from far away and concerning a person one doesn't know.' He insisted that on the arrival of the wooden mansion or palace that was on the way, better measures could be taken; that the coming ship carried many pieces of furniture and eatables supposed to be desirable; that the government made all kind of efforts to soften his situation.

The Emperor replied that all these efforts were but little things. That he had begged to be subscribed to the Morning Chronicle and the Statesman to read about the matter (sic) in less unpleasant terms and nothing had been done; that he had asked for books –his only consolation– and, after nine months, nothing has been received; that he had requested news about his son, his wife and nothing had been said.

'Regarding the eatables, the furniture, and the lodgings' –he continued– *'you and I are soldiers, monsieur; we know the real value of these things. You have been in my birth city and perhaps even at my home. Without being the worst on the island, with no reason to be ashamed of it, you have seen what little thing it is. Well, despite having had a throne and given crowns, I have never forgotten my original condition: my canapé, my camp bed, that's all that I need.'*

The governor remarked that the wooden palace and all the rest was at least an attention.

'**Perhaps to keep you satisfied in the eyes of Europe,**' –replied the Emperor– '**but for me all of them are unfamiliar and irrelevant. It is not a mansion; it is not furniture what should be sent to me, but rather an executioner and a shroud! The one would seem like an irony, the other would be a favour. I repeat, your minister's instructions lead to that, and I demand it. The Admiral, who is absolutely not a bad man, I believe, has softened them. I don't complain about his acts; only his manners disturbed me**'. Here the governor inquired if he, ignorantly, could have incurred in some faults too. '**No, monsieur, we don't complain of anything since your arrival. However, one fact hurt us: that of your inspection of our servants, in as much as it was injurious to monsieur de Montholon, whose good faith is questioned and mean, painful, and offensive towards me; perhaps even for an English general that came to meddle between my valet and me**'

Hudson Lowe interrogating the domestic staff at Longwood. (Bombled. ©Andrea Press).

*The governor was seated on an armchair facing the Emperor, who was stretched out on his canapé. It was shadowy, the evening had fallen and visibility was not good. '**So,**' –remarked the Emperor– '**it was just to no avail that I tried to study the expression on his face to know the impression I could have made on him at that moment**'*

In the course of this conversation, the Emperor, who had read that morning the campaign of 1814 by Alphonse de Beauchamp, in which all the English bulletins are signed Lowe, asked the governor if it was him. This prompted him to answer, certainly embarrassed, that they were his, and that had been his point of view.

On leaving, Sir Hudson Lowe, who during the conversation had many times offered the Emperor his doctor –that he said to be very skilled– repeated to him at the door his plea to accept his offering, but the Emperor, who saw it coming, repeatedly refused it.[1]

There weren't any witness for this dialectical duel between Napoleon and Lowe: the prisoner and his gaoler. Las Cases' account, as told directly by the Emperor, renders a vibrant picture of Napoleon the 'tactician'. How the setting is arranged with him in informal room attire, lying nonchalantly on his canapé while Lowe, in uniform, is seated in a oblique position towards Napoleon. The Emperor tried to scrutinize his inscrutable opponent.

Very interestingly sir Hudson Lowe left a personal account of this second interview:

'Having received an intimation from Captain Poppleton, the orderly officer attached to Longwood House, that General Bonaparte had not been visible the day before, but that either he or Dr. O'Meara would certainly endeavour to see him in the course of that evening, to be enabled to make his report as usual to me, I immediately repaired to Longwood, in order to prevent any unpleasant intrusion on him, however warranted by the instructions given to the orderly officer, which require that he should either see General Bonaparte twice during the day, or ascertain his being on the spot and report accordingly.

I met General Montholon at the door of the house, asked how General Bonaparte was, and, on being told he was indisposed and suffering, said I wished to offer him the assistance of a medical officer, but begged him to wait on General Bonaparte and acquaint him I was there, imagining, as it was after four o'clock, when he usually received people, he would probably see me. General Montholon went in, and returned shortly afterward, saying General Bonaparte would see me.

1.   *Le Memorial de Sainte-Hélène. Le Comte de Las Cases. Garnier Frères. Paris 1895.*

I passed through his dining-room, drawing-room, another room in which were displayed a great number of maps and plans laid out on a table, and several loose quires of writings, apparently memoirs and extracts, and was then introduced into an inner apartment, with a small bed in it and a couch, on which latter Bonaparte was reclining, having only his dressing-gown on, and without his shoes. He raised himself up a little as I entered the room, and, pointing out a chair to me close to the couch, desired I would sit down. I seated myself, and commenced the conversation by saying I was sorry to hear he was suffering from indisposition, and had come to offer him the assistance of a medical officer of respectability[1] who had come out with me from England, that he might have the benefit of his advice as well as that of Dr. O'Meara, should he require it. **'I want no doctors,'[2]** *was his reply.*

He then, after some indifferent questions, asked me whether the wife of Sir George Bingham had arrived. She had not arrived, I replied; and I had reason to regret on another account the Adamant transport had not yet come in, as she was laden with several articles that might be useful to him, such as wines, clothes, furniture, etc.

He said it was all owing to the want of a chronometer; that it was a miserable piece of economy on the part of our Admiralty not to give every vessel above 200 tons a chronometer—he had caused it to be done in France; that, exclusive of the value of the ship, the lives of the persons in it merited that consideration. I said they were not vessels employed under the direction of the Admiralty, but of another board.

This made no difference, he said. After some other general and unimportant questions a short interval of silence ensued. He lay reclined on his couch, his eyes cast down, apparently suffering a good deal from an oppression in his breathing (which had been particularly observable, so as to cause an occasional interruption to his voice while in discourse), and his countenance unusually sallow and even bloated. He recovered himself after a little while to ask me what was the situation of affairs in France at the time I left Europe. I said, every thing, I believed was settled there.

'Beauchamp's Campaign of 1814 was lying on the floor near him. He asked me if it was me who had written the letters referred to in the appendix to his work. I replied 'Yes.' **'I recollect Marshal Blücher at Lübeck,'** *he said:* **'is he not very old?'** *'Seventy-five years,' I replied, ' but still vigorous, supporting himself on horseback for sixteen hours*

---

1. Dr. Baxter.
2. 'Je ne veux pas de médecins.'

in the day, when circumstances render it necessary.' He sat reflecting a few moments without any observation. He resumed: ' **The Allies have made a convention declaring me their prisoner: what do they mean? They have not authority to do so (ni en droit ni en fait). I wish you to write to your Government and acquaint it I shall protest against it. I gave myself up to England, and to no other power. It is an act of the British Parliament alone which can warrant the proceedings against me. I have been treated in a cruel manner. I misunderstood the character of the English people. I should have surrendered myself to the Emperor of Russia, who was my friend, or to the Emperor of Austria, who was related to me. There is courage in putting a man to death, but it is an act of cowardice to let him languish, and to poison him in so horrid an island and in so detestable a climate.'**[1]

I said the island of Saint Helena had never been regarded in that light; that, except so far as related to the precautions necessary for his personal security, it had been the desire of the British Government to render his situation as comfortable as possible. That the house, furniture, and effects of every kind coming out for his use, certainly indicated as much regard as it was possible to show him consistent with the main object for which this place of residence had been selected.

'Let them send me a coffin; a couple of balls in the head is all that is necessary. What does it signify to me whether I lie on a velvet couch or on fustian? I am a soldier, and accustomed to every thing. I have been landed here like a convict, and proclamations forbid the inhabitants to speak to me.'[2] *attributing a great deal of all this to the Admiral; but concluded with saying.* **'It is not that the Admiral is a bad man.'**[3]

The conversation then turned on the localities of Longwood House. He inveighed bitterly against it; said he was excluded from all communication with the inhabitants; that many persons in the town would willingly come to see him, but that they were afraid to ask for

1. *NOTE FROM THE ORIGINAL TEXT: 'J'ai mal calculé; l'esprit du peuple Anglais. J'aurais du me rendre a l'Empereur de Russie, qui était mon ami, ou a l'Empereur d'Autriche, qui était mon parent. II y a du courage a faire tuer un homme, mais c'est une lâcheté de le faire languir et empoisonner dans une île si affreuse et sous un climat si détestable.'*
2. *NOTE FROM THE ORIGINAL TEXT: 'Qu'on m'envoie un cercueil! Deux balles dans la tête, voila ce qu'il faut. Qu'importe à moi si je me couche sur un canapé de velours ou de basin? Je suis un soldat, et accoutumé a tout. On m'a débarque ici comme un galérien. Proclamations défendent aux habitants de me parler.'*
3. *NOTE FROM THE ORIGINAL TEXT: 'Ce n'est pas que l'Amiral soit un méchant homme.'*

passes; that he had no trees about him; that this alone rendered the spot detestable; that he could not ride to any extent; that he wished to have a greater range for his exercise without being accompanied by an officer; that unless I gave him a greater range I could do nothing for him. I told him the range of Longwood was greater than any other piece of ground on the island. He said perhaps so; but that there was the camp on part of it. He did not want to see the camp always; he could not ride where that was. He wished the people of the island might be allowed to come and see him. He recurred frequently to the hardship there was in depriving him of all intercourse with them. His addresses to me on this point were humble and artful; they obtained no assent from me.

He spoke of my having insisted on seeing his servants; that it was a strange thing to interfere between a man and his valet-de-chambre; that personally seeing and examining the servants after having received their declaration was as much as to say, **'in good French, that they had lied.'**[1] *I told him that it was Count Bertrand's fault. I had pointed out to him the way in which I intended to receive their declaration; he wished it to be otherwise, but I had insisted upon receiving it in the manner I had indicated.'* **Ah! This is now over.'** *he replied.*[2]

He said he would recommend to the four who had signed their declaration to leave him whenever he found his situation more precisely defined, and should make application for their being permitted to do so. He said, **'Repeat every thing I have mentioned to you to your Government. I wish them to know my sentiments.'** *On going away I again offered him medical assistance.* **'I want no doctors,'** *he replied. These were the last words he addressed to me.'*[3]

These two versions of the same episode exemplify very well the dual character of Saint Helenian's large bibliography. Notwithstanding, both renditions are coincidental in illustrating the clash between these two incompatible men. At the end of this meeting the Emperor should have definitively set his course of action for the coming years, once he became completely aware of the fact that Lowe wouldn't be seduced by the allure of 'Napoleon the Great' nor would budge an inch regarding the conditions of his captivity...

1.   *NOTE FROM THE ORIGINAL TEXT: 'En bon Français, qu'on avait menti.'*
2.   *NOTE FROM THE ORIGINAL TEXT: 'C'était la faute du Général Bertrand. Je lui avais indiqué la manière que je comptais recevoir leur déclaration; il l'avait voulu faire d'une autre, mais j'avais insiste pour la recevoir de la manière que j'avais indiquée.' 'Ah! c'est une chose passée.'*
3.   *History of the Captivity of Napoleon at Saint Helena. From the letters and journals of the late Lieut. Gen. Sir Hudson Lowe and official documents not before made public by William Forsyth, MA. Harper Brothers. 1853, New York.*

Once he relayed this meeting to Las Cases he kept silent, in a reflexive mood, for a while before producing the following remark:

> *'What ignoble and sinister figure is that of this governor! I have seen nothing like that in my whole life! One shouldn't drink from a cup of coffee left alone with such a man for a moment!... My dear, they couldn't send me anything worse than a gaoler!'*[1]

May 1816

On Monday 6th May, the Adamant arrived to Saint Helena loaded with the much praised 'wooden palace' the furniture and goods which, in turn, failed to arouse any enthusiasm from Napoleon and his company. Also this month Lt. Colonel Skeleton boarded on the way back to Britain after promising the exiles to carry news of them to Europe; which he eventually did.

On Saturday 11th, at four in the afternoon, a card addressed to *'le Général Bonaparte' was* delivered to Longwood inviting the Emperor for dinner at Plantation House. In this way Lowe, by clumsily trying to please the Emperor, opened the can of worms infuriating the whole French party; always ready to exploit any deviation from the etiquette on which the point of Napoleon's imperial character was quintessential.

As the saying goes, 'it never rained but it poured' when a satisfied, confident Lowe arrived at Longwood on Thursday 16th, to present Napoleon with good news: the palace, furniture and the goods arrived with the Adamant, and of course his 'complimentary' invitation to Plantation House. Let Sir Hudson Lowe render this detailed account of what happened in the course of this 3rd encounter between the two men:

> *'It being necessary to come to some decision in respect to the house and furniture which had been sent from England for the accommodation of General Bonaparte and his followers, I resolved, on waiting on him, communicating to him the arrival of the various materials, and asking his sentiments in respect to their appropriation before I made any disposition of them. I previously called on General Bertrand to ask if he thought General Bonaparte would be at leisure to receive me, and on his reply, which was in the affirmative, proceeded to Longwood House, where, having met Comte Las Cases, I begged he would be the bearer of my message to the General, acquainting him of my being there, if his convenience admitted of being visited by me. I received a reply, saying the 'Emperor' would see me.*

---

1. *Le Mémorial de Sainte-Hélène. Le Comte de Las Cases. Garnier Frères. Paris 1895.*

I passed through his outer dining-room into his drawing-room. He was alone; standing with his hat under his arm, in the manner he usually presents himself when he assumes his Imperial dignity. He remained silent, expecting I would address him. Finding him not disposed to commence, I began in the following words:

- Sir, you will probably have seen by our English newspapers, as well, perhaps, as heard through other channels, of the intention of the British Government to send out hither for your accommodation the materials for the construction of a house, with every necessary furniture. These articles have now for the most part arrived. In the mean time, Government has received information of the building prepared for your reception at this place, and I have instructions for appropriating the articles as may seem best, whether for making a new building, or adding to the conveniences of your present one. Before making any disposition on the subject, I wished to know whether you had any desires to communicate to me regarding it.

He stood as before, and made no reply. Observing his silence continue, I again commenced by saying:

- I have conceived, Sir, that possibly the addition of two or three good rooms (deux ou trois salons) to your present house, with other improvements to it, might add to your convenience in less time than by constructing a new building.

He then commenced, but spoke with such rapidity, such intemperance, and so much warmth, that it is difficult to repeat every word he used. Without apparently having lent an ear to what I had said, he began:

- I can not understand the conduct of your Government toward me. Do they want to kill me? Are you come here to be my executioner, my jailer?

Posterity will judge of the way in which I have been treated; the sufferings I experience will recoil upon your nation. No, sir, I will never allow any one to enter the interior of my house, to penetrate into my bed-chamber, as you have ordered to be done.

When I heard of your arrival on this island, I thought that, as an officer of the army, I should find you possessed of politer manners than the Admiral, who, as a naval officer, might have had a rougher bearing.

I have no fault to find with his heart. But how do you treat me? It is an insult to invite me to dinner, and to call me General Bonaparte. I am the Emperor Napoleon. Are you come here to be my executioner, my jailer?[1]

While speaking in this manner his right arm moved backward and forward, his person stood fixed, his eyes and countenance exhibiting every thing which could be supposed in a person who meant to intimidate or to irritate. I suffered him to proceed, though not without a strong feeling of restraint upon myself, until he was nearly out of breath, when, on his stopping, I said:

- Sir, I have not come here to be insulted, but to treat of an affair which concerns you more than it does me. If you are not disposed to speak about it, I will retire.

- I had no intention to insult you, sir, but how have you treated me? Has it been in a way becoming a soldier?

- Sir, I am a soldier to perform the duties I owe to my country in conformity with its customs, and not according to the model of other countries. Besides, if you think you have any cause to complain, you have only to write, and I will transmit your representation to England by the first opportunity.

- What will be the use of sending it to your Government? It will not be attended to there any more than here.

---

1. *NOTE FROM THE ORIGINAL TEXT: 'Je ne conçois rien à la conduite de votre Gouvernement envers moi. Est-ce qu'on veut me tuer? Est-ce que vous êtes venu ici pour être mon bourreau—mon geôlier? La postérité jugera de la manière dont j'ai été traite. Les malheurs que je souffre retomberont sur votre nation. Non, monsieur; je ne permettrai jamais qu'on entre dans l'intérieur de ma maison, qu'on pénètre dans ma chambre-a-coucher, comme vous en avez donné l'ordre. Lorsque j'ai entendu parler de votre arrivée dans cette île, j'ai cru que, comme militaire de l'armée de terre, je vous aurais trouvé d'un caractère plus honnête que celui de l'Amiral, qui, comme officier de marine, aurait pu avoir des manières plus dures; je n'ai pas à me plaindre de son cœur. Mais de quelle manière me traitez-vous? C'était une insulte de m'inviter a dîner et de m'appeler le Général Bonaparte. Je ne suis pas le Général Bonaparte—je suis l'Empereur Napoléon. Est-ce que vous êtes venu ici pour être mon bourreau—mon geôlier?'*

- I will have it published in all the papers of the Continent, if you wish it. I am performing my duty, and am indifferent to any thing besides.[1]

Then adverting, for the first time to the matter which had brought me to him, he said:

*- **Your Government has made me no official communication of the arrival of this house. Is it to be constructed where I please, or where you may fix it to be?***

- I am now come, sir, for the express purpose of announcing it to you. I have no difficulty in replying to the other point. If there is any particular spot which you might have thought of to erect it upon, I will examine it, and have it erected there, if I see no objection to it. If I see any objection to it I will acquaint you of it. It was to combine this matter in some degree of concert with you that I am now come.

*-**Then you had better speak to the Grand Maréchal about it**, he replied, **and settle it with him.***

- I prefer, sir, addressing you upon it. I find so many mésintelligences happen when I adopt the medium of other persons, particularly as in the instance of the orders which you mention I had given for forcing an entrance into your private apartments, that I find it more satisfactory to address yourself.

He made no particular reply to this, walked about for a moment, and then, working himself up apparently to say something which he thought would appal me with extraordinary surprise or dread, he said:

---

1. NOTE FROM THE ORIGINAL TEXT: - *Monsieur, je ne suis point venu ici pour être insulté, mais pour traiter d'une affaire qui vous regarde plus que moi. Si vous n'êtes pas dispose d'en parler, je vais m'en aller.*
    - Je n'ai pas voulu vous insulter, monsieur; mais de quelle manière m'avez vous traité! Est-ce de la manière d'un militaire?
    - Monsieur, je suis militaire a la manière de mon pays, pour faire mon devoir envers lui, et non pas d'âpres celle d'un autre. D'ailleurs, si vous croyez avoir raison de vous plaindre de moi, vous n'avez qu'à écrire: j'enverrai votre représentation en Angleterre par la première occasion.
    - A quoi bon l'envoyer à vôtre Gouvernement? Elle ne sera pas plus écoutée qu'ici.
    - Je la ferai publier dans toutes les gazettes du continent, si vous me le demandez. Je fais mon devoir, et suis indifférent pour le reste.

- Shall I tell you the truth, sir? Yes, sir, shall I tell you the truth? I believe that you have received orders to kill me. Yes, to kill me. Yes, sir, you have received orders to do any and every thing.[1]

He then looked at me as if expecting a reply. My answer was:

- You remarked, sir, at the last interview I had with you, that you had misunderstood the character of the English people, and you now equally misunderstand that of the English soldier.[2].

Our conversation here terminated. He stood a little while, and, as if neither of us had any thing more to say, we mutually separated. Not seeing, however, any motive in what had passed to prevent me from saying what I had intended to do when I first came into the room, I addressed him again by the word 'Monsieur,' and, on his turning his head, said:

- There is at present an officer of my staff with me, who I am desirous, on this occasion, of presenting to you. It is a Lieutenant-Colonel of the King's Guards[3] (Lieutenant-Colonel Wynyard)[4].

He replied,
- I can not receive him at present. When one is insulted, one is not in a humour to see any one.[5]

---

1. NOTE FROM THE ORIGINAL TEXT: - *Voulez-vous, monsieur, que je vous dise la vérité! Oui, monsieur, voulez-vous que je vous dise la vérité ? Je crois que vous avez les ordres de me tuer. Oui, de me tuer; oui, monsieur, vous avez les ordres de faire tout, tout.*

2. NOTE FROM THE ORIGINAL TEXT: - *Vous avez observe, monsieur, dans la dernière entrevue que j'ai eue avec vous, que vous aviez mal calculé l'esprit du peuple Anglais; vous calculez aussi mal à présent l'esprit d'un militaire Anglais.*

3. NOTE FROM THE ORIGINAL TEXT: - *Il y a un officier de mon État-major avec moi a présent, que je désirerais dans cette occasion vous présenter. C'est un Lieutenant-Colonel des Gardes du Roi.*

4. *Lieutenant-Colonel (afterward Major-General) Edward Buckley Wynyard, C.B., arrived at Saint Helena in the Adamant store-ship on the 6th of May, and became Military Secretary to the Governor.*

5. NOTE FROM THE ORIGINAL TEXT: - *Je ne peux pas le recevoir á présent; lorsqu'on est insulté, on ne peut tenir société à personne.*

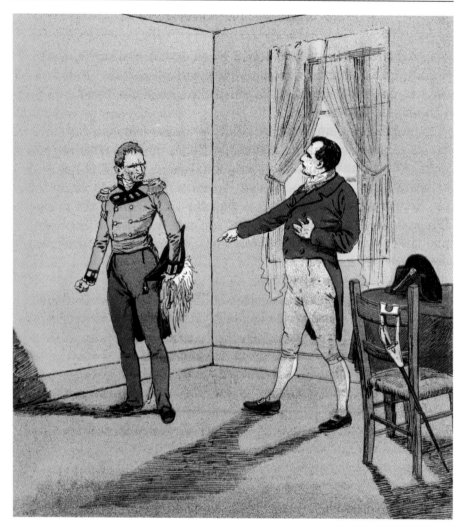

Heated discussion between Napoleon and Hudson Lowe. (Bombled. ©Andrea Press).

I made an inclination of my head, and retired. On quitting the room I found two of his servants close to and listening at the outside of the door, and Count Las Cases walking in a contemplative mood at the other end of the room[1-2]

1.   NOTE FROM THE ORIGINAL TEXT: *According to Forsyth 'Montholon, Las Cases, and O'Meara concur in saying that this interview took place on the 16th instead of the 17th of May, and they have all more or less misrepresented what took place. Not one of them, it must be remembered, was present; and they must all have derived their knowledge of the conversation from Bonaparte.'*
2.   *History of the Captivity of Napoleon at Saint Helena. From the letters and journals of the late Lieut. Gen. Sir Hudson Lowe and official documents not before made public by William Forsyth, MA. Harper Brothers. 1853, New York.*

Some days later Lowe sent the following report on this 3rd meeting to Bathurst:

'It would be difficult to account for the extraordinary resentment he displays at the most common precautions which are taken for his personal security on any principle of common reasoning. It must be, therefore, affectedly put on, or spring from a great delusion in his own mind as to the degree of faith and confidence to be reposed in him.

Under either point of view, I feel it more and more difficult to reconcile the exercise of my duty with the high respect, regard, and attention which he seems to require. His objects evidently are a greater degree of personal liberty, and greater opportunity of personal intercourse with that class of persons who are the most likely to be worked on by him. **'If you can not extend my limits, you can do nothing for me,'** was a remark he made in my second conference with him. All the rest, I apprehend, he considers as a specious illusion, if not an insult, and feels irritated at the same time his designs should have been seen through, and his applications prove abortive. It has been very remote indeed, however, from either my intention or practice to give him any additional motive of irritation.

The precautions for his security are precisely the same as those established by Sir George Cockburn. The communications I addressed to your Lordship on the 13th instant, and the memoranda of conversations referred to in them, will show that no additional measures have been taken beyond what the attempts to produce relaxation, and to establish precedent thereupon, have too evidently required. In every other respect I have been solicitous to add to his comforts and convenience; and on the occasion of informing him of the arrival of the materials for his house, was prepared, if I had found the objections to establish his permanent residence at Longwood absolutely irremovable, to have offered to him the selection of another spot, incomparably the most eligible in point of air, trees, and verdure, on the island, and which I had already in a certain degree for this purpose insured the occupation of. The violence of his manner, however, prevented his receiving any other communication than that which is detailed in my conversation with him.

In relating the particulars of this conversation to your Lordship, I think it a duty to myself to mention that General Bonaparte's anger drew forth, no violence of language or expression from me.

I said precisely what is stated in the memoranda and nothing else; and what I did say was uttered with a tone of composure. I understood he was in an exceedingly ill-humour after I quitted him, but that *the following morning (during which interval he had seen General Bertrand, and probably heard the conversation I had with him) he had recovered his temper, so much so as to send for Dr. O'Meara to breakfast with him, when his conversation almost entirely ran on the accusations which had been brought against him by Sir Robert Wilson for his conduct in Syria, and what he had been accused of in respect to Captain Wright, alleging the injustice of both, and saying he doubted not Sir Robert Wilson would, during his late residence in France, have ascertained upon what slight foundation his accusations stood.'[1]*

Profoundly irritated by Lowe's impassibility, the Emperor certainly lost his temper confronting this new governor who was absolutely not that *'class of persons who are the most likely to be worked on by him'*. He had clearly overreacted and probably thought that this kind of emotional outburst –so strikingly contrasting with Lowe's dignified coolness– didn't fit with the imperial condition so dear to him. On the last day of May he would go over the incident regretting his behaviour, even though any apology had to be discarded, given the 'circumstances'...

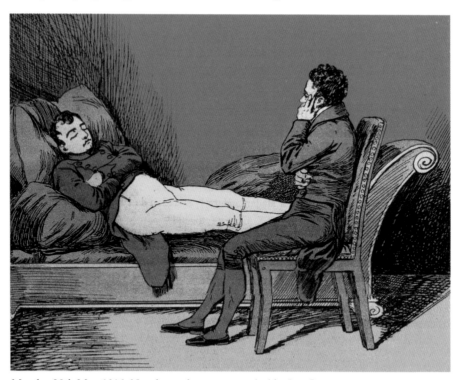

Monday 20th May 1816. Napoleon takes a nap watched by Las Cases.
(Bombled. ©Andrea Press).

---

1. *History of the Captivity of Napoleon at Saint Helena. From the letters and journals of the late Lieut. Gen. Sir Hudson Lowe and official documents not before made public by William Forsyth, MA. Harper Brothers. 1853, New York.*

Tuesday 28th May 1816. When riding by the British camp, every soldier ran to fall in before Napoleon. (Bombled. ©Andrea Press).

June 1816

Napoleon entered June in a depressive mood which would only be alleviated by taking three-hours-long hot baths and engulfing himself in long conversations and digressions on a variety of topics –mainly literature and history– so reflecting and examining his past with a sharp critical eye. He pondered the alternative choices to wrong decisions made in the past and projected what could have happened had he moved differently. However, this critical analysis was mostly referred to tactical decisions that could perhaps have been better. Or, in other words, regarding the means of his political and military activity, but never the ends, by which he resolutely always stood.

French dragons in Spain under the watching eye of a group of relaxing Spaniards.
(Bombled. ©Andrea Press).

A significant example for these mediations took place on Friday14[th] concerning the war in Spain, that he judged to be a crucial point in his career and the beginning of his end, according to the following excerpt from Las Cases' memorial:

'In any case', he said, 'Charles IV was over for the Spaniards, and the same should be done with Ferdinand. The plan best fitting me and my purposes would have been mediation, like that of Switzerland. I should have given the Spanish nation a liberal constitution and have Ferdinand putting it into practice. Had he performed it in good faith, Spain would prosper in harmony with our new customs. In this way the great goal would be achieved, and France would acquire a close ally, a tremendous increase in power really. If Ferdinand, on the contrary, didn't honour his

new commitments, the Spaniards wouldn't fail to suppress him and would come to me to be given a new master.'

   'Whatever it may be', finished the Emperor, 'this unfortunate Spanish war has been a veritable calamity, the first cause for the misfortunes of France. Following my meetings with Alexander, Britain should accept the peace by reason or by force. It was lost and discredited on the continent; its affair of Copenhagen[1] had appalled all the spirits. As for me, on the contrary, I gleamed full of advantage. Then the unfortunate Spanish affaire suddenly reversed the opinion against me and restored the British prestige. They could then follow on with the war; the resources of South America were at their disposal; a British army could be assembled on the Peninsula and from then on they became the victorious agent and the redoubtable core of any possible intrigue in the continent, etc. The war of Spain is what has lost me!'[2]

Hot baths and conversations of balsamic effect with Las Cases strolling around and inside the house... God, religion, agnosticism, Voltaire, Gil de Blas... an incessant flow of ideas and words alternated with long, ominous long silences while June slowly slipped by.

On Monday 17th admiral Sir Putney Malcolm arrived to Saint Helena. Reported to be a likeable and perceptive man, he was presented to Napoleon at 3 in the afternoon this very same day. Malcolm would play a positive role in refreshing and easing a little the increasingly oppressive atmosphere by this time. In addition, it was not only Malcolm who disembarked on the 17th, as he had sailed in the company of three extravagant characters: Balmain, Stürmer and Montchenu, the respective commissioners of Russia, Austria and France detached to Saint Helena to keep a watching eye on Napoleon. The Emperor greatly despised this bunch and, adamantly, refused to receive any of them. They would never meet him...

On Wednesday 19th the Northumberland set sails to Europe, which didn't leave the French unmoved, as they had shared the long crossing from Europe in the company of Cockburn and his officers, by whom they had been reasonably well treated aboard. There was a sad feeling of solitude and abandonment when this ship –their last direct connection with Europe– weighed anchors and disappeared on the horizon...

---

1.   *The British bombardment of Copenhagen in 1807 during the Napoleonic wars.*
2.   *Le Memorial de Sainte-Hélène. Le Comte de Las Cases. Garnier Frères. Paris 1895.*

Saturday 22nd and Tuesday 25th should have been joyful days for the Emperor, as two consecutive book shipments arrived to Longwood. He rushed to open the boxes, leafing through the books eagerly. As a consummate reader he knew books were the best way to escape from harsh realities by letting his mind fly across the universe, to strengthen his inner world, to reinforce his will...

Napoleon remains silent for a while. Then, as if perking up; exclaims: **'Quel roman pourtant que ma vie!'** *(What a novel my life has been!) (Bombled. ©Andrea Press).*

July 1816

Any court worthy of this name is expected to display some degree of magnificence and abundance. It was no different in the case of Longwood. Despite the constrictive circumstances or its insignificant size, there was plenty of food and beverages at disposal for Napoleon and his guests; at least by Saint Helena's standards. That was a permanent conflict between the French and Hudson Lowe, who made his first approach to the subject this month of July by announcing a reduction of expenses that were –not surprisingly– angrily protested by the Emperor's retinue which, in turn, were then free to abandon the isle and so escape their miseries. In fact, the exodus would soon begin while Napoleon's grievances, sadness and loneliness grew.

In the first days of July the Emperor is in good enough spirits as to take Montholon's son Tristan on his knees and relate him some tales. (Bombled. ©Andrea Press).

However, the reduction of the household wouldn't end the pressure for cutting the expenses as, peculiarly enough; Napoleon had no free access to his funds abroad and had to maintain his household depending on British allowances rigorously –or meanly– administered by Lowe.

Spirits were rather hot when the fourth meeting between the Emperor and Lowe took place on Tuesday 16th. For two hours Napoleon devoted himself to delivering a stormy philippic that, basically, stressed on the same arguments exposed during the previous interviews... to the same effect: none. In fact there is a striking contrast between Napoleon's overexcited demeanour and Lowe's perfect temperance. By the time of this fourth meeting Napoleon should overly have known that he had no way with Lowe and, for this reason, this meeting was perfectly dispensable... He would learn in time.

A fire breaks out in the sitting room. (Bombled. ©Andrea Press).

Days went by slowly and routinely until Friday 19th, when a fire in the sitting room broke during the night. They went out to the garden to escape the fire that threatened with devouring the whole building. When in the haste a silver buckle from the Emperor's shoe fell onto the ground, everybody around prompted to fetch it, which led Las Cases to included the following remark on the Longwood's etiquette in his memoirs:

> 'The Emperor was always the most and best familiar of all men for us. We were around him the most respectful courtesans, always ready to anticipate his desires, watching for his needs. A simple gesture pushed us on the move.
>
> None of us entered his room without being called. If there was something important, an audience was requested. When he was strolling with any of us by his side nobody else joined him without being called. At the beginning all of us had our hats off in his presence, which puzzled the English, who had orders to put their hats on once they had been addressed. This contrast seemed so ridiculous to the Emperor that he ordered us to proceed just like them. Nobody save the two ladies sat in his company without being so ordered by him. He would never be approached without his request, unless there was a conversation going on, that was always and in all cases directed by him.'[1]

On Monday 22nd the weather is fine and the Emperor, in good and talkative humour, enjoys a carriage ride in the morning and has lunch outside. The fire damage is still being repaired, and they have to remain in the dinning room for a lively after-dinner conversation that soon drifts into the world of fortune-tellers and necromancers, on whom Napoleon –still loquacious– would produce the following remarks:

> '**All this charlatanism and so many others, like those of Cagliostro[2], Mesmer[3], Lavater[4], etc. are destroyed by this only and very simple reasoning: All that might be, but it is not.**

1. *Le Memorial de Sainte-Hélène. Le Comte de Las Cases. Garnier Frères. Paris 1895.*
2. *'Count Alessandro di Cagliostro' (1743–1795) was the alias of the Italian occultist Giuseppe Balsamo. An adventurer and magician, he was a glamorous figure associated with the royal courts of Europe, where he exhibited various occult arts. Even though his reputation lingered for many decades after his death, he would be finally regarded as a charlatan and impostor, dying imprisoned.*
3. *Franz Friedrich Anton Mesmer (1734–1815) was a German physician believing that there was a natural energetic transit between all animated and inanimate objects that he called 'animal magnetism' or mesmerism.*
4. *Johann Caspar Lavater (1741–1801) was a Swiss priest mostly known for his work in the field of physiognomy, introducing the idea that there is a direct relation between the physical and psychological traits of individuals.*

Man loves the marvellous, which attracts him with an irresistible enchantment. He is always ready to neglect the immediate reality and run after the contrived. He gives himself to be fooled. The truth is that all is marvellous around us. There is no phenomenon properly speaking: everything is a phenomenon in nature. My existence is a phenomenon; the firewood that burns in the fireplace and warms me up is a phenomenon; the sunlight here, that sheds light on me is a phenomenon; all the first causes, my intelligence, my capacities, are phenomena, as all these exist but we don't know how to explain them.

I leave you here, and then there I am now, in Paris, coming into the opera. I am greeting the spectators, hearing the ovations, watching the actors, listening to the music. Well, if I can cross the distance from Saint Helena, why couldn't I see the future as I see the past? Would any of them be more extraordinary than the other? No; simply there is not such a thing. Such is the reasoning that will destroy always, indisputably, any imaginary wonder. All the charlatans talk about very spiritualistic things. Their reasoning may be right and alluring but the conclusion is wrong, because facts are missing.

Mesmer and the mesmerism have never recovered from Bailly's report[1] in the name of 'Académie des Sciences'. Mesmer produced effects on an individual by magnetising him face to face. The same person, when magnetised from behind and unaware experimented no effect at all. It was thus for his part a failure of his imagination, a feebleness of his senses. It was like the somnambulist that runs across the roofs safely because he is scared of nothing, but in daylight he would break his neck because his senses would be troubled.

I approached once during one of my public audiences the charlatan Puységur[2] in relation with his somnambulist girl. He wanted to praise her highly but I laid her low just with these words: if she is so wise; have her saying something new. In two hundred years, men would have made many advances; let her speak about just one. Let her say what I will be doing in eight hours. Tell her to announce the winning number for tomorrow's lottery; etc.

---

1. Jean Sylvain Bailly (1736-1793) was a French scientist and politician from the early French Revolution. He was mayor of Paris and died guillotined during the Reign of Terror.
2. Amand-Marie-Jacques de Chastenet, Marquis de Puységur (1751–1825) was a French magnetizer remembered as one of the pre-scientific founders of hypnotism.

I did same way with Gall[1] and contributed greatly to his demise. Corvisart[2] was a great sectarian of his. He and his kind had a great penchant for materialism, which supposedly should increase their science and domain, but nature is not so poor. Had she been so rough as to show herself by her outward appearance, we would be faster and wiser.

Her secrets are finer and more delicate, more fleeting and –until now–, escape everybody. A little hunchback happens to be a great genius while a big, handsome man can be just a fool. A big head containing a large brain sometimes cannot produce one single idea but a little brain may enclose a huge intelligence.

Note Gall's imbecility: he attributes to some humps tendencies and crimes that are not in nature but derive from society and conventionalism. What would be of the theft humps if there were no property? Or of the drunkenness hump with no fermented liquors? Or the ambitions if there were no society at all?

It is the same thing with the remarkable Lavater and his accounts on the physical and the moral. Credulity is in the weakness of our character. We are immediately open to positive ideas when we should, on the contrary, be very careful about them. Immediately upon seeing a man's traits we claim to know his character. The right thing would be to reject the idea, to neutralise the misleading aspects. Somebody robbed me. He had gray eyes, so I will never look into grey eyes without the idea and fear of being robbed. That is a weapon that has hurt me and scares me whenever I see it. But, did the gray eyes really hurt me? Reason and experience –and I have lived quite a lot through that– show that all those outward features are deceitful, that you can't be too careful and that you can only measure men for sure by watching them; by trying them out; by talking with them.

---

1. *Franz Josef Gall (1758–1828) was a German scientist considered as a pioneer for the localization of mental functions in the brain. Controversial at his time, his studies are not seriously regarded nowadays. According to Las Cases, Gall repeatedly assured that Napoleon's skull structure was the most extraordinary thing he had even seen: something marvelous. Upon a long and detailed study of the Emperor's head, Gall arrived at the conclusion that his head should have been growing larger very late, even after adultness. Eager to produce evidence for his theory, he collected from Napoleon's hatter astonishing testimony stating that Napoleon's hats had to be enlarged even during the Empire.*
2. *Jean-Nicolas Corvisart-Desmarets (1755–1821). A significant figure in the history of French medicine, he was the primary Napoleon's doctor from 1804 until the exile to Saint Helena.*

However, there are hideous faces[1] in front of which the most powerful reason vanished and condemnation is pronounced prevailing against reason."[2]

The next day, Tuesday 23rd, Napoleon's humour has changed for worse. Depressed and uneasy, anything seemed to disturb him: the repairs still going on, the British soldiers around him... it was a sort of 'emotional rollercoaster' in which days or moments of relative relief were followed by others of profound displeasure, all surrounded by the inescapable boredom...

A couple of days later Admiral Malcolm came to visit him. They chatted for three hours of which the Emperor took advantage to repeat once again his long list of complaints. Malcolm seemed to agree to most of them which, at least, should appease a little the unbearable anxiety of this formidable jailed lion.

On Monday 29th the weather was still no good and bad blood feelings roamed around Longwood against the Governor, who continued applying his instruction to the letter. Possessed by an outburst of wrath and fanatical devotion to his Emperor, Santini makes plans to kill Hudson Lowe, by then the embodiment of every possible evil for the French. When Napoleon is told about Santini's plot he reprimanded the poor man and obliged him, reluctantly, to renounce to his purpose.

Needles to say, had Santini carried out his plans successfully this story would have continued differently. It is clear anyway that Napoleon totally disliked the idea, taking for granted that things wouldn't have improved if Lowe had been killed...

---

1.   *Here Las Cases remarks that Napoleon pointed out Hudson Lowe as an example of hideous face and everybody laughed.*
2.   *Le Memorial de Sainte-Hélène. Le Comte de Las Cases. Garnier Frères. Paris 1895.*

Monday 29th July 1816. When a tent is raised outside to provide some shade (admiral's courtesy) the Emperor converses with the officer and sailors at work and gives instructions to gift the men with one napoleon each. (Bombled. ©Andrea Press).

August 1816

Wind, clouds, rain... This was the month of Napoleon's first birthday at Saint Helena. On the 15th of August 1816, Thursday, he is 47 years old. A nice party and a plentiful dinner are arranged that day under a huge tent assembled outside the house. Napoleon seemed to be very pleased.

Next day, as if to break the monotony, a forerunner of present-day coolers or fridges arrives to Longwood: it is a contraption supposed to produce ice chemically that creates great expectation: Unfortunately it only worked poorly and would be soon forgotten...

Napoleon and Las Cases entertaining one of his many conversations during a stroll while being followed by their carriage at hearing distance. (Bombled. ©Andrea Press).

Napoleon spent most of his time with Las Cases dictating, chatting and reflecting on great variety of subjects that, occasionally, revealed his inner thoughts about profound questions like, for example, the ideas of God and religion in which he digressed on the evening of Saturday 17th. According to Napoleon, the notion of God is natural to any man, but distorted and used by the many different religions manipulating mankind into a troubled existence... most probably he was just an agnostic.

In all, a most significant event happened on Sunday 18th. Bad weather had not receded yet. Napoleon was in a prankster mood, pulling the leg of Mme. de Montholon when the Governor, unexpectedly, arrived in the company of Admiral Malcolm. Immediately upon seeing them the Emperor fled into the back yard but, when Montholon arrived and informed that these two gentlemen earnestly requested to see him to discuss a very important matter, he finally consented. This would be the fifth and last time Hudson Lowe met the great man alive. The conversation evolved with the three men strolling around the house while Las Cases, Montholon and some British officers walked behind them at a respectful distance. Among any possible flaw in Lowe's personality should not be found inaccuracy or lack of rigour; especially regarding official matters. So I think his account on this last conversation is worthy of being reproduced here[1]:

'Having called at Longwood in company with Sir Pulteney Malcolm, we found General Bonaparte was walking in his garden. He went off immediately as he saw us; but having inquired for Count Montholon, and sent a message by him to say we were there, Bonaparte returned to the garden, and the Admiral and myself joined him. He spoke solely to the Admiral, in which I made no attempt to interrupt him, but, profiting by the first interval of silence, I commenced and addressed him as follows: That I was sorry to be under the necessity of saying any thing which tended to incommode him, but I was placed under such peculiar circumstances, from the conduct toward me of General Bertrand, that it became a matter of indispensable necessity I should make known the details of it to him, and endeavour to establish some rule for my future communications in regard to his affairs. He was aware of the instructions I had received from my own Government in regard to the expenses of his establishment.'

Lowe referred to a recent quibble (one of many others) regarding protocol involving Counts Montholon and Bertrand, and complained about Count Bertrand's behaviour before following on addressing Napoleon.

'It was obvious, after this, I could have no further communication with General Bertrand, and I thought it proper to call and acquaint him of it; that, whatever might have been General Bertrand's personal feelings toward me, I called upon him by the desire of the person whom he acknowledged as his Emperor to speak of his business; that it was a failure of respect to him as well as to me; that I wished in consequence to learn with whom it was his desire I should in future communicate on questions of such nature in regard in his affairs. General Bonaparte made no reply for so considerable a space of time that I thought he did not mean to speak at all; but, finally, in a hollow, angry tone of voice, commenced a string of remarks to the following purport, addressing himself entirely to the Admiral:

1.   See Malcolm's own report of this last interview in page 91.

'General Bertrand is a man who has commanded armies, and he treats him as if he were a corporal; he is a man well known throughout Europe, and he (the Governor) had no right to insult him. He did perfectly right in speaking about the prohibition against sending letters, and was justified in engaging in a discussion on that subject. He (Sir Hudson Lowe) treats us all as if we were deserters from the Royal Corsican or some Italian regiment; he has insulted Marshal Bertrand, and he deserved what the Marshal said to him.'

I repeated what I had said in a former conversation—that General Bertrand had first insulted me; that in the conversation which had passed nothing could be more temperate and moderate than my language to him, as could be testified by my military secretary, who was present at the interview; that I had said nothing which, in tone or manner, could justify the reply he gave to me. He recommended his reproaches of my having written insulting letters to General Bertrand, and provoked him to say to me what he did. I again referred to his having first written an insulting one to me; that he had said I rendered his (Bonaparte's) situation 'affreuse'; had accused me of 'abus de pouvoir et injustice.' I then added: 'I am a subject of a free government. Every kind of despotism and tyranny I hold in abhorrence, and I will repel every accusation of my conduct in this respect as a calumny against him whom it is impossible to attack with the arms of truth'. He stopped a little on my making this observation, but soon resumed, addressing himself to the Admiral, and with language more bitter than before:

'There are two kinds of people,' he said 'employed by Governments: those whom they honour, and those whom they dishonour; he is one of the latter; the situation they have given him is that of an executioner.'

I answered: 'I perfectly understand this kind of manoeuvre-endeavour to brand with infamy, if one can not attack with other arms. I am perfectly indifferent to all this. I did not seek my present employment; but, it being offered to me, I considered it a sacred duty to accept it.'

'Then,' said he, 'if the order were given you to assassinate me, you would accept it?'

'No, sir'. He again proceeded (to the Admiral), and said I had rendered his situation forty times worse than it was before my arrival; that, though he had some disputes with Sir George Cockburn, he always treated him in a different manner; that they were content with *each other, but that I did not know how to conduct myself toward men of honour; that I had put General Bertrand under arrest in his own house; and had taken away from him the permission to give passes to Longwood. The Admiral said it was Sir George Cockburn who had done this. Bonaparte replied,* **'No, sir; he told you so'** *(alluding to me),* **'but it is not true.'** *The Admiral again told him it was not me, but Sir George Cockburn, had told him so. Bonaparte then said he could not even write a billet de galanterie to my Lady Malcolm without my seeing it; that he could not now have a woman come to see him without my permission; and that he could not see the Lieutenant-Colonel and the officers of the 53*[rd]*. I interrupted him here by saying he had refused to see the Lieutenant-Colonel and the officers of the 66*[th] *regiment. If they wanted to see him, he answered, why did they not apply to the 'Grand Maréchal'?*

'I had mentioned it to General Bertrand,' I observed. **'But the Lieutenant-Colonel ought to have spoken to him, and not to you.'** *He again broke out into invectives on my mode of treatment; said I had no feeling; that the soldiers of the 53*[rd] *looked upon him with compassion, and wept (pleuraient) when they passed him. Continuing, he said to the Admiral:* **'He kept back a book which had been sent to me by a Member of Parliament, and then boasted of it.'** *'How boasted of it?', I exclaimed, struck with the falsehood of the assertion.* **'Yes, sir'** *(interrupting me),* **'you boasted of it to the Governor of the island of Bourbon;**[1] **he told me so. You took hold of him'** *(he said)* **'on his arrival here, and made him believe that you were on the best footing with us all, and treated us all particularly well; but this was not true.'**

He was proceeding with a further repetition of what had passed between Colonel Keating and him, when the Admiral interrupted him with a defence of my not having sent the book to him; saying that a book with such an inscription on it I could not send, and that I ought not to have been made the instrument of delivering it to him. The Admiral added, 'Colonel Keating was wrong in mentioning such a thing to him.' **'Yes,'** *he said,* **'in one to boast of it, and the other to repeat it.'** *He then remarked that I had sent letters to him with the title of Emperor. 'Yes,' replied I, 'but they came from the Secretary of State's office, and were from your own relations or former subjects, and not from English*

---

1.   *NOTE FROM THE ORIGINAL TEXT:'Colonel Keating, who is here alluded to, denied in the strongest terms that he had made any such communication to Napoleon. It was one of O'Meara's accusations against Sir Hudson Lowe that he reported this affair to Earl Bathurst unknown to Colonel Keating. This is untrue. In a dispatch to Lord Bathurst, dated August 29, 1816, Sir H. Lowe, speaking of that officer, said, 'I enclose a letter to inform him of what Bonaparte said.'*

persons. *I am personally acquainted with the gentleman who sent the
book; he left it to my choice to send it or not, and I am certain he will
fully approve of what I did in not sending it.' He paused at this, and
dropped the topic. He again addressed himself to the Admiral; accused
me of having published the contents of a letter he had received from his
mother. The Admiral defended me; said he knew I never published the
contents of any private letters received from his family. I replied, it was
not me that had done so; it must have been his own people that did it;
that every thing was misrepresented to him.*

*Lowe, Malcolm and Napoleon in the course of the last interview between the Emperor and the
governor. (Bombled. ©Andrea Press).*

'*You have* bad people about you *sir,*[1] *I said. The Admiral shortly afterward repeated a similar remark, saying,* 'You have bad people around you.'[2] *He appeared to me struck at both our observations in this respect, and made no attempt to reply, but went on again in his strain of invective, general and personal; he told me, as he had done once before,* **'You are a Lieutenant-General, but you perform your duty as if you were a sentinel; there is no dealing with you; you are a most intractable man. If you are afraid that I should escape, why do you not bind me?'** *I answered, I merely executed my instructions; that, if my conduct was disapproved of, I might be readily removed.* **'Your instructions are the same as Sir George Cockburn's'** *he replied;* **'he told me they were the same.'** *He said he was to be treated as a prisoner of war; that the Ministers had no right to treat him in any other way than as prescribed by the Act of Parliament; that the nation was disposed to treat him well, but Ministers acted otherwise; accused me of being a mere instrument of the blind hatred of Lord Bathurst. I remarked,* 'Lord Bathurst, sir, does not know what blind hatred (haine aveugle) *is. He talked about our calling him General; said he was* 'Empereur'; *that, when England and Europe should be no more, and no such name known as Lord Bathurst, he would still be Emperor. He told me he always went out of the way to avoid me, and had twice pretended to be in the bath that he might not see me.* **'You want money; I have none, except in the hands of my friends; but I can not send my letters.'** *He attacked me about the note which had been sent back to Count Bertrand, saying,* **'You had no right to put him under arrest; you never commanded armies; you were nothing but the scribe of an État-Major. I had imagined I should be well among the English, but you are not an Englishman.'** *He was continuing in this strain, when I interrupted him with saying,* 'You make me smile, sir.' **'How smile, sir?'** *he replied, at the same time turning round with surprise at the remark, and, looking at me, added,* **'I say what I think.'** *Yes, sir,* 'I answered,' *with a tone indicative of the sentiment I felt, and looking at him,* 'you force me to smile; your misconception of my character and the rudeness of your manners excite my pity. I wish you good-day;' *and I left him (evidently a good deal embarrassed) without any other salutation. The Admiral quitted him immediately afterward with a salute of the hat."*[3]

---

1.   *NOTE FROM THE ORIGINAL TEXT: 'Vous êtes mal environné, Monsieur.'*
2.   *NOTE FROM THE ORIGINAL TEXT: 'Vous êtes mal entouré.'*
3.   *History of the Captivity of Napoleon at Saint Helena. From the letters and journals of the late Lieut. Gen. Sir Hudson Lowe and official documents not before made public by William Forsyth, MA. Harper Brothers. 1853, New York.*

At this point Napoleon threw out the towel with Lowe. He finally acknowledged to himself that Lowe would never be cajoled into anything; that his play of high-worded admonishments and exhortations to honour, etc., had produced no effects. Lowe was no fool and there was no point in prolonging such an awkward situation. Besides, that man´s coolness and inaccessibility infuriated him so jeopardizing his dignity and his honour.

Shortly after this rather stormy meeting, the Emperor announces to Las Cases that he will never meet the governor. Next time that the latter would see him he would be dead... (see page 83)

Bad weather outside the house. Bertrand and Napoleon kill the time playing chess.
(Bombled. ©Andrea Press).

SEPTEMBER 1816

Bad weather still going on. Heavy rain...

The battle between the exiles and the governor about the ever discussed problem of Longwood's squander with supplies reach a climax this month. On one side the constant complaining of the French about the poor quality of their nutrition. On the other side is Lowe's determination to reduce the expenses. He fixes a limit and declares that any excess should be covered with Napoleon's personal funds. The Emperor maintains that what's left of his fortune is in the hands of his friends abroad, to whom he is not free to write with instructions. This is a jumble with apparently no way out, as no party is prepared to compromise a solution.

Sunday 15th September 1816. Taking advantage of one of the scarce sunny days this month the Emperor goes alone for a stroll in the garden. (Bombled. ©Andrea Press).

*Prompted upon reading in a British newspaper about the 'big Napoleon's hidden treasures'
the Emperor dictates a long list of the great civil works executed all across Europe under his
ruling. (Bombled. ©Andrea Press).*

The waste at Longwood is no way Lowe's invention, but a
reality sustained by the facts and numbers of the immoderate French
consumption of eatables and –very especially– spirited drinks; which
on the other hand might be quite understandable, considering the
idleness and the boredom borne by the captives.

Napoleon, now decided to give his battle till the end, is prepared
to take advantage of any opportunity to leave perfectly clear to the
world the humiliation and crudeness he and his party are subjected
to on the island. He could very probably have implemented a proper
solution by defraying the extra cost himself but, instead, chose to
play a rather theatrical effect by ordering to break down part of his

magnificent silver ware in pieces and sell them at Jamestown. Then Lowe, aware of the move and its potential propagandistic effect blocked the operation...

Uneasiness and hatred increase each day but now there is no way back and just two possible ways ahead for Napoleon: eventual deliverance from Saint Helena after nearly a year of seclusion, not entirely impossible depending on the evolution of the political affairs in Europe, or just remaining there to the end of his life. In both cases the magnification of this privations and miseries, and the emphasis on blaming the British in the figure of Hudson Lowe were the best course of action as, even if there were no release ever, these vexations and sufferings would consecrate his figure and political system for many centuries to come...

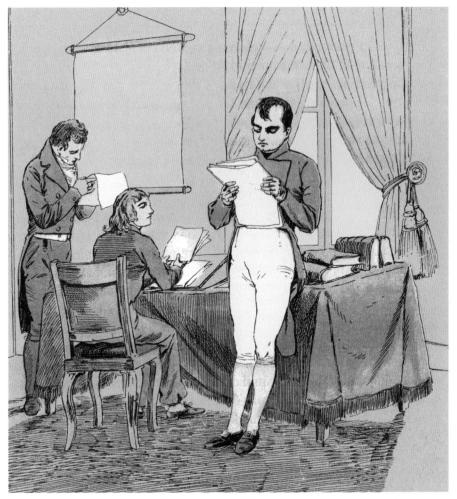

In the course of a work session with Las Cases and his son the Emperor recognises he is not able to 'decipher' his own writing… (Bombled. ©Andrea Press).

October 1816

On Tuesday 1ˢᵗ, Lowe came back to Longwood. He wanted to explain personally to the Emperor the new regulations imposed to the exiles. The Emperor, firm in his decision of never meeting the man again, didn't receive him. That, of course, wouldn't stop Lowe from putting into practice a series of extreme measures including an increase of controls, partly dissuading eventual British visitors from coming into the enclosure. On top of that, servants Archambault, Santini and Rousseau; together with captain Piontkowski would be ordered to leave the island heading for Britain. From there the first two would later sail to the United States, where they met King Joseph informing him first hand regarding the situation at Saint Helena. Piontkowski for his part tried –unsuccessfully– to meet Marie-Louise, being detained in Austria until 1821, when he vanished pursuing his adventurous life...

According to Lowe's new regulations which arrived to Longwood on October 19th; British sentinels should be posted during the night beside the house. (Bombled. ©Andrea Press).

But Lowe's most outrageous measure, heavily hitting the pride for the captives, was putting Napoleon's staff between the devil and the deep blue sea by demanding them to sign affidavits of total submission to British law and the restrictions in force at Saint Helena, or to abandon the island. Among these regulations was death penalty in case of evasion; accessories included.

On Tuesday 15th the crisis reached its peak. Amidst great sadness and anxiety the captives had to make a decision... time was running out. The Emperor, surrounded by his loyal companions declares:

'The outrages that those devoted to my person must bear daily, these outrages that apparently are wanted to be multiplied more and more, form a spectacle that I mustn't and cannot stand for any longer. Sirs, you should part, getting away from me. I couldn't stand seeing you submitted to the restrictions that they want to impose on you now and that will be increased tomorrow. I want to be alone. Go to Europe and let people know the hideous machinations against me. You will tell how you have watched me going down into my tomb. I don't want any of you signing that imposed statement. I forbid it. It won't be said that the faithful people at my disposal served to degrade me. For they expel you for refusing a completely absurd formality[1] that means that you would be expelled tomorrow one after another for any similar insignificant reason. Well! I'd rather have you all going at once. Maybe this sacrifice could bring some results'.[2]

Napoleon's orders, however, wouldn't be followed this time as, finally, all of them signed the 'infamous' declaration addressed to 'General Bonaparte' pondering that their humiliating pledge was the lesser of two evils. But, even when they opted to stay there beside their beloved master, that marked a turning point in this story at which Napoleon's retinue begun to shrink. The two servants and the Polish officer that left the island this month would be the first, but not the last. Others would soon follow...

---

1. *The 'completely absurd formality' was the treatment of 'General Bonaparte' given to Napoleon implying the denial of his imperial title that became a central issue between the two parties all along the captivity as the French, adamantly, would never accept his Emperor being simply addressed as a general.*
2. *Le Memorial de Sainte-Hélène. Le Comte de Las Cases. Garnier Frères. Paris 1895.*

NOVEMBER 1816

Nice weather. The Emperor seems to be in good health, but the atmosphere at Longwood rarefies. Idleness and boredom are taking their toll at Longwood. Envy and jealousy are commonplace. Especially, Montholon and Gourgaud couldn't stand the closeness between Las Cases and the Emperor. There was a lot of quibbling like questioning who of them should precede the others when entering the dining room, the quality of their respective lodgements and so on... Only Bertrand seemed to stand above all that pettiness. This was only the beginning of a degradation process around the figure of Napoleon as the radiating centre of this minuscule, artificial world.

Las Cases is estranged from Longwood. (Bombled. ©Andrea Press).

Hudson Lowe seizes Las Cases's papers. (Bombled. ©Andrea Press).

But Las Cases wasn't the only one hurting sensitivities at Longwood as Cipriani, the Corsican valet and factotum, was also greatly envied because of his particular and mysterious bond with the Emperor, to whom only he could speak in Corsican (see page 113).

November's days slipped away with a conciliatory Napoleon always trying to bring his party together; which proved to be a strenuous and mostly fruitless effort that often drew him into gloomy moods at which he shut himself in his inner rooms.

Friday 15th November 1816. Las Cases and Napoleon watch the fortifications in progress surrounding Longwood prescribed by Lowe. (Bombled. ©Andrea Press).

Suddenly, on Monday 25th, a new crisis broke out that would cast a long shadow all along the forthcoming years. When Las Cases tried to smuggle a clandestine letter written on silk sewn inside the lining of a mulatto servant and this is intercepted by Lowe, events rushed. He and his son are arrested, estranged from Longwood and moved to a little house nearby. Even though Las Cases earnestly claims that the governor is not entitled to, his papers and luggage are seized and scrutinized...

Under the tensions, seclusion and lack of exercise Napoleon's health declines…
(Bombled. ©Andrea Press).

DECEMBER 1816

The Emperor, dispirited and indifferent takes refuge in his apartments.

The perspective of losing Las Cases' company obviously worries him. All this affair of arresting the count and his estranging from Longwood is a favourite conversational and gossiping topic at Saint Helena. Suddenly on Wednesday 18th, after many comings and goings, Lowe changes his mind, leaving Las Cases free to return to Longwood. Surprisingly enough, the latter discarded going back beside his 'beloved' master and asks to leave Saint Helena supporting his decision with a series or rather alembicated reasons, among which the precarious health of his young son might be the only fully credible one… (see page 65).

Las Cases dining with the British duty officer in the early days of December.
(Bombled. ©Andrea Press).

There was constant unease and uncertainty this whole month, with letters coming back and forth between Las Cases, Longwood and the governor. Probably Las Cases had mixed feelings about his final resolution; including a sense of guilt for leaving the Emperor, as the following excerpt from his memorial of Sunday 29th might suggest. The die is then cast already but, apparently, he tries to justify himself alluding to a final remark made by Napoleon:

> *'About six the governor appeared unexpectedly and, after delivering his customary preamble, told me that he had brought the Grand Marshall in, whom he allowed to bid me farewell. Then he drew me to the next room where I could in fact embrace this honourable Longwood companion. He would transmit to me the following statement from the Emperor, 'That he would see me staying with* pleasure, *and see me leaving with* pleasure".[1]

---

1.   *Le Memorial de Sainte-Hélène. Le Comte de Las Cases. Garnier Frères. Paris 1895.*

Tuesday 10th - Sunday 15th. Lowe interrogates Las Cases. (Bombled. ©Andrea Press).

The next day, Monday 30th, Las Cases and his son would leave the island heading towards Cape Town, where they remained for ten months before being allowed to return to Europe...

Las Cases' departure marked a turning point at Longwood. For Napoleon it was another twist of the screw. Las Cases was the most cultivated man in Napoleon's inner circle and, as such, able to provide the Emperor with intelligent and varied conversation, a need for a loquacious man like Napoleon holding a phenomenal inner world that demanded continuous movement: physically and mentally. Gourgaud was a hot-headed, primary young man that most of the time enervated Napoleon; especially after Las Cases' parting. Montholon, a dubious character, was also a family man at least partially devoted to his own interest. Finally there was Bertrand. He was an honourable but rather tepid personality with a family too, that kept a respectful distance from Napoleon and even the others. He lived out of Longwood and would not mingle in the frequent petty conflicts occasioned by the difficult Longwood cohabitation.

On a more practical side, it should be noted that Las Cases was the only man close to the Emperor with a good command of the English language, a crucial skill given the circumstances...

Las Cases and son bid farewell to Longwood. (Bombled. ©Andrea Press).

1817

January 1817

Wednesday 1st. Life goes on after Las Cases' leaving and the year 1817 is welcomed at Longwood with the usual exchange of gifts amidst an atmosphere of harmony and concord: a full Christmas spirit hiding underlying tensions that would soon be back.

In following Napoleon's steps at Saint Helena the interruption of Las Cases' memorial at the end of 1816 should be accounted as a loss. From now on we should mainly rely on Gourgaud's and Marchand's accounts that cannot match Las Cases in terms of profundity and scope because of his superior education and closer proximity to the Emperor. Quite the opposite, Gourgaud sprinkles his journal with odds and ends that, being always obsessed with the fair sex, included some salacious remarks like the following one recorded on Saturday 4th dedicated to Mme. Montholon:

> *'I assure Mme. Bertrand that I don't tell anybody about this Montholon, that she would be very pleased of my doing so, that she gets along well with His Majesty, bed, etc. Poor Montholon, what role does he play? The Emperor calls for us. He plays billiards with the Montholon. This latter does all she can to attract His Majesty: sweet eyes, enticing, and tight fitting dress at the waist. In short, she tries to look beautiful and that is not easy. His Majesty has some oranges coming and gives them to us. He is very friendly with Mme. Bertrand and pays little attention to the Montholon.'[1]*

Or this one from Wednesday 14th:
> *'I will never abide at Saint Helena going behind M. de Montholon and even more behind his wife. She may be a whore if she wants, but I find vile the man that lets himself be forcibly persuaded by a woman and especially by a scheming and ugly woman'[1]*

Or yet another one from Saturday 18th:
> *'At seven I am called to the salon. The Emperor is with O'Meara and received me coldly. His Majesty welcomed the Montholons, he pinches her... (sic)'[1]*

It seems as if Gourgaud, once his most hated Las Cases was gone, concentrated himself on Albine Montholon. She, together with her husband would become a veritable *bête noir* for the usually over-the-

---

1.   *Général baron Gourgaud. Journal de Sainte-Hélène 1815-1818.*

top young officer. Despite the insistence displayed by Bertrand and Napoleon to get him on good terms with the couple, things would only worsen.

On his side, Napoleon battles one day after another. Baths, dictation, chatting, strolling, some visits, reading... monotony. Curiously enough, as recorded by Gourgaud, God and religion were a recurrent topic in Napoleon's conversation at the beginning of this New Year...

February 1817

Morale at Longwood begins to crack. Bertrand is considering going back to London or, at least, to send his family there. That greatly displeases Napoleon and diminishes his trust in the human condition that, by the way, should never have been too much according to an annotation in Gourgaud's journal from Wednesday 12th as follows:

> 'I left the Emperor at 5, half glad, half sad. He has talked to me with affection, but he doesn't appreciate the real attachment, he only considers the external signs and, when I pointed out that he judges the human species too devious, he replied: **'I am not paid to find it better.'**'[1]

A rather cynical remark quite unfitting Napoleon's true character. It could just be an irate response to Gourgaud's pestering company. In truth Napoleon would be more a sceptic than a cynic; a positivist than a believer. Like any other leader of men, there could be little doubt that he was well acquainted with human nature; for good and for bad. And, for that reason, he rarely would be surprised by anybody's behaviour. Besides, lack of loyalty wasn't an issue he could moan of at Saint Helena. He had sufficient examples of devoted people around. No, the real problem was the mediocrity and predictability of his whole inner circle; especially now that Las Cases was gone. From a psychological point of view, for an intellect like Napoleon's, that could represent a constriction far more acute and painful than the physical limitations imposed on him at Longwood. Simply, there was no chance of a suitable conversational partner any more in his proximity. Out of it, gents like Malcolm or O'Meara, even though they might provide some temporary relief, weren't and couldn't be reliable interlocutors...

In consequence a double and simultaneous process started: mental introspection and physical self reclusion within his last abode on this earth: the dull, unsubstantial and pathetic Longwood House. His gigantic past fell upon him unmercifully, hidden in the dark rooms,

---

1   *Général baron Gourgaud. Journal de Sainte-Hélène 1815-1818.*

stalking him, haunting him during those moments of disturbing gazes and weird, troubling silences, more and more frequently every day...

Wednesday 5th February.

His majesty, in very bad mood, engrossed, retires at half past ten mumbling: 'Moskowa... five hundred thousand men.'[1]

Days pass by with no remarkable events. Horse races at Deadwood begin with the assistance of Gourgaud and Montholon, who would take the opportunity to meet the foreign commissioners while Napoleon tries to make them out with his spyglass, hidden behind the window blinds of Bertrand's house; a visit from the Balcombe family and little more. O'Meara pointed out the first signs of Napoleon's declining health. The latter, still contemplating religious affairs declares that the religion of Mahomet is the most beautiful[1] ...

MARCH 1817

The slow and boring passing of the time at Longwood was broken on Tuesday 5th, when O'Meara arrived at the house announcing that Dr. Warden's 'Letters Written on Board His majesty's ship the Northumberland...' (see page 95) had been published in Britain amidst a great commotion. This event would mark the rest of the month. Upon reading Warden's account, a series of reactions –or better overreactions– erupted. Even though Napoleon's judgment swung at the beginning he finally got irate about Warden for betraying the confidence bestowed on the doctor aboard the Northumberland and the falseness of certain statements.

In fact, although this account displeased both pro and anti Napoleonic parties, it worked more for than against Napoleon's cause, which was no impediment for everybody there talking about and against the book practically on a daily basis. Not surprisingly the most thunderous response would be staged by Gourgaud on Sunday 9th as follows:

'I am pretty much enraged by Warden, who pictures me as a braggart and I declare to the grand marshal that I want to present a complain for slander to the governor. It is Las Cases who committed all the evil. He tells a lot of nonsense, is self-important and nobody will believe the conversations reported in this work, because he cannot speak a single word in French and his Majesty cannot understand a word in English!'[1]

1. *Général baron Gourgaud. Journal de Sainte-Hélène 1815-1818.*

In fact Gourgaud was progressively losing the command of himself, constantly complaining about trifling, domestic matters and especially obsessed with Montholon. Neither Bertrand, nor even the Emperor escaped from his broadsides (see page 71).

Finally the Emperor wouldn't resist the temptation of producing a detailed refutation of Warden's work and would spend the whole morning of Sunday 9th working on that[1]. Besides being a good way to keep himself occupied, it was clear that this was also a good opportunity to expose his predicaments before the public gaze. Most likely entirely authored by Napoleon, who probably considered replying personally to his critics beneath his dignity, two anonymous books were published in English: 'Letters From the Cape' (1817) and 'Letters from the Island of Saint Helena' (1818).

Authorship open to speculation, some maintain these letters could have been written by Las Cases, but the following excerpt from Gourgaud's journal suggests it was effectively the Emperor:

> *'Friday 20th June,*
>
> *His Majesty assures me that he has not replied to that work. He says that it is rumoured that it was Las Cases who wanted to respond from the Cape. To this I object to the Emperor that I had seen more than ten letters dictated by him to the Grand Marshal to be printed. One of them even written upon the same desk I am writing. The Emperor cannot deny it any longer and asks me if I have been visiting Mme. Bertrand.'*[1]

So, most probably, the Emperor having decided upon giving to Warden's letters a personal –though anonymous– reply and not involving Gourgaud or O'Meara in this decision, he dictated the text to Bertrand and his wife translated into English.

APRIL **1817**

Bad weather and rain… Quite a few people inside and around Longwood are ill from stomach cramps and dysentery, from which some British soldiers would die. There is a sort of dead calm amidst the overwhelming boredom only alleviated by the upcoming horse races that, even though hindered by the rough weather, provide some relief for the islanders and very especially the captives, who take advantage for socializing and gossiping. As for the Emperor, also suffering from

---

1.   *Général baron Gourgaud. Journal de Sainte-Hélène 1815-1818.*

stomach cramps, he remains mostly indoors fighting one long day after another; still missing Las Cases' conversation and barely bearing Gourgaud's pestering, and the annoyance of the constant squabbling among most of his companions. A dense atmosphere emanates from Gourgaud's pages dedicated to these days of April sprinkled with some of Napoleon's remarks illustrative of his inner feelings:

Monday 7th

Being fifty years old, one cannot love anymore. Berthier still loved but I, I have a seasoned heart. I have never really loved except perhaps Joséphine; a little. And that because I was just twenty seven when I met her. I felt a deep friendship for Marie Louise. I feel a bit like Gassion, who told me that he didn't love life enough as to give it to another being.[1]

May 1817

May 6th, 1817

The Emperor has told me:
I am losing my strength; I will be dead in two years. I no longer enjoy restful sleep; I drowse. I remember my mistakes. That's like a continuous nightmare as soon as I close my eyes. M. Lowe is killing me by preventing me from wearing my body out through severe exercise. He wants to humiliate me, but he will not succeed; I'd rather die from his tortures than be humiliated. Maybe working at night would do me some good, but it would be quite strenuous for you and Gourgaud, so both of you have the nights, but the day? No, that's not possible. Come on, let's go to work![2]

By giving up the exercise and the outings he was used to, Napoleon condemned himself to a premature death. Hard work was now his only and veritable relief. Until Las Cases' departure he had benefited from the learned conversation that pleased him so much, but now his closest companion was Gourgaud, who of course couldn't compete with Las Cases in terms of intelligence or education. In addition, his constant outbursts, arrogance and childish behaviour exasperated the Emperor. However, and considering the fact that completing his diminishing inner circle were just the dubious Montholon and the

1. *Général baron Gourgaud. Journal de Sainte-Hélène 1815-1818.*
2. *Said by Napoleon to Montholon as quoted in 'Le Drame de Sainte Hélène'. André Castelot. Perrin.*

cold, distant Bertrand it is no surprise that an imbecile like Gourgaud, who in other circumstances would have passed perfectly unnoticed by the great man, succeeded in getting so close to him.

Napoleon's malaise continued this month during which he remained inside the home most of the time. Probably tired of so many long sessions dictating his memoirs, and having advanced considerably in this work, he indulged at this time in some trivial chatting alternating the company of Montholon and the mercurial Gourgaud, thereby exciting the jealousy of the latter. This rarefied atmosphere reigned at Longwood all through May, with no remarkable events except perhaps a tiny glimmer of hope when the captives learned from the British gazettes that a possible relaxation of their conditions was being considered in Britain but, unfortunately, any hope vanished thereafter, when later news arrived to the island making clear that Lord Bathurst had ruled out any change...

June 1817

As if for breaking the dull monotony of the previous month, June would provide some novelties like de arrival of a shipment of books from lady Holland[1] or a bust of Napoleon's son that soon would 'unleash the hounds'...

Royal Navy gunnery chief Redwith had arrived on board the Baring to Saint Helena in the last days of May. With him he had brought a marble bust of the King of Rome intended to be presented as a gift to the Emperor. It was indeed a mediocre sculpture supposedly made at Livorno in 1816, where the little boy would have stayed accompanied by his mother. However, it seems that Napoleon's son never left Austria[2] and the bust was created in London by a not very learned artist that even represented the boy sporting the order of the Legion of Honour, that he had only used a long time ago. Furthermore, it could doubtfully be labelled as a gift, as the author recommended himself to the Emperor's generosity in a cover letter annexed to the piece...

At Saint Helena even a trivial matter like that could stir the boring, dead calm normally reigning all over the island and especially at

---

1. *Elizabeth Vassall Fox, Baroness Holland (1771-1845) was an English political hostess and the wife of Henry Vassall-Fox, 3rd Baron Holland. Both Lord and Lady Holland were great admirers of Napoleon, sending to Saint Helena supplies of food and hundreds of books. The Emperor didn't forget her in his will and following his death Bertrand and Montholon delivered to Lady Holland a gold snuffbox.*
2. *'Le Drame de Sainte Hélène'. André Castelot. Perrin.*

Longwood, where the Emperor remained pretty anxious as, topping the miseries and pains inflected on him by the captivity was the separation from his beloved son and heir who –hopefully– would some day be crowned as his successor, so continuing the dynasty whose survival had became his ultimate reason for staying alive. He had known of the existence of the bust immediately upon its arrival but, eight days later the bust had not yet been delivered. Regardless of whether Hudson Lowe's reasons to keep him waiting so long were mere stupidity or just pure hatred, the anecdote is illustrative of the state of affairs at that time.

When the Emperor finally received it; staring at the bust made the following remark:

> *'How it is that on this rock there is a man wild enough to order this bust to be thrown into the sea?*[1] *He is surely not a father. For me, this bust is worth more than millions. Put it on the console so that I can see it every day'*[2]

July 1817

Books and the King of Rome bust were not the only new arrivals to the island in June as Lord Amherst, British ambassador to China arrived at Saint Helena during those days. Napoleon, reluctant to receive him at first stance, later changed his mind and conceded Amherst an audience. The Emperor entertained a long conversation with Amherst about the Chinese civilization that had always interested him so much. Perhaps it was on this occasion that the famous remark *'Quand la Chine s'éveillera, le monde tremblera'* (see page 57) originated.

Lord Amherst's secretary, Ellis, depicted the Emperor in the course of this audience as sporting a dignified and pleasant appearance. Not too fat and in good health and walking back and forth as customary while uttering a torrent of concise statements. His upper lip would protrude in a pursed expression and, when silent, Ellis observed a convulsive trembling; as if holding inside a torrent of thoughts anxious to be delivered and keeping at all time the same attitude as he would have had at the peak of his glory[3]. Amherst and the Emperor empathized during the interview and the first even made himself available for

---

1. *Lowe's chief of staff: Sir Thomas Reade, proposed just tossing the bust into the sea; a suggestion possible derived from Napoleon's prior refusal to receive one of the superior British judges of Calcutta, Sir Thomas Strange, in his passing by Saint Helena.*
2. *Mémoires de Marchand. Libraire Plon. Paris 1952.*
3. *'Le Drame de Sainte Hélène'. André Castelot. Perrin.*

intercession with Hudson Lowe; which Napoleon kindly refused. He would keep his hat all the time under his arm, now deprived of its cockade that Marchand had removed some days earlier following his orders...

In the first days of July Napoleon would sink deeper into his disgrace and isolation when Admiral Malcolm reached Longwood to bid his farewell. Malcolm had been always sympathetic to the Emperor and even tried –unsuccessfully– to ease to some extent the ever increasing pressure exerted by Hudson Lowe upon the Longwood captives. Malcolm also introduced his successor Rear Admiral Robert Plampin who, much unlike Malcolm was a rather coarse man prejudiced against Napoleon who, in his turn, remarked about Plampin:

> *'This little man of about 60 years has an unpleasant appearance. He resembles one of those fat Dutch sailors that are always drunk that I have seen in their country, seated at a table, pipe in mouth, with a piece of cheese and a bottle of gin in front of them'*[1]

Napoleon and Plampin would indeed never get along...

Also this month of July the 53rd infantry regiment would be relieved by the 66th. Before leaving the island the officers of the outgoing unit would present their respects and good byes to Napoleon. Among them was captain Poppleton who, having been the duty officer at Longwood, managed to fulfill his unpleasant work as watchman and gain the affection of the Emperor at the same time.

On another level, the relationship between O'Meara and Hudson Lowe worsen even more when the first, requested by the governor to report about the state of Napoleon's health, refused on the grounds of professional secrecy.

August **1817**

Rumours about an eventual repatriation circulate boosting for a while the captives' morale but... they are soon belied. Napoleon's profound deliberations about Religion and particularly the figure of Jesus Christ are interspersed in the extensive chronicle of his campaigns and political memoirs. These remarks show him rather as a pragmatic agnostic. Still, these philosophical concerns don't prevent him from playing at every opportunity the role of the unjustly

---

1. *Mémoires de Marchand d'après le manuscrit original par Jean Bourguignon. Plon, Paris 1952.*

oppressed captive, deprived of the most basic needs. So, when one of his frocks wore out, in a rather theatrical fashion bordering upon the ridiculous, he has the fabric turned around rather than using a British made cloth for a new one...

On Friday 15th Napoleon is 48 years old. For the occasion of his 3rd birthday in captivity –and according to Gourgaud– he wears the 'brown frock of the Malmaison' while receiving the compliments of his officers and their respective wives. The Emperor presented the children and the ladies with gifts, which contributed to cheer up his guests in a similar way as he did the previous year when, as now, the phantom of the sumptuous birthday parties of their bygone past lingered in the minds of them all.

In a permanent fight against idleness and monotony events and affairs that in normal circumstances would receive little or no attention at all become recurring topics. Such is the case of Warden's letters which had appeared in March of this year that have Napoleon, four months later, still dictating explanatory or refuting communiqués. Soon a more intriguing business would come up...

SEPTEMBER 1817

'My life has been so amazing that the admirers of my power have thought my childhood was equally extraordinary. They are wrong. There was nothing special in my early years. I was just a curious and stubborn boy. My first education was pitiful; as any other thing in Corsica. I learned French easily in the company of the garrison officers. I succeeded in what I started because so I wanted. I had a strong will and a resolute character. I have never hesitated, which puts me in advantage over any other. Ultimately, the will depends upon moral fibre; not everybody has command of himself.

My mind detests illusion. I have always made out the truth at once. That's the reason why I have always seen the bottom of things better than others. The world has been always for me in the facts; not the law. So, there is hardly anybody like me. By my nature, I have always been isolated. I have never understood the benefit of studying. In fact only the methods I learned were useful to me. Only mathematics has been fruitful to me. The rest was good for nothing. I only studied out of pride.'[1]

---

1.   *Le manuscrit de Sainte-Hélène. Une énigme napoléonienne. Michèle Brocarde. Cabédita.*

The text above is an excerpt from the libel published in Britain in 1817 under the title *'Le manuscrit de Sainte-Hélène'* supposedly written by Napoleon himself. This booklet had a remarkable repercussion in Europe at the time, opening an animated debate about the alluded –and boasted– Napoleon authorship which, as is today generally accepted, was not true. In fact the real author was Lullin de Châteauvieux[1], a noble in the inner circle of Mme. de Staël[2].

According to Gourgaud, it was Plampin who brought a copy of the *'manuscrit'* to Longwood on Friday 5th so providing the captives with many hours of conversation around this work pointing out errors and misconceptions and –above all– speculating about who had written it. Constant, Mme. de Staël or de Sieyès[3] were mostly suspected. On the evening of Monday 8th Gourgaud, after reporting some lengthy observations on the topic by the Emperor, finishes this day's entry in his journal with the following, enigmatic remark: *'On parle encore de l'ouvrage ont je crois bien à présent connaître l'auteur. On se couche à 10 heures'*[4].

Weather was not good that month and the Emperor suffered from swollen legs and bleeding gums that he believed to be consequence of a scurvy outbreak derived from the poor nutrition. The constant horse-trading over Longwood's expenses would ease after Bertrand made an agreement with Lowe to have the Emperor's domestic expenses settled against his personal bank in London. In that way, the official inquiries about the origin of funds spent at Longwood ceased. Unfortunately that was hardly enough to alleviate the stifling atmosphere in which the French were immersed. There was constant gossiping and intrigues to gain Napoleon's favour, especially in the form of pecuniary allocations and pensions, which Gourgaud would really pursue with unbearable insistence that exasperated Napoleon. To his well known feud with Montholon he had added by then Cipriani's enmity and is gradually losing his nerve. At one point he suggested –threatened– leaving the island.

---

1.   *Jacob-Frédèric Lullin, marquis de Châteauvieux (1772-1841)   was a liberal Swiss agronomist and scholar friend of Mme. de Staël and author of the 'Manuscrit venu de Sainte-Hélène d'une manière inconnue' (1817) apocryphally attributed to Napoleon.*
2.   *Anne Louise Germaine de Staël-Holstein (1766-1817) was a French writer of Swiss origin; writer and socialite of the Napoleonic era. Her independence of thought and reluctance towards the Napoleonic system induced an ambivalent relationship between them; half way between admiration and aversion.*
3.   *Emmanuel Joseph Sieyès (1748-1836) was a French clergyman, political writer and theorist of the French Revolution who also played a significant role in the Napoleonic period.*
4.   *'We talk about the work, of which I believe I know the author. We go to bed at 10'*

The following fragment from Gourgaud's journal illustrates the mood reigning over Longwood at the time:
Tuesday 16*th*.

'Montholon visits me. He is sad and tells me that his Majesty is in a peculiar mood; that currently all of us dream of leaving, which has never happened before... His Majesty will never change. He and Bertrand imagine the throne will be soon recovered, hence their thirst for novelties. His wife has not seen his Majesty since long ago. Apparently his Majesty always wants to dine alone in his apartments. His Majesty listens only to his valets. I meet the grand marshal. His wife is mad from boredom and sadness. He would like to draw me out; there is something I can't figure out. He assures me he had not seen the Emperor for more than 15 minutes in the whole day. We all have dinner separately in our places.'[1]

With the passing of time, keeping composure at Longwood was increasingly difficult. And very especially for Napoleon, as the epicentre of any conflict arising from the meanness and pettiness of most of his misfortuned companions, who obviously at that time felt the exile was lasting too long... in exchange for too little. In fact, in this overwhelming psychological stress, it was him against the rest, with the commendable exception of his servants; like Marchand, Ali –or possibly even Cipriani– who remained perfectly loyal until and after the end.

Still, nobody around could offer intellectual intercourse the way Las Cases did. Deep thinking was only natural in a man like him and verbalizing his thoughts an indispensable outlet even in the worst moments. So, even in that sad evening of Tuesday 16*th* after everyone had dined separately, immediately after he still called for Gourgaud (for lack of a better interlocutor) and unleashed the following meditation:
'No matter what they say, all is just but more or less organized matter. When hunting, I have deer opened in front of me and I see the same insides as in men. They are just a more perfect being than trees or dogs; and living better. Vegetables are the first link of the chain and men the last. I know very well that it is against religion but, well, this is my opinion: we are no more than matter. Man has been created by a certain temperature of the atmosphere. Men are young and the earth is old. Human race is no more than six to seven thousand years old and in thousands of years from now men will be very different. Then, sciences would

---
1.   *Général baron Gourgaud. Journal de Sainte-Hélène 1815-1818.*

so advance that perhaps the way to live forever could be found.
Vegetal and farming chemistry are just in their infancy. In some
centuries we'll have discovered the extraordinary proprieties of
elements that our present knowledge cannot explain: magnetism,
electricity, galvanism. So many discoveries will be made in
thousands of years!"[1]

OCTOBER 1817

Napoleon's health keeps falling down the long decline that will
only end with his death. When O'Meara diagnoses hepatitis Lowe,
never trusting the young doctor, insists on having Dr. Baxter[2] check the
Emperor, which he formally and adamantly refuses. Actually, O'Meara
is now in the middle of an unsustainable crossfire between Lowe, who
blames him of being bribed by the French to produce alarmist reports,
and the Emperor, who suspects the doctor is keeping the governor
updated on the state of his health.

On the other hand Gourgaud is at this point flying off the handle.
He argued that his room door had been forced and suspects Cipriani
of spying on him. He even dares to produce some risqué remarks on
Mme. de Montholon´s pregnancy and the notorious kindness showed
by the Emperor to this lady... Napoleon, now completely fed up, begins
to consider that Gourgaud leaving the island is a good idea.

Sporadic visits of the Balcombe family including an attractive young
Betsy, who naturally would be immediately spotted by Gourgaud;
or the gossiping and unfulfilled expectations[3] of an eventual visit to
Longwood of the three foreign commissioners is a meagre counterpart
to the tedious passing of these October days...

NOVEMBER 1817

Tensions keep growing among the captives. Gourgaud is now
exasperating everybody around and begins to consider challenging
Montholon to a duel. He simply cannot stand the presence of the
dubious officer and his wife. When he tried in despair to gain Bertrand´s
confidence in his feud against Montholon he only gets cold gazes and

---

1. *Général baron Gourgaud. Journal de Sainte-Hélène 1815-1818.*
2. *Main medical officer at Saint Helena, Alexander Baxter had long served under Lowe's*
   orders.
3. *The captives believed that a formal meeting with these commissioners could help to*
   improve their conditions on the island and even perhaps pull the strings in Europe for a
   future release.

conciliatory or evasive answers. Only Fanny Bertrand escapes to some extent Gourgaud's acrimony perhaps because she is also fed up with Saint Helena and this captivity that probably was lasting at this point much longer than she could reasonably have expected. Even though she managed to live separately with her husband, spoke fluent English and frequented the company of other ladies of position on the island –Lady Lowe included– she complained about having her children so far from Europe and deprived of a proper education. She is becoming more and more uneasy everyday...

The Emperor on his side tries to avoid sterile and exasperating discussions with the raging Gourgaud who turns 33 this month, but nothing seems to appease this fanatical man who, considering himself badly mistreated, is fast losing the due respect of the great man:

'*Saturday 8th*

His Majesty calls for me at nine. The Emperor harasses me repeating that I complain of Longwood. I can, if I am not happy, leave or wait until hearing that Las Cases has arrived and to appreciate the welcome given to him in Europe. Besides, his Majesty will not live longer than a year and, here or there, he will think of me, but I am too earnest. Montholon suits him better, as he takes care of him down to the last detail. I am bad tempered and will end badly.

I ask the Emperor what he means by these words. I have always conducted myself honestly and I will.

'**What do you have against us?**' *interrupts the Emperor.*

I reply that, according to Montholon, his Majesty has decided not to dine at the table anymore. '**That's not true**'- *Then, sire, call for Montholon, who will not dare to maintain that in front of me. The Emperor becomes indignant and treats me harshly:* '**You hate all of us. I can clearly see that you hate me; you love just my enemies. You attack those that are loyal to me: Bertrand! Montholon!** -*Sire, because I defend the artillery against the engineers, his Majesty presumes I attack General Bertrand. In front of the English, I always defend all of us whereas because of perfidious insinuations there are bad feelings about me. As I am not fairly treated here I rather leave. Let's find an honourable way out for me and I will leave Saint Helena'.*

The Emperor thinks that I am happy here by having room and board. '*Oh! Sire, in prison, anywhere I should go, I would have room and board without the humiliation I have here. I will never accept being*

*considered at the orders of M. and Mme. de Montholon; I'd rather
die. He, Montholon, regards himself as much as Bertrand. -**And he is
right; he takes care of my household. Were the grand Marshall
in charge, his wife would be served better than I. At the isle of
Elba I was well aware of what they did. Bertrand is gifted with
great features but they are ruined by plebeian shortcomings. He
is most of all a pretender...**'*

*I am greatly moved even if his Majesty regards me as being very
selfish. '**I am very selfish too and if you walk out on me, that
would mean that there is no nobility or devotion to my person
in your heart.** – And his Majesty wants to expel me or that I obey
Montholon? I cannot, I despise him too much for that!'*

*His majesty gets mad then and says he had often swallowed his
feelings when he was master of the world. He was equally compromised
by his wife and siblings, and I wouldn't accept to do the same! I reply
that it is for the sake of frankness that I always want to be frank... His
majesty, on noticing that I was almost decided, becomes a little milder
and tells me off with sweetness, goes to bed and repeats that in less than
a year his liver malady will take him away, converses peacefully with
me until midnight and then tells me: '**Go to bed and try to have a
good night**'.[1]*

So, the man to whom Beethoven had dedicated a symphony[2]; who was admired by Goethe[3], had descended to a point in which his more dedicated interlocutor was little more than an insolent madcap: Gourgaud...

On a more prosaic level, Napoleon's wisdom tooth that would be years later exhibited in O'Meara's dentistry office at London (see page 87) would be arduously and painfully extracted by the doctor on Sunday 16th this month.

DECEMBER 1817

December elapsed with no remarkable events to be consigned, while Gourgaud's hatred keeps growing spiced with some malicious

---

1. *Général baron Gourgaud. Journal de Sainte-Hélène 1815-1818.*
2. *Beethoven originally dedicated his third symphony to Napoleon in the belief that he embodied the ideals of the French Revolution, but renamed the piece in 1804 extremely disappointed upon learning that his up-to-then hero had crowned himself Emperor.*
3. *Goethe met Napoleon in Erfurt in 1808 where they entertained a cultivated conversation before parting with mutual admiration. The illustrious writer would always keep a bust of the Emperor in a prominent place in his study.*

comments questioning the fathering of the baby that Mme. de Montholon is about to deliver and his insistence in duelling with Montholon: which the Emperor would strictly forbid. Unable to make Gourgaud see reason, he would invite him to leave the island upon settling with Bertrand the 'honourable conditions' he had asked for (meaning money, of course).

A dull ominous atmosphere shrouds Longwood and its dwellers that, probably, couldn't avoid fueling bad premonitions for the New Year...

1818

JANUARY 1818

New Year opens gloomily. There are rumours of an invasion of Saint Helena prepared by French exiles in America but nobody takes them seriously.

On Monday 26th Mme. de Montholon finally delivers a girl that would be baptized as Josephine. Continuing the speculations about this lady being Napoleon´s mistress, Fanny Bertrand, the servants and of course Gourgaud, find a resemblance between the newborn and the Emperor. Tensions keep growing.

FEBRUARY 1818

This was a really troublesome –and pivotal– month in this story, marked by Gourgaud´s imminent departure and Cipriani's death, of whom Gourgaud in one of the last entries in his journal on Saturday 28th wrote: '(...) *selon moi, Sa Majesté regrettera plus Cipriani que n'importe qui de nous tous.*'[1] The scarce, fleeting presence of Cipriani in the annals of the captivity doesn't correspond to the importance of the person veiling darker, mysterious aspects of this drama that perhaps won't ever be disclosed. His sudden, unexpected death or the fact that the corpse has never been located feed many theories about the surreptitious activities of this peculiar character as commented in other parts of this work (see pages 113 and 292).

On Monday 2nd, Gourgaud asks the Emperor for permission to leave. The insolent officer wouldn't miss this late opportunity to return again to his recurrent complaints and impertinence:

---

1.   '(...) *in my opinion, his Majesty will miss more Cipriani than any of us.*'

*'I beg his majesty permission to leave. I can't stand the humiliation
he wants me to submit to. I have always done my duty; I displease
his majesty, I don't want to bother anybody; just that the Emperor
allows me to go.' He rouses claiming that he can treat M. and Mme.
de Montholon as he pleases, that I suppose he has fathered her a child.*
' Well, and if I sleep with her, what's the matter? *- None, sire, but I
have never said to his majesty anything about that. I don't suppose that
his majesty has such a pervert taste.'*[1]

When Gourgaud formally challenges Montholon to a duel the
latter refuses following Napoleon's orders. Gourgaud's departure is
then questioned no more: the dice is cast. On 11th Wednesday he bade
farewell to the Emperor parting from Longwood on 14th Saturday.
Escorted by Basil Jackson (see page 101) he would be welcomed with
open arms by Lowe and the foreign commissioners. Once freed from
the oppressive environment of Longwood he would give free rein to
the dissatisfaction and rancour accumulated during his stay at Saint
Helena by revealing intimate details about the difficult cohabitation of
the French party. Lowe learns then that the Emperor has been keeping
regular correspondence with Europe or that, apparently, an eventual
evasion was not discarded.

Gourgaud is indeed very disappointed; very especially with
Napoleon from whom he would have expected a significant monetary
compensation for his devotion and support during and before the
seclusion at Saint Helena. Obviously following Napoleon's instructions
Bertrand had offered him 12,000 francs; an amount that would be
certainly far from Gourgaud's expectation as he, greatly offended,
refused to take the money... He would embark a couple of weeks later.

The loss of Cipriani and Gourgaud set a turning point in Napoleon's
long ordeal. There is little doubt that Cipriani was his confidant and
only real 'friend' there. On the other hand Gourgaud, despite his
terrible character was able to arouse real affection in the Emperor, at
least to some extent. He certainly enjoyed his company and liked to
converse with him about a huge variety of topics in a similar way he
had done with Las Cases even though in fact there is no comparison
between these two men in terms of education or personality. Now
he has to rely on just his two remaining high officers: the cold, rather
inaccessible Bertrand and the shady, slimy Montholon.

---

1.   *Général baron Gourgaud. Journal de Sainte-Hélène 1815-1818.*

MARCH **1818**

Hudson Lowe decides, on his own, to send Gourgaud directly to Britain skipping the customary quarantine at the Cape. The mischievous officer would finally embark on the 14th Saturday. True to his style till the very end, he would spend his last days on the island fussing about his penniless situation and some trivial matters like a bundle of books that the Emperor would rather keep at Longwood than letting him have them. He even borrows from Lowe 100 pounds posturing himself as a poor, pitiable outcast.

But Gourgaud wouldn't be the only person in Napoleon's entourage parting this month as the Balcombe family would also leave Saint Helena on Wednesday 18th apparently because of some differences between Mr. Balcombe and the governor and the poor health of his wife. One ultimate reason could be the amiable relationship existing between this family and the Emperor. Betsy left the following, rather weepy account of his farewell to Napoleon in her memoirs:

'In consequence of my mother's health declining, from the enfeebling effects of the too warm climate of St Helena, she was ordered by her medical adviser to try a voyage to England, as the only means of restoring her shattered constitution. The Winchelsea store-ship having arrived from China, my father took our passage on board, obtaining first, from Sir Hudson Lowe, six months' leave of absence from his duties as purveyor to Napoleon and his suite, etc.

A day or two before we embarked, my father, my sister, and myself rode to Longwood, to bid adieu to the Emperor. He was in his billiard-room, surrounded by books, which had arrived a few days before. He seemed saddened by our leaving the island, and said he sincerely regretted the cause; he hoped my dear mother's health would soon be restored, and sent many affectionate messages to her, she being too ill to accompany us to Longwood. When we had sat with him some time, he walked with us in his garden, and with a sickly smile pointed to the ocean spread out before us, bounding the view, and said, 'Soon you will be sailing away towards England, leaving me to die on this miserable rock. Look at those dreadful mountains - they are my prison walls. You will soon hear that the Emperor Napoleon is dead.' I burst into tears, and sobbed, as though my heart would break. He seemed much moved by the sorrow manifested by us. I had left my handkerchief in the pocket of my side-saddle, and seeing the tears run fast down my cheeks, Napoleon took his own from his pocket and wiped them away, telling me to keep the handkerchief in remembrance of that sad day.

We afterwards returned and dined with him. My heart was too full of grief to swallow; and when pressed by Napoleon to eat some of my favourite bonbons and creams, I told him my throat had a great swelling in it, and I could take nothing.

The hour of bidding adieu came at last. He affectionately embraced my sister and myself, and bade us not forget him; adding that he should ever remember our friendship and kindness to him, and thanked us again and again for all the happy hours he had passed in our society. He asked me what I should like to have in remembrance of him. I replied, I should value a lock of his hair more than any other gift he could present[1]. He then sent for Monsieur Marchand, and desired him to bring in a pair of scissors and cut off four locks of hair for my father and mother, my sister, and myself, which he did. I still possess that lock of hair; it is all left to me of the many tokens of remembrance of the Great Emperor.'[2]

APRIL 1818

Napoleon's circle grows gradually smaller. After the departure of Gourgaud and the Balcombes Lowe tightens the grip on O'Meara, whom he blames for spreading the idea of Longwood's climate being the cause of Napoleon's ill health.

The new commissary substituting Balcombe was an interesting personage called Denzil Ibbetson (1788-1857). This British officer had been aboard the Northumberland with Napoleon and was at Saint Helena until the latter died. Being an amateur artist, he rendered an interesting little collection of portraits of the Emperor as well as a number of evocative Saint Helena landscapes; he even kept a diary that his descendants only released as late as 2010 containing, among other things, this literary depiction of the great man complementary to his drawings: *'very corpulent, about 5ft 6 inches high; short brown hair, sallow complexion, broad shoulders and has at times a very ferocious countenance.'* From a more professional point of view it seems that Ibbetson, now in charge of providing Longwood's supplies, did a better job than his predecessor as the regular complaints of the French about this particular ceased from now on.

---

1.   *Betsy omits here that, according to Marchand, the Emperor bestowed Balcombe with a draft on London for 72,000 francs as a yearly pension of 12,000 francs.*
2.   *To Befriend an Emperor. Betsy Balcombe's Memoirs of Napoleon on St. Helena. (Originally published in 1844). Ravenhall Books.*

May 1818

If during the first years the sporadic visits to Longwood of British officers and significant passengers arriving to the island acted as a sort of outlet alleviating the prevailing boredom and oppression, now the situation worsens after Lowe's new orders restricting visits and the removal of British personnel serving at the house.

Quite probably, these regulations were due more to the Governor's pathological fears than to a conscious desire to punish, as they would be perceived by the captives. Whatever the case, the result was just a severe increase in the already unbearable isolation of the sad Longwood dwellers and very specially the Emperor, now remaining for days in a row secluded in his tiny private rooms.

June 1818

Counting now just on two officers and Bertrand living separately, it would be Montholon who would have the largest share of work. In fact Montholon would become his closest aide until the day he died. It goes without saying that he always had the help of the loyal Marchand –and to a lesser extent Ali– to carry out the daily intellectual work besides their many other, more domestic, chores.

But the flow of leavings that had marked the prior months of 1818 wouldn't stop. Now it is the turn to go of the sophisticated cook Lepage and his wife Catherine Sablon (see page 122). Pierron (see page 116), who was by then doubling his own responsibilities by assuming the work of the deceased Cipriani triples now taking the role of Lepage too.

But it is not all. As if to demonstrate that anything can get worse Lowe, by no way open to O'Meara´s diagnostics on Napoleon, seeks permission from London to remove the adventurous doctor from Longwood... and the isle.

Darker clouds of misery and oblivion cast over Longwood house. Cloistered away in his paltry rooms on the stark plateau, lost in the middle of the South Atlantic Ocean, the man even deprived of his birth name –'General Bonaparte' according to his merciless guardians– takes a new step every pitiful day into his grave, that he feels now is getting closer and closer...

July 1818

When Hudson Lowe has Longwood's duty officer captain Blakeney replaced by Colonel Lyster, Bertrand strongly refuses on the grounds that Lyster served as a commanding officer in the Corsican battalion at Ajaccio, and for this reason Napoleon considers his appointment a grave personal offence. That's the beginning of a new, harsh dispute with the Governor involving Lyster's duel challenge to Bertrand. The opposition was strong enough to force Lowe to remove Lyster from the post after two weeks, but Bertrand and the governor wouldn't speak to each other until Napoleon's death.

Finally giving up in his multiple –and unsuccessful– efforts to meet the Emperor, the Austrian commissioner von Stürmer, sent to Saint Helena to check Napoleon's movements, leaves the island on the 11th. The presence of Stürmer and his Russian and French colleagues (Balmain and Montchenu) was never welcomed by the French or the British who considered Napoleon's capture exclusively a British affair.

Upon receiving Bathurst's letter for the expulsion of O'Meara on the 25th, Lowe orders him to leave Longwood the very same day.

Before being finally arrested and shipped off the island at the beginning of August 1818 the doctor would bid his farewell to Napoleon. The scarce or null faith professed by the Emperor to medical science, didn't impede him from developing a real affection for O'Meara who could speak Italian and really cared about his health. In the course of their last meeting the doctor was instructed on how to proceed once in Europe in relation to his cause and was gifted with a generous stipend and a small bronze figure of the Emperor. Then, he shook his hand and embraced him before adding these final words: *'Adieu, O'Meara, nous ne nous reverrons plus, soyez heureux!'*[1].

August 1818

After the parting of so many people, a dull stagnation looms over Longwood. The Emperor's health deteriorates and now he suffers from severe and frequent vomits. Once O'Meara was no longer available Lowe had appointed Doctor Verling (see page 97), but Napoleon wouldn't accept him as the governor had sent Verling to Longwood without any prior notice. Verling had sailed to Saint Helena

---

1.   *'So long, O'Meara, we will not see each other again, be happy!' From: 'Napoléon en Exil a Sainte-Hélène. Barry E. O'Meara. Plancher, Paris 1822.'*

with Napoleon in the Northumberland and now, despite the fact that he could only observe the Emperor from a distance he was struck to see the change apparent in our man, whom the British doctor depicts as showing signs of a chronic disease: with sunken eyes and a sallow complexion.

> '*Since long ago the Emperor had complained of pain in his side and even a sharper one in his right shoulder that I should massage with cologne, which I then dried by passing my hand rapidly on the skin. He did the same for his side rubbing it first with a soft brush, and then I poured a little cologne in the hollow of his hand, which he applied and rubbed himself on the pain he was feeling. All these were just palliatives. When stronger remedies were required, I dared one day to tell the Emperor I had prepared pills that the doctor had left me, and about what would be necessary for rubbing his legs.* '**As for that**'*, he said,* '**right; but for everything intended to enter my stomach, you can throw it into the fire.**'*[1]

September 1818

Nothing changes, time seems suspended... Napoleon remains secluded for weeks and can only rarely be spotted, which greatly disturbed Lowe, now pondering the possibility of entering Longwood by force to check if the Emperor is still there. Captain Nicholls (see page 100) had a difficult time trying to get sight of the Emperor and bearing the growing anxiety and pressure exerted upon him by the enraged governor...

October 1818

On September 4th Lowe informs that the foundation layout for 'Longwood New House', the intended new residence for the Emperor, was ready on the 'best place' at Longwood, on a lower level than the old house and better sheltered from the wind and rains.

The first steps to build a new residence for Napoleon and his 'court' were taken in 1815, but it was only this month that the works began after many comings and goings. When it was ready in 1821 the Emperor's life was almost extinguished. The new mansion was an ample one floor prefabricated building, with a total floor area of approximately 22,600 sq ft (2.100 m²) and a facade 118 feet (36 metres) long. It was certainly

---

1. *Mémoires de Marchand d'après le manuscrit original par Jean Bourguignon. Plon, Paris 1952.*

of a far superior quality and better located than the old Longwood House, but in all probability Napoleon never considered for a moment moving to it. This building would be later serving different uses until its complete disappearance in 1949.[1]

About to complete his third year at Saint Helena he is an ill, weakened man who can barely keep going on with the routine work on the account of his campaigns. He stays at home all day long, carelessly sporting a dressing gown with his iconic madras scarf around his head. Sometimes he can be seen in this attire engrossed, silently wandering around the garden...

NOVEMBER 1818

In the autumn of 1818 the four allied powers Britain, Austria, Prussia and Russia held the Congress of Aix-la-Chapelle primarily to decide about the withdrawal of occupation forces and some other related matters including the future treatment of Napoleon at Saint Helena. Nothing changes: he will remain there...

Napoleon's health seems to improve a little. He finds some relief working at his memories and doing some gardening. In addition, the fact that Madams de Montholon and Bertrand, surely worried about his obvious decline, increase their visits to him mitigates his downheartedness; at least to some extent. After struggling for a time with the bureaucratic jumble prescribed for any publication arriving to the island intended to be delivered at Longwood, the Emperor can, at last, lay his hands on a new bundle of books. He spent the whole night perusing some of them...

DECEMBER 1818

> 'Eh bien, mon cher Bertrand, sortirons-nous d'ici? Finirons-nous dans ce misérable pays ? Je ne le crois pas, mais la question est compliquée...'[2]

The signs of improvement in Napoleon's health were just apparent. After exposing himself carelessly to the coolness of the evening his fragile health falls again and vomiting and fever return. Nothing remarkable breaks the leaden monotony as the end of 1818 approaches.

---

1. *Sainte-Hélène. Île de Mémoire. Fayard.*
2. *'Well, my dear Bertrand, will we leave from here? Will we end in this wretched country? I don't think so, but this is a complex matter...' Napoleon to Bertrand in December of 1818. Cahiers de Sainte-Hélène 1818-1819. General Bertrand. Èditions Albin Michel. 1959.*

Sequestered at Longwood; tucking himself away inside the house; dodging the regular visits of Lowe and his officers always eager to catch a glimpse of him; writing elaborated –and useless– complaint letters signed by Montholon or Bertrand, the year ends silently...

1819

JANUARY **1819**

The Emperor was still ill when the 1ˢᵗ of January arrived and was really not ready to celebrate this day with the customary, plentiful meal. He just gave away some gold coins to the children as New Year's gifts.

On the 6ᵗʰ he passed out in the presence of Montholon. Some days later, on the 16ᵗʰ, he was bad enough as to accept Dr. Stokoe (see page 98) going to Longwood, which he did on the following morning checking on the Emperor and confirming O'Meara's previous diagnostic: hepatitis.

It has been speculated that this episode in Napoleon's illness could have been triggered by his learning about the decision made at Aix-la Chapelle to retain him indefinitely at Saint Helena which in its turn, would have caused the stomach perforation later observed in his autopsy. A peculiar notion whatever the case, if only considering the perilous and hazardous life carried out by this exceptional man; his nerves of steel and command of himself that make him doubtfully susceptible of contracting a stomach ulcer out of an event that, in any case, he would have probably anticipated and perhaps even desired.

FEBRUARY **1819**

'He[1] has learned that M. Jackson (see page 101) met frequently with Mme. de Montholon. It is said that she is crazy about him. Apparently she is madly in love because, being a little flighty, she keeps needing love, which creates a lot of trouble at Longwood and destroys everything else; she speaks carelessly; after mindlessly disclosing many things she immediately repents; Jackson takes notice of everything and has two-hours-long conversations with the governor everyday ; that this happens with nobody else, even though he can be very talkative in extraordinary cases; that we should tell Montholon to not trust Jackson at all; that the Governor praised him very much today; that

---

1.   *Balmain.*

Jackson should be repatriated; that the grand Marshall did quite right not receiving him; that his movements were just an ambush.'[1]

So the scatterbrained, 40 year old Albine de Montholon delighted the many busybodies at the boring Saint Helena with this spicy romance set around Longwood between the young lady and the 'gallant' British officer. As for the Emperor, whose health has been slowly improving this month, he was back at work, frequenting the company of the Betrands and indulging in reading and conversation and cheering up when he learned about the affaire. Upon summoning the Montholon couple he admonishes them to cut immediately all this business. Montholon –not surprisingly– complies, but his whinging wife reluctantly replies that Jackson is a fine man and that, after all, distractions are hard to find at Longwood. According to Bertrand she was still meeting Jackson at the end of the month although in a more surreptitious way...

MARCH 1819

Even though Napoleon should probably have known in advance about the decision made at Aix-la Chapelle to have him indefinitely retained at Saint Helena; it is now officially communicated. Possibly giving up his last tiny hopes for an eventual deliverance, he dictates the first known draft of his testament.

Health condition seems stable this quiet month in which he keeps up with his regular routine. There are rumours for a forthcoming departure of the foreign commissioners, whose stay at the island seems more and more unnecessary everyday. Rumours about the Jackson affaire don't cease. Then on the 18th the Emperor requested Montholon, under his word of honour, to stop this relationship once and for all or to leave the island, which the couple seriously weighs. Upon Bertrand's advice to stay –and probably the notion that there was by then too much at a stake– they calm down and reconsider...

APRIL 1819

Ships arriving to Saint Helena were always due to create great expectation. Very specially to Napoleon who liked to watch the vessels approaching the island with his spyglass and even had a so called

---

1.   *Cahiers de Sainte-Hélène 1818-1819. General Bertrand. Albin Michel. 1959.*

'Chinese Pavilion' built in Longwood's gardens for that purpose[1]. One of these ships was the Aslett, which reached the island from Bengal bound for London on 26th March 1819. Upon knowing that Lord Liverpool's[2] cousin, Mr. Ricketts, was onboard the Emperor took advantage by inviting him to Longwood entertaining a long interview recorded by Hudson Lowe as follows:

> 'On the 2nd of April, in the afternoon, Mr. Ricketts, a cousin of Lord Liverpool, was presented to Napoleon by Count Bertrand, and remained in conversation with him for four hours. Napoleon entered fully upon the subject of his grievances, and gave his visitor the following memorandum in writing, as containing a short abstract of his wishes and complaints:
>
> 1°- Sortir de l'île, parce que j'ai une hépatite chronique.
>
> 2°- Qu'en quelque position où je sois, la raison politique est de mettre près de moi un homme d'honneur qui ait des formes.
>
> 3°- M'envoyer mon médecin O'Meara, m'en donner un François, ou m'en envoyer un Anglais civil qui n'ait aucun lien militaire, et bien famé.
>
> 4°- Ne pas me contraindre à habiter la nouvelle maison, parce qu'il n'y a pas d'arbres, parce qu'elle est trop près du camp, et qu'elle est dans la position de l'île où il n'y a pas d'arbres; que c'est un chêne que je désire.
>
> 5°- Que si Lord Liverpool envoie l'ordre qu'on ne viole pas mon intérieur, qu'on ne m'en menace point.
>
> 6°- Qu'il autorise une correspondance directe avec lui cachetée, et qui ne passe pas par Lord Bathurst; ou avec un pair du royaume qui soit notre avocat près du ministère, tel que Lord Holland: c'est le moyen que le public ne s'occupe plus de cela.[3]

1. This 2x2 meters Chinese Pavilion was built under Napoleon's request in Longwood garden by Chinese workers on top of a platform intended as an observatory but, due to the fact that it would be ready just one year short of Napoleon's death it wasn't much used.

2. Robert Banks Jenkinson, second Earl of Liverpool, (1770-1828). Britain's Prime Minister from 1812 to 1827.

3. 1°- To leave the island: because I have chronic hepatitis.
   2°- That in my position, the politically correct (thing to do) is to place by my side a man of honour and in keeping with formalities.
   3°- Send my doctor O'Meara back to me or provide me with a French or a civil Englishman with no military connection and well reputed.
   4°- I refuse to live in the new residence because there are no trees; because it is too close to the camp and is located on a part of the island where there are no trees: it is an oak what I desire.
   5°- That if Lord Liverpool has given the order to not break in into my apartments, I shouldn't be threatened with that in any way.
   6°- That he authorizes a private direct correspondence; no passing through Lord Bathurst; or a peer from the kingdom being our counsel with the ministry, like Lord Holland: that is how to keep the public away from this.

Napoleon also desired Mr. Ricketts to give his 'remercîments' (sic) to Lord and Lady Holland for their attention in sending him books, and presents to Bertrand's children; his 'remercîments' (sic) also to the Duke of Sussex, and his 'souvenirs' (sic) to Lord Amherst."[1]

The Chinese Pavilion built on Longwood's gardens to watch ongoing vessels.

A view from the inside of the Chinese Pavilion.

---

1.   *History of the Captivity of Napoleon at Saint Helena. From the letters and journals of the late Lieut. Gen. Sir Hudson Lowe and official documents not before made public by William Forsyth, MA. Harper Brothers. 1853, New York.*

As it can be noticed Napoleon, never ready to give up fighting, was still trying to induce a change of mind at London regarding his situation. It seems that he had received Mr. Ricketts in bed in the attempt of exciting his pity; a rather clumsy move suggesting a loss of faculties or extreme despair that, in any case, wouldn't work out...

First glimpse of a forthcoming crisis arises when Mme. de Montholon, probably still convalescent from a recent miscarriage, receives medical advice to leave the island for the sake of her health. Her husband ponders going back with her too. They are in a swoon of doubts...

A new session of the always welcomed Deadwood races takes place. The Montholons and the Betrands hang out with Saint Helena's socialites relieving themselves from the growing tension and the overwhelming presence of their master secluded at Longwood.

May 1819

Together with some other books and back magazines and newspapers sent by the governor to Longwood Gourgaud's work 'La Campagne de 1815' is included providing a conversational topic for another quiet month in which the Emperor feels good enough to keep going with his dictations and digressions on a variety of subjects such as the appraisal of the Corsican soldiers, Hannibal, Egypt, Louis XIV, Moscow, Spain, Rogniat[1] or Waterloo. Gourgaud's book, mostly composed on Napoleon's dictations, fails to shake the dull mood prevailing at Longwood; the Emperor just points out that Grouchy and Soult were not fairly treated in this rather irrelevant work.

Lowe, in accordance with the agreements made at Aix-la-Chapelle, formally requests that the foreign commissioners be received at Longwood. It was doubtless a mere formalism, as by then it should be quite clear that they will never be received by the Emperor. On visiting the works in progress for Longwood New House the governor, in an unusual benevolent mood, accedes to enlarge the openings on the surrounding fence, as requested by the French...

June 1819

Mme. de Montholon´s departure approaches. Regardless of what could have been the real, ultimate nature of the relationship between

---

1.   *Joseph, viscount of Rogniat, 1776 - 1840. General of engineers in Napoleon's army.*

Napoleon and this lady, her significant role in this story is beyond any doubt. Albine de Montholon not only supplied mundane distractions and the consequent relief from the heavy atmosphere of Longwood; she was also projecting an affection that –at least to some extent –could have been real.

Now, the decision is made and it only remains to settle the last details before the ultimate and definitive farewell. The Emperor takes care to ensure that she and her children will have everything needed for the long trip back to Europe and Pierron (see page 116) is in charge to place plenty of provisions aboard. But there is still a last important detail: her 'compensation'. According with Marchand[1] she was given 200,000 francs in letters of credit plus an additional pension of 20,000 francs: a considerable sum in striking contrast with Gourgaud, who was only offered 12,000 francs. Her husband, either on his personal decision or perhaps ceding to Napoleon's pressure; stays.

On another level, and as a response to Bertrand's repeated requests in the past months to get additional personnel to fill the gap produced at Longwood by the succession of departures, on the 26th it is at last known that two priests and a new doctor –Madame Mère's choice– had left Rome four months ago and were en route to Saint Helena...

July 1819

The final send-off took place in the sitting room; the same chamber that would be eventually converted into his mortuary chapel. Albine and her children met him there for the last time. He thanked her kindly for letting her husband remain by his side; presented her with a splendid gold box sporting his portrait encircled by large diamonds and wished them all great happiness. She was already in tears when the Emperor started pronouncing a series of instructions for his family. The children affected great sorrow too and, at this point, the illustrious prisoner who probably is trying to restrain his own emotion, embraced them one after another and, not wanting to prolong the pitiful scene, retires to his apartments. While undressing to take one of his customary hot baths, the coach carrying Mme. de Montholon and her offspring starts moving. Then, through an aperture in the curtains he, unnoticed, catches Albine de Montholon´s last glance at Longwood house and the so many memories left behind...

---

1.   *Mémoires de Marchand. Libraire Plon. Paris 1952.*

They boarded the 'Lady Campbell' on Friday 2nd. It was a very fine day overall until late in the evening, when a heavy rain began falling. That night Napoleon went to bed in fever and aching from a pain in his side. The departure of Albine de Montholon surely was a strong blow culminating a series of departures over the last months: a point of no return marking the beginning of the end of his irremediable decline to death[1]. General Montholon, on this side, falls ill too in these days.

But even in the worst moments there is somebody around enjoying the pleasure of living, as was the case of Noverraz (see page 111) who married his beloved Joséphine Brulé this month (see page 121).

In order to protect the garden from the strong winds, perhaps as a first sign of the interest in gardening that would be developed by the Emperor in the near future, and surely out of his uncontainable, dynamic nature he contrives the building of a tall, lawn-covered embankment...

August 1819

When Napoleon is teaching mathematics to Bertrand's son Hudson Lowe unexpectedly arrives and, upon noticing the embankment works in process, and for the first time in three years, his eyes and Napoleon's fleetingly meet just before avoiding each other. The incident revives the ridiculous epistolary war with the habitual communiqués addressed to 'General Bonaparte' coming to and fro.

On Saturday 21st, the unfortunate Dr. Stokoe (see page 98) arrived to Saint Helena. He had been previously expulsed from the island due to the unambiguous sympathy shown to the Emperor and subsequently shipped back from London to face a court martial in situ. Napoleon, who had by this time relapsed, tried to take advantage of the doctor's return and requested his services but Lowe, being absolutely not fond of the idea, delays Stokoe's visit to Longwood on futile excuses until the doctor is again repatriated. This, and new threats to force an entrance to the Longwood residence to finally ascertain that the captive is still there rarefied even more the difficult relationship between the prisoners and their guards...

---

1. *Basil Jackson would follow his flirt six days later loaded with Lowe's correspondence. They would later rejoin at Brussels where, free at last from the gossips and restrictions imposed to them at Saint Helena, the romance could have been continued.*

SEPTEMBER **1819**

Doctor Stokoe is finally discharged from the Royal Navy on Thursday 2nd.

Countess Bertrand barely can stand her long stay at Saint Helena and starts talking about going back to Britain... In the meantime, there is great expectation at Longwood because of the arrival of the long awaited group nicknamed the '*petite caravane*', composed by the priests Buonavita and Vignali, doctor Antommarchi, the butler Coursot and the cook Chandelier that are finally lodged there on Sunday 21st. After a first checkup Antommarchi confirms his predecessors' diagnosis recommending leg rubbings to reduce swelling and to change his sedentary lifestyle by introducing physical exercise and horseback and carriage rides.

Montholon is now fully recovered and ready to resume the role he took on after Gourgaud's parting as the closest person to the Emperor at Longwood. Now 'his majesty' tells him that from now onwards they would dine together.

OCTOBER **1819**

Antommarchi should have projected a good impression on the Emperor as, by following the doctor's sound advice, a notorious improvement in his health is soon noticed. He carries now a more regular life; the pain in his side disappears –at least for now– and, reenergised, he sits at the table on Sundays and plays chess with Montholon and Bertrand. On Thursday 14th Buonavita marries Ali and Mary Hall (see page 123).

NOVEMBER **1819**

'*Quand je ne serai plus ici, les voyageurs anglais feront le dessin de ce jardin fait par Napoléon. Il n'en est aucun qui ne veuille le visiter.*'[1]

With his health restored –at least momentarily– Napoleon is in good enough spirits as to undertake the last 'great project' of a life full

---

1. '*When I am no longer here, English voyagers will make drawings of this garden made by Napoleon. There will be nobody not wanting to visit it.*' Said by Napoleon to Bertrand in December 1819. '*Cahiers de Sainte-Hélène 1818-1819*'. Général Bertrand. Editions Albin Michel.

of extraordinary feats: the development of Longwood's gardens that would be referred to as the period of the *'jardinage'*. Donning a cool nankeen outfit, touched with a wide brimmed straw hat, red slippers[1] and brandishing a pool cue, the Emperor sported the determination and energy of former times giving orders, spurring all the others and even executing some manual work himself.

Paths laid out in a grid pattern; a couple of ponds linked by a cascade; a channel leading to an artificial and refreshing cave; an arbour providing some intimacy from the ever-present and inevitable watchers and even a beautiful aviary made by Chinese carpenters completed the ensemble that, carefully reconstructed, can be admired at Longwood house nowadays. Lowe, who had previously taken steps to assure Longwood was supplied with plenty of water – making these gardens possible– put no impediment to their creation and even offered supplementary help. Perhaps he thought anything leading to the Emperor being visible outside the house would make his unpleasant work easier...

Longwood garden.

---

1. *He had Ali and Noverraz dressed in a similar fashion to make himself less conspicuous.*

December **1819**

*On the 19ᵗʰ Sir Hudson Lowe wrote to Lord Bathurst, -'General
Bonaparte continues to occupy himself with improvements in his
garden. He caused three large reservoirs to be dug in different forms,
within a few paces from one another; it being found they did not retain
the water, Count Montholon applied to have them lined with lead. It
was calculated by Major Emmett of the Engineers this would create
an immediate expense of near 300 l. for an appurtenance merely to
the old building. I proposed, therefore, that a stone reservoir should be
commenced in the first instance, which would be always found useful.*

*In the meantime General Bonaparte has himself caused a second one
to be constructed of wood, in the form of an immense vat, and has given
up the project of the third. He shows himself a good deal in his garden,
and I have myself lately seen him twice, but not at such near distance
as to observe anything further than that he appeared to walk as strong
and as well as I have ever seen him.'*[1]

So, the year 1819 would be gone with Napoleon engrossed in
the building of his garden. His health was declining, but he had still
some spells of apparent improvement and by the end of the year had
at least acquired the habit of strolling in the gardens according to
Antommarchi's advice.

The progressive shrinking of his diminutive court during the year
and especially the parting of Albine de Montholon and her children
probably cast a thick cloud of sadness over Longwood impeding the
cheerful Christmas spirit fitting the closing festivities at the end of the
year of which the main recorders at that time; Marchand and Bertrand,
left no significant remarks...

1820

January **1820**

*'My actions and events answer all the libellous remarks
made against me. I am free from the usual crimes of dynasty
heads. I have nothing to fear from posterity, possibly history
will accuse me of having been too good. Montholon, my son,'*

---

1.   *History of the Captivity of Napoleon at Saint Helena. From the letters and journals of
the late Lieut. Gen. Sir Hudson Lowe and official documents not before made public by
William Forsyth, MA. Harper Brothers. 1853, New York.*

he said to the general pinching his ear, **'I can present myself with confidence before the court of God.'**[1]

On the 1st of January the habit established in the previous year stands and the Emperor gathers all his retinue for a celebration dinner gifting the children with the customary gold Napoleons.

Longwood at the beginning of 1820. (Bombled. ©Andrea Press).

1. *Mémoires de Marchand. Libraire Plon. Paris 1952.*

As now the duty officer has no problem in checking Napoleon during his frequent outings in the garden, a 'benevolent' Hudson Lowe voluntarily extended the free circulation limits but the Emperor, mostly occupied with his garden takes no advantage of it. Instead, he found it more amusing to shoot the chickens and goats unfortunate enough to graze or peck his flowerbeds.

FEBRUARY **1820**

Captain Nicholls (see page 100), the orderly officer who never personally met the Emperor at any time, is substituted by Captain Engelbert Lutyens[1] on the 10th of this month. This is a significant event if only because Lutyens produced a series of letters[2] that even being of a, rather boring, laconic military style, shed some light on this somewhat obscure year in which Bertrand's journal –perhaps the most reliable account at this phase– became short of clear entries. Marchand's memories, on the other hand, are focused on more domestic aspects

Captain Engelbert Lutyens.
(KGM. ©Andrea Press).

of Longwood life. Lutyens' regular letters picture Napoleon spending those quiet days mostly strolling in the garden and shooting fowl.

When Angelo Gentilini –a Corsican sailor and footman already in the Emperor's service at the time of the exile at Elba– is noticed entertaining an affair with the wife of a British sergeant, gossips are delighted and the leaden monotony of Saint Helena recedes... a little.[3]

---

1. *Captain Engelbert Lutyens (1784-1830). Orderly Officer at Longwood from February 10th, 1820 to April 15th, 1821. He produced a series of official letters covering these fourteen months, except for a few days, preceding Napoleon's death.*
2. *'Letters of Captain Engelbert Lutyens. Orderly officer at Longwood, Saint Helena: Feb. 1820 to Nov. 1823. Edited by Sir Lees Knowles'. LONDON—John Lane, The Bodley Head. New York- John Lane Company. MCMXV.*
3. *- Sainte-Hélène. Île de Mémoire. Fayard.*

March 1820

> Hot weather... slow time...
> *'Longwood, 10ᵗʰ March, 1820.*
> *Sir,*
> *About six o'clock yesterday evening. General Bonaparte undressed and plunged into the stone-reservoir in the garden. Count Montholon was with him and two servants attended to wipe and assist the General in dressing. I saw him for some time in the garden.'[1]*

A sad communiqué, probably bringing back moving memories, reached Longwood on the 9ᵗʰ, when news arrived of the misfortunes of Mme. de Montholon in Europe, where her residence had been almost destroyed by fire, her children were about to die and the luggage, jewellery and souvenirs carried from Saint Helena lost...

April 1820

> *'Longwood, 16ᵗʰ April, 1820.*
> *Sir,*
> *About seven o'clock last night General Bonaparte was walking in the gardens, with Count Montholon, when he discovered some cattle belonging to the farm, in the outer garden. He immediately ordered his two fowling-pieces to be brought out, loaded with ball, both of which he fired and killed one of the oxen. The ball passed through the neck. I believe there is another slightly wounded in the leg.'[1]*

The dedicated –and polite– captain Lutyens kept Lowe quite aware of Napoleon's movements... in the garden. What happens inside the house was another question on which he couldn't provide satisfactory report. There was now a different environment and routine at Longwood house that included Sunday masses and 'spiritual comfort' provided by the newly arrived priests while Antommarchi, the loquacious and outgoing new doctor mitigated, at least to some extent, the dull and depressing atmosphere of the last months. On the other hand, the intellectual tone of the earlier Las Cases era was now sensibly debased as none of the newly arrived were men of highbrow thought. In such circumstances the closest man to Napoleon from now to the end would be Montholon who, unlike Gourgaud, sustained a rather opaque relationship with the great man...

---

1. *'Letters of Captain Engelbert Lutyens. Orderly officer at Longwood, Saint Helena: Feb. 1820 to Nov. 1823. Edited by Sir Lees Knowles'. LONDON—John Lane, The Bodley Head. New York- John Lane Company. MCMXV.*

May 1820

> 'Longwood, 29th May, 1820.
> Sir,
> General Bonaparte this morning at six o'clock walked out through the gate of the new building and went towards the farm-fields, alone, where his horse was taken to him. He rode into the wood accompanied by Archambeau (sic), and did not return until a quarter-past eight o'clock. The General then took a warm bath.'[1]

Regenerated by the physical exercise and the excitement of building up his gardens, Napoleon is now in a cheerful mood. Even though he still feels a slight pain in his side, he takes horseback rides again and is in good appetite. Perhaps too good in fact, as judging by the stoutness he had by then attained. Lunch was served by Ali and Noverraz at ten o'clock in some shady and fresh spot of the gardens: soup, vegetables, chicken or lamb and over-sweetened coffee. He is usually accompanied by Montholon and sporadically by Bertrand, when he was around. The priests and Antommarchi are only rarely invited. There are animated table talks where he, freely and relaxed, often tells stories of his youth...

June 1820

> 'Longwood, 19th June, 1820.
> Sir,
> General Bonaparte was in the garden this morning with Count Bertrand.'[1]

While the Emperor was still enjoying this parenthesis of relative peace and quietness in his gardens, Hudson Lowe wouldn't relax his watch on him. Unable –or not daring enough– to penetrate the privacy of Napoleon's inner rooms, he relied in Lutyens´ reports and struggles to extract additional information through the foreign commissioners, like the garrulous Montchenu who would tell him about the bad manners and hatred for the Bourbon royalty showed by Bertrand's son; or about Montholon´s calculations on the real size of Napoleon's fortune that, in due time, would turn him rich. There is a sad tone of moral baseness in these reports that reflects the mediocrity and pettiness of most of the people connected with Napoleon at Saint Helena and speaks poorly about the human condition. A dull premonitory feeling of the proximity of death floats around...

1. 'Letters of Captain Engelbert Lutyens. Orderly officer at Longwood, Saint Helena: Feb. 1820 to Nov. 1823. Edited by Sir Lees Knowles'. LONDON—John Lane, The Bodley Head. New York- John Lane Company. MCMXV.

July 1820

> *'Longwood, 7ᵗʰ July, 1820.*
> *Sir,*
> *General Bonaparte was out last evening shooting. Count Montholon*
> *mentioned to me about half an hour ago, that the General was taken*
> *very unwell yesterday with a severe cold, accompanied by fever. He*
> *has not quitted his bed this day. I have seen Saint Dennis (sic) go for*
> *Antommarchi twice this morning.*[1]

Napoleon's health declines. He again stays mostly indoors and recurs to frequent and long hot baths to ease his pains.

On the 24ᵗʰ a rather humorous incident takes place when Vignali *'dressed in a nankeen-jacket, something like the one worn by General Bonaparte, black breeches, with brown top-boots, a straw-hat, but not in the least like the hat worn by the General'*[1] left Longwood on horse back accompanied by Archambault for a ride, being immediately spotted by Lutyens. It is not clear if the joke was Vignali's own idea or it was suggested by the same Napoleon.

August 1820

> *Longwood, 10ᵗʰ August, 1820.*
> *Sir,*
> *Between three and four yesterday afternoon, General Bonaparte rode*
> *into the wood, accompanied by Count Montholon, Archambeau (sic),*
> *and Novaraz (sic). The latter was dressed in uniform, with a silver-*
> *flask and a telescope slung round his body. They returned the same way*
> *about half-past five o'clock. I was riding through the wood from the*
> *piquet. Immediately they saw me, they rode off in another direction.*[1]

During this month of August there are frequent outings on horseback. Napoleon used to ride in full dress uniform; his horse harnessed in scarlet and gold livery and usually accompanied by Montholon and Bertrand. Sometimes Mme. Bertrand is in the party too. Never giving up his aspiration to extend the limits for the sake of a wider freedom of action, he has Montholon pushing the issue with Lowe, who respectfully denied the petition as being beyond his competence, but gladly acceded to several other suggestions as a more convenient way of posting some sentries keeping them out of sight or making some repairs to a road

---

1.   *'Letters of Captain Engelbert Lutyens. Orderly officer at Longwood, Saint Helena: Feb. 1820 to Nov. 1823. Edited by Sir Lees Knowles'. LONDON—John Lane, The Bodley Head. New York- John Lane Company. MCMXV.*

called '*le chemin militaire*', so giving the Emperor and his party access to a more varied landscape. Montholon takes advantage then of the governor's good faith and draws the attention of Gorrequer (see page 88) to the defective quality of the provisions supplied to Longwood: bread and beef, are not good; fish is not enough and the wine is bad... The British understand there are grounds for these complaints and some measures are taken.

September 1820

> '*Longwood, 10th September, 1820.*
> *Sir,*
> *General Bonaparte was in the garden with Count Montholon today at twelve o'clock. He is not going to ride this afternoon.*'[1]

On the 2nd of this month Bertrand sends a letter to the Governor on behalf of the Emperor addressed to Lord Liverpool complaining of the state of Napoleon's health. Stating that he had been suffering from chronic hepatitis since October of 1817 because of the defective conditions and extremely poor climate of Saint Helena, his coming back to Europe is demanded as the only way to restore his highly deteriorated health after a stay of five years on the island. As customary, the imperial title is used all through the letter and, for that reason, it is sent back to Bertrand, but not before making a copy to be forwarded to London...

October 1820

All during this month Lutyens can only briefly spot Napoleon three times. A deadly calm reigns over Longwood...

On the 4th the Emperor left the house on horseback accompanied by Montholon and Bertrand towards Mount Pleasant (see page 54) and had a picnic at Sir William Doveton's place, who finds his guest as being '*in good health; his face is astonishingly fat, and his body and thighs very round and plump. He looked as fat and as round as a China pig*'[2]. But despite the evident overweight he was seriously ill and just short of a few months from his death. This would be the last time he would go out of Longwood. Extenuated after the visit he travelled back in the carriage.

---

1. '*Letters of Captain Engelbert Lutyens. Orderly officer at Longwood, Saint Helena: Feb. 1820 to Nov. 1823. Edited by Sir Lees Knowles*'. *LONDON—John Lane, The Bodley Head. New York- John Lane Company. MCMXV.*
2. *History of the Captivity of Napoleon at Saint Helena. From the letters and journals of the late Lieut. Gen. Sir Hudson Lowe and official documents not before made public by William Forsyth, MA. Harper Brothers. 1853, New York.*

Now it is Bertrand and family who are considering going back to England. The grand Marshall proposes sailing there too and returning once his family is properly accommodated. Napoleon pretendedly agrees.

November 1820

'Longwood, 9th November, 1820.

Sir,

Yesterday evening at half-past four the phaeton drove up to the garden-gate, when General Bonaparte came out, leaning on the arm of Count Montholon, and walked a little below the stables. They then got into the carriage, and took an airing in the wood for about an hour. The General appeared very feeble when walking. He wore a greatcoat and a round hat. He has not been out this morning.'[1]

The symptoms of his fatal disease are now completely evident: frequent vomiting and stomach pains; pale and chilly limbs denoting insufficient blood circulation and a strong drowsiness that often keeps him in bed. Salt-water baths provide some relief while Antommarchi watches out.

However, he still occasionally drove out in his carriage and on one of these occasions Lowe bumps into him:

'I was returning through the grounds of Longwood, towards Longwood House, when I observed a phaeton drawn by four horses with General Bonaparte and Count Montholon in it. As soon as they saw me, the drivers were ordered to turn off by another road, but this could not be done so soon as to prevent my having a good view of General Bonaparte's side face, at about thirty yards distance. He wore a round hat, and green surtout buttoned close over his breast. He appeared much paler than when I had last seen him, but not gaunt. I should have inferred, however, a looseness of fibre and inability at the moment of any active exertion. A sallow, colourless look is characteristic of his appearance in general, and any degree of indisposition would naturally add to it.'[2]

1.   'Letters of Captain Engelbert Lutyens. Orderly officer at Longwood, Saint Helena: Feb. 1820 to Nov. 1823. Edited by Sir Lees Knowles'. LONDON—John Lane, The Bodley Head. New York- John Lane Company. MCMXV.

2.   History of the Captivity of Napoleon at Saint Helena. From the letters and journals of the late Lieut. Gen. Sir Hudson Lowe and official documents not before made public by William Forsyth, MA. Harper Brothers. 1853, New York.

December **1820**

> '*Longwood, 4ᵗʰ December, 1820.*
> *Sir,*
> *General Bonaparte was not seen out yesterday, or today. I heard his bell ring about an hour ago. I have seen the Doctor go to the house, and Saint Dennis come for Count Montholon. I have this morning seen Count Montholon. He informed me that General Bonaparte was getting weaker every day, and that now Dr. Antommarchi thought seriously of the General's state of health; that he fainted the last time when he returned in the carriage; that whatever he ate he immediately threw off; that he, Count Montholon, had the greatest trouble to get the General to move off his bed, or sofa. He was going in, and hoped he might persuade him to go out, if fine, in the carriage.*'[1]

Despite the unequivocal signs that Napoleon is seriously ill, the British still fear a possible evasion and lord Bathurst would even instruct Lowe by letter to take any necessary steps to prevent it. As illness aggravates Antommarchi is found to be a rather whimsical, negligent man who is frequently absent in town. The end of 1820 is made even sadder when the news of the decease of Napoleon's sister Elisa reaches Longwood. The Emperor is desolated...

1821

January **1821**

> '*Longwood, 11ᵗʰ January, 1821.*
> *Sir,*
> *General Bonaparte has not been observed out this day. Richards was in the dining-room this morning about twelve o'clock, when General Bonaparte passed through the room. He says the General looked very bad, that his eyes appear almost sunk in his head, and that he is continually coughing. The Doctor was sent for last evening, when he was at dinner. He has been frequently at the house this day.*'[1]

Bertrand, possibly feeling that the end is near decides to stay. Now it is Buonavita who begins to consider leaving... Despite some interspersed amelioration spells –less frequent each day– the gravity of the situation is clear. Anything thought useful to improve Napoleon's health is tried; like a seesaw installed in the parlour expected to help

---

1. '*Letters of Captain Engelbert Lutyens. Orderly officer at Longwood, Saint Helena: Feb. 1820 to Nov. 1823. Edited by Sir Lees Knowles*'. *LONDON — John Lane, The Bodley Head. New York- John Lane Company. MCMXV.*

the Emperor in taking some exercise that, probably judged as rather incompatible with his 'imperial dignity', is soon removed. In the meantime Antommarchi's frivolity and immaturity exasperate the Emperor to the point that Bertrand and Montholon suggest calling on Dr. Arnott[1].

FEBRUARY 1821

> 'Longwood, 28th February, 1821.
> Sir,
> A short time before seven o'clock this morning General Bonaparte and Count Montholon walked part of the way across the lawn leading to the stables. The phaeton was in readiness; but, a shower of rain came on at that moment, which obliged them to return.'[2]

Short spells of apparent improvement alternated with relapses keeping Napoleon indoors and in his dressing gown most of the time. Montholon tried to encourage him to take some outings, which he only accepted with reluctance. He always returns to the house exhausted, anxious to throw himself onto his settee...

MARCH 1821

> 'Sir,
> Last night there was a light visible in the bath and dressing rooms. Saint Dennis was at the General's bedroom window this morning. Count Montholon has informed me, that the Doctor does not think General Bonaparte is any better, that when the Doctor gave him some medicine this morning the General threw it away, that he had passed a quiet night, but had slept but very little. I again spoke to the Count about the necessity of my seeing General Bonaparte. He made the same sort of reply as yesterday, adding that he should be very happy if he could assist; but, the General kept his room so dark, that it would be impossible for me to see him from the window; for, when he or Count Bertrand went into the room from the light, they could not see anything for a short time, and the General, to prevent any light coming to his eyes, had his bed removed from between the windows. I then requested Count Montholon to come up with a plan whereby I might see the General'.[2]

---

1. *Archibald Arnott (1772-1855) was a British Army surgeon most remembered for being Napoleon's last physician at Saint Helena. He was present at the autopsy.*
2. *'Letters of Captain Engelbert Lutyens. Orderly officer at Longwood, Saint Helena: Feb. 1820 to Nov. 1823. Edited by Sir Lees Knowles'. LONDON—John Lane, The Bodley Head. New York- John Lane Company. MCMXV.*

Unreachable for Lutyens, what was happening inside the house at that time is quite well illustrated by Marchand in his diary containing vivid scenes like this:

'The days of the 28th and 29th were pretty much like the prior ones. The shutters were closed. Day and night the Emperor often moved from his bed to his settee or armchair. He had the door to the garden open and told Bertrand to go for a flower; a pansy that the Emperor placed on his table.

The grand marshal and count de Montholon pleaded the doctor's case[1] remarking how worried he was by the big responsibility laid on him. He only wanted to mitigate the Emperor's suffering and would be happy when allowed by the Emperor to bring in a doctor deserving of confidence which he couldn't inspire. **'That's all right; tell him that I shall see him tomorrow.'** The Emperor received him the next day exclaiming: **'Doctor, I'm a dead man'-**If your Majesty refuses any help!

The doctor came to the bedside, took his pulse, palpated his stomach, found it bloated and advised the use of some pills that would eliminate this condition. **'Doctor'**, the Emperor replied laughing, **'you are a great ignorant my friend, you know that Hippocrates said yes and Galen said no. In such circumstance, here is the best medicine:'** and he showed a little bottle filled with liquorice water, which he preferred to all the other drinks laid on the table.'[2]

A compassionate Fanny Bertrand now spent many moments by the Emperor's bed side. On the 17th Buonavita is leaving Saint Helena and comes in the morning of this day to bid farewell to the Emperor, who attends mass from his bed before instructing the priest what to tell to his family once he had arrived to Rome.

April 1821

'Longwood, 18th April, 1821.
Sir,
Doctor Arnott was with General Bonaparte this morning. He found the General very low and not any better. Count Montholon mentioned to me that he did not think General Bonaparte could survive more than three or four weeks. He added, the strength of the General's body appeared to have gone from his body to his head, that he now recollected

---

1. *Tired of Antommarchi's absences Napoleon had angrily dismissed the futile doctor some days ago.*
2. *Mémoires de Marchand d'après le manuscrit original par Jean Bourguignon. Plon, Paris 1952.*

*everything of former days, that the stupor and forgetfulness had left him,
and he is now continually talking of what will take place at his death.'[1]*

On the 1ˢᵗ of April Napoleon, after great insistence from his
companions of misfortune finally gives up and accepts receiving Dr.
Arnott. In the evening of the same day the British Doctor enters the
Emperor's bedroom. Upon examining the patient he concluded that
it is an inflammation of the stomach, not affecting the liver at all, and
attributes the pain in the intestines to gases. As remedies he suggests
poultices and some beverages to be taken every hour...

He is perfectly aware that the end is near; very near. Stoically
bearing Arnott's erratic diagnostics and remedies and barely able to
cope with Antommarchi's stupidity he withdraws and, starting on the
11ᵗʰ, dictated his long and exhaustive last will aided by Montholon and
Bertrand. He signs it on the 15ᵗʰ even though he would still produce a
series of codicils until the 27ᵗʰ, when the lucidity he enjoyed all his life
begins to vanish.

Probably in the absence of a better choice, he commissions
Antommarchi to perform his autopsy. Montholon and Marchand take
shifts by his bed side...

May 1821

*'All along the forty-odd days that the Emperor had been in bed,
we who had been constantly at his service beside him were so tired,
and desperately in need of some rest that, in the night, couldn't control
our sleepiness. The quiet of the apartment helped to it. Everybody, on
chairs or sofas, took some moments of rest. If we woke up, we ran to
the bed listening attentively to hear the breathing and pouring into
the Emperor's mouth, which was a little open, a spoonful or two of
sweetened water to refresh him. We scrutinised the sick man's face as
much as permitted by the reflection of the candlelight hidden behind the
screen which was before the door of the dining room. That was the way
we spent the night.'[2]*

That's the end. A persistent hiccup exhausts the dying man. Dr.
Arnott, probably feeling insecure confronting the imminent outcome,

---

1. *'Letters of Captain Engelbert Lutyens. Orderly officer at Longwood, Saint Helena: Feb.
    1820 to Nov. 1823. Edited by Sir Lees Knowles'. LONDON—John Lane, The Bodley
    Head. New York- John Lane Company. MCMXV.*
2. *Souvenirs du Mameluck Ali sur L'Empereur Napoléon. Payot, Paris 1926.*

calls in his colleagues Shortt and Mitchell[1]. In the afternoon of the 3rd, Vignali gives the Emperor the extreme unction. Then the three British physicians agree to administer the vanishing Emperor a strong dose of calomel[2] resulting in the final death blow to the moribund and drawing him into a comatose condition.

At 5.50 p.m. on Saturday May 5th 1821, the prisoner of Saint Helena finally gives up by, semi-consciously, pronouncing his last words: *'France. Armée, tête d'armée, Josephine'*[3].

The next day at dawn Lowe, escorted by his staff, could at last penetrate into the Emperor's abode and contemplate his lifeless body...

1. *Respectively chief medical officer on St Helena and Navy surgeon.*
2. *Calomel was a mercury compound that was used in medicine at that time as a diuretic and laxative before its toxicity was discovered and its medical uses discontinued.*
3. *'France –the Army– Head of the Army– Josephine'. This is Montholon's version; others slightly differ. According to Marchand for example the last words were '... France... mon fils ...armée.' (France, my sons, army). By most accounts these last words were muttered in a series of rather unintelligible expressions.*

The road to the burial place...

THE ILLNESS

he stomach appeared, at first sight, in a perfectly healthy state; no trace of irritation or phologosis[1], and the peritoneal membrane exhibited the most satisfactory appearance: but, on examining that organ with care, I discover on its anterior surface, near the small curve, and at the breadth of three fingers from the pylorus[2], a slight obstruction, apparently of a scirrhous nature, of little extent, and exactly circumscribed. The stomach was perforated through and through in the centre of that small induration, the aperture of which was closed by the adhesion of that part to the left lobe of the liver.

The volume of the stomach was smaller than it is usually found.

On opening that organ along its large curve, I observed that part of its capacity was filled with a considerable quantity of matter, slightly consistent, and mixed with a great quantity of glairous substances, very thick and of a colour resembling the sediment of coffee, and which exhaled an acrid and infectious odour. These substances being removed, the mucous membrane of the stomach was ascertained to be sound from the small to the large cavity of this organ, following the great curve. Almost the whole remainder of the internal surface of the stomach was occupied by a cancerous ulcer, whose centre was in the upper part, along the small curve of the stomach, whilst the irregular digital and linguiform borders of its circumference extended both before and after that internal surface, and from the orifice of the cardia[3] to within a good inch of the pylorus. Its rounded opening, obliquely cut in the shape of a basil at the expense of the internal surface of the organ, scarcely occupied a diameter of four or five lines[4] inside, and at most two lines and half outside.

The circular border of that opening was extremely thin, slightly denticulated, blackish, and only formed by the peritoneal membrane of the stomach. An ulcerous, greyish, and smooth surface lined this kind of canal, which, but for the adhesion to the liver, would have established a communication between the cavity of the stomach and that of the abdomen. The right extremity of the stomach, at the

1. Tumour, with inflammation, heat and pain.
2. The lower orifice of the stomach.
3. The upper orifice of the stomach.
4. Old English unit of uncertain length most frequently understood as 1/12 of an inch.

distance of an inch from the pylorus, was surrounded by a tumour, or
rather a scirrhous annular induration, a few lines in width. The orifice
of the pylorus was in a perfect state. The lips of the ulcer exhibited
remarkable fungous swellings, the bases of which were, hard, thick,
and in a scirrhous state, and extended also over the whole surface
occupied by the cruel disease.[5]

Nearly 200 years after Napoleon's death the discussion about its causes is still going on and nothing today gives grounds to expect this to change in the near future. The first thing to take into account when approaching this subject is that medical profession was a far cry then from what we have at present time. If medicine nowadays could be depicted as an amazing, and extremely sophisticated mixture of science and art, it was quite different in Napoleon's time, when a considerable deal of ignorance and even superstition was still part of this old and noble profession. That of course was no significant impediment for the arrogance and self assurance sported by some of its members. These facts were indeed not strange to Napoleon´s understanding who, with some remarkable exceptions like Corvisart[6] or Larrey[7], projected very little confidence and appreciation on the real capabilities of most of his contemporary doctors.

In addition there seem to be little doubt that all the doctors intervening in Napoleon's illness would rate rather poorly in terms of knowledge, judgment or care. The Corsican Francesco Antommarchi was selected in 1819 by Napoleon's uncle, Cardinal Fesch, to be the Emperor's doctor after the dismissal of the precedents O'Meara and Stokoe. Unfortunately, this young man of 30 was not at all up to the task as, besides any personal consideration commented in other parts of this book, he was just an anatomist and a pathologist short of clinical experience. Needless to say Napoleon despised Antommarchi and even at a given point refused to take any medication prescribed by him[8]. In addition Dr. Arnott, the British doctor that was called in at the last phase of the illness, was certainly no better, diagnosing the Emperor's condition as just something of physiological nature and not really serious, just a few days before his death...

---

5. *Excerpt from Antommarchi's autopsy of Napoleon. 'Napoleon's Exile' by F. Antommarchi.*
    London. Henry Colburn, New Burlington Street. 1826.
6. *Jean-Nicolas Corvisart-Desmarets (1755 –1821). An important figure in the history of*
    French medicine and primary physician of Napoleon from 1804 to 1815.
7. *Dominique Jean Larrey (1766 –1842).Surgeon in Napoleon's army often considered as the*
    first modern military surgeon.
8. *Antommarchi gave Napoleon a strong dose of 'tartaric emetic', a purge that had the*
    Emperor rolling on the floor in great pain.

All the above considered, any retrospective study of Napoleon's pathology forcibly has to rely on the autopsy performed on the 6th of May. It took place in the parlour, where the Emperor's body had been laid on a table covered by a sheet. Besides Antommarchi the British physicians Arnott, Shortt, Mitchell, Burton and Livingstone were present along with a couple of assistants and several British and French personalities. Marchand, Saint Denis and Pierron, who had brought in the corpse, were present too.

From an attentive study of the autopsy report emerge some remarkable statements useful for reaching a reasonable knowledge on the real pathology that caused Napoleon´s death.

First are the clear signs of tuberculosis noted in Napoleon's lungs and the striking fact that Antommarchi made no prior mention of that disease in the nearly two years he was treating Napoleon.

Then is the contradiction observed in regard with the state of the liver between Arnott's and Antommarchi's reports, which respectively state that 'there was not unhealthy appearance in the liver' and that 'the liver was very large and distended with blood and affected by chronic hepatitis'.

Last is the surprising fact –too– that neither the British nor Antommarchi arrive to a clear final conclusion explaining the cause of death. Antommarchi noted 'abnormalities' of the stomach of cancerous (scirrhous) nature that, together with other remarks shown in the opening quote of this chapter, would lead to a stomach cancer diagnosis...

All in all, and leaving aside conspiracy theories as that of a gradual poising with arsenic (see page 291) or even a plain murder executed by Arnott by administering a massive dose of calomel (most probably a shameful mistake) no conclusive diagnostic is affordable yet. The most likely guess would be a gradually weakened health involving tuberculosis, chronic hepatitis and, most of all, stomach cancer. All of that accelerated and aggravated by an extremely defective medical care; even for that time.

Napoleon's tomb.

DEATH AND BURIAL

ow and when Napoleon was certain that he wouldn't ever leave Saint Helena cannot be exactly determined. After all he knew very well the great changes one can expect from life, especially in times of great political turbulence as those he had lived through. In any case, however, the chance of dying there was within the realm of possibilities and even of high probability with the passing of years and the stiffness of the British government, which was never really willing to risk loosing the still relatively young and restless 'General Bonaparte'. In consequence, dying at Longwood House should have been always on his mind, determining his course of action.

It was not only living imprisoned on the island by keeping his rather mocking, pathetic court and his royal status, but also being able to project his historical persona and his legend beyond physical death. In the middle of 1819, after nearly four years of captivity, it was pretty clear that lord Holland's theoretical sympathy to his cause and the evolution of British politics was putting the wind up on him. It could be then when he abandoned all hopes and began to think of death as the only possible, and desirable, deliverance.

Before travelling to Saint Helena, Napoleon had enjoyed sound health and a strong, resilient body. He had lived through hardships and fatigues on little food and extremely physical and brain work that few other men could possibly bear but, once at Saint Helena, and coincidental with the arrival of Hudson Lowe six months after moving to Longwood, his health began to decline.

The arguably harsh climate of the island and the restrictions imposed by Lowe that drew the Emperor to drastically reduce his outings on foot and horseback are commonly mentioned as more or less direct causes of his illness and premature death.

Of course there is no doubt about the great influence of the state of the mind on physical condition and, very probably, the alluded factors contributed to some extent to the development of his illness but, one way or the other, the year 1816 was almost ended when O'Meara set off alarm bells about the poor state of his health.

From then on his general attitude changed. As a man of war he had been living next to death all his life. Death was nothing for this man. He was not afraid to die but quite possibly glad to; and the sooner the better... He wouldn't worry anymore about his health and consecrated the last phase of his life to working on the memories of his incredible life and the building of his legend that he thought would ultimately survive his mortal existence on earth. His death so taken for granted, it is no surprise that he frequently announced to all around the proximity of his end and the meticulousness exerted in dictating his will, setting the details for his funeral or choosing the right place where his body should be buried...

The last ordeal begins towards the mid-February in 1821. From then on he suffered almost constantly frequent lapses of memory and acute pains. He throws up practically any food and lives mainly on meat jelly. As stated before, no doctor succeeded in providing him any satisfactory relief. All through those last painful months he had no doubt that his was a fatal disease and, even though by no means trusting the doctors around him, he just let them administer their absurd remedies sporting most of the time an indifferent, stoic attitude; as if he was already dead.

When dictating his will he declared that he dies in the Catholic, Apostolic and Roman faith and expressed his desire of resting on the banks of the Seine. Then he produces a detailed list of recommendations and bequeaths and, upon finishing this last and exhausting work he sank again. He even took trouble to dictate a letter with blank date to be delivered to the governor upon his death...

Weather is gloomy on the evening of Sunday 5th May of 1821 at Longwood House. Rain falls persistently and there are thick, somber clouds above while the south-east wind blows sharply and the night comes. Ten minutes before six the body of the tireless battler shivers from head to toes. His eyes are turned upwards and wide open and there is foam on his lips when he, at last, is free of himself and finally becomes part of eternity...

'The Emperor visiting the grand marshal while he was living at Hutt's Gate happened to descend with some difficulty down the valley extended in front of that house and arrived to a small plateau from where the ocean could be seen. There were three willows and a spring of cool water providing shade and refreshment. He found this water to be excellent and, on leaving the place said to Bertrand: **'Bertrand, if after my death my body remains in the hands of my enemies, put**

it here.' Once back at Longwood, he demanded going there every day to fetch his water from this spring. A Chinese was given that task, and then the Emperor only drank that water which he had found so beneficial and which was brought to him in two large silver containers used in the field. So His Majesty had been to this place only once, but he had kept a pleasant memory of it and he liked the quietness. In consequence this place was designed as his grave on the advice of Count Bertrand."[1]

The protocol ruling at Longwood house, so scrupulously followed all during the captivity, would still be enforced after the death. The corpse is reverentially handled by Ali and Marchand, who state that Napoleon appeared in death no older than thirty and showed a countenance of calmness and even of satisfaction. His figure being controversial even in death, there were some discussions during and after the autopsy[2]. According to the Emperor's instructions his heart was removed to be delivered to Marie-Louise, which didn't happen because of Lowe's objection. But the heart was not the only piece of Napoleon's corpse in dispute as Lowe, on his side, wanted to send the stomach to London[3]. This time Bertrand and Montholon earnestly opposed it. At the end both organs, conveniently stored in wine-filled containers, would be deposited with their original owner in the coffin.

Once the autopsy was completed and this strange 'war of relics' settled, the loyal Marchand and Ali proceeded to dress their master in full regalia with his legendary uniform *of 'chasseurs de la garde'* and wearing his unmistakeable hat. A makeshift 'mortuary chapel' is swiftly assembled in the sitting room. By this time, probably because of the attention drawn by the unusual quantity of black cloth purchased at Jamestown, the towners soon became aware of the news. A veritable multitude would arrive at Longwood to see the 'greatest man in the world' in the words spoken by a father to his son when confronting the Emperor's corpse.

His body would be finally placed in a tin coffin lined with white quilted satin. As there was not enough room to keep his hat on, this would be placed on his legs. Once soldered this first coffin would be placed inside another one of mahogany and this in turn into a leaden casket sealed with silver-headed iron screws.

---

1. *Mémoires de Marchand d'après le manuscrit original par Jean Bourguignon. Plon, Paris 1952.*
2. *Antommarchi wanted to examine the brain for the sake of scientific interest, which he finally couldn't do because of the firm opposition of Bertrand and Montholon.*
3. *Which eventually gives some food for thought...*

The burial couldn't take place until the morning of the 9th, once the masonry works for the grave were completed. Finally, on the 9th at 10 a.m. he could be buried.

Napoleon's hearse, draped in violet velvet was preceded by Vignaly and followed by the whole household of Longwood headed by Bertrand and Montholon. Hudson Lowe and Admiral Lambert came after them together with General Coffin[4] and Montchenu. The islanders, wearing their best attires, watched the procession pass in silence and the garrison paid honours to the Emperor as corresponding to the highest rank in the British army. Three salvoes salute 'General Bonaparte'.

As if to confirm his narrow-mindedness and shameful stinginess, Hudson Lowe insisted that the surname 'Bonaparte' should be added to the simple 'Napoleon' suggested by Bertrand and Montholon in a last –and unsuccessful– attempt to overcome this ridicule quibble about names. At the end, the tombstone would remain void of any name as a silent testimony to the greatness of a man whose simple name was feared even in death and the clumsy lowliness of his enemies...

---

4.   *Major-General John Pine Coffin (1778–1830). Lieutenant-Governor of Saint Helena (1819-1823).*

(KGM. ©Andrea Press).

THE MYSTERIES

NAPOLEON AND LOVE

t was, I believe, about this time[1] that the First Consul became ardent about a young and smart woman full of grace, Madame D...[2]. Madame Bonaparte, suspecting this intrigue, was jealous; and her husband did all within reach to dispel her conjugal concerns. He would wait until everybody in the palace was asleep before moving into his mistress' chamber and took care enough as to go barefoot in his night gown.

Once I notice that the day was about to break before his return and fearing trouble, I proceed as the First Consul had instructed me to do in such a case by informing the chambermaid of Madame D... to tell her mistress what time it was. Hardly five minutes after this sound advice had been given, I saw the First Consul coming back in great excitement for reasons I immediately learned.

On returning, he had spotted one of Madame Bonaparte's maidens, watching him through the casement of a closet overlooking the corridor. The First Consul, after being greatly annoyed about the curiosity of the fair sex, sent me to the young scout from the enemy's camp to intimate to her his orders to hold her tongue, unless she wished to be discharged for good. I do not know whether he added a more amiable argument to these threats to buy the silence of the nosey girl; but whether out of fear or because of compensation, she had the good sense not to talk. In any case, the joyful lover, fearing another surprise, commissioned me to rent in the 'Allé des Veuves' a little house where he and Madame D... met now and then.

Such were, and kept being, the First Consul's measures preventing his wife being aware of his loving affairs. He was very fond of her and took all the necessary steps preventing his infidelities coming to her

1. Apparently 1805 even though Napoleon was already Emperor and not first consul by that time.
2. Madame Duchâtel, born Adèle Papin. A blue-eyed beautiful brunette that enchanted Napoleon, who would gift her plenty, which eventually wouldn't impede Adele to make the acquaintance of Monsieur (future Charles X) in 1814.

knowledge. Besides, these brief flirts did not detract from his tenderness
for her and, although being attracted by other women, none of them could
compete with the trust and friendship devoted to Madame Bonaparte.

In regard to his supposed harshness and brutality towards women,
it is the same in the case of the uncountable slanders said about him.
He was not always gallant but I have never seen him being coarse and,
regardless how surprising it may seem after what has here been reported,
he greatly appreciated a woman of exemplary conduct, speaking in
admiring terms of happy couples; and he didn't like cynicism either in
morals or in language. When he entertained illegitimate affairs he kept
them aside, and concealed them with great care[1].

This fragment from Constant's memoires serves well to illustrate
Napoleon's views on love and/or sex. It is clear that he made a clear
distinction between fidelity and loyalty and that, the latter being of
paramount importance, the first was just another thing which he felt
free to look for and entertain any sexual relationships with no other
moral restriction than keeping them unknown out of 'respect' for his
beloved wives.

Although not really being a womanizer, he nevertheless enjoyed
having sex all during his life helped by his valets that discretely arranged
his amorous encounters. That of course wouldn't be a problem when
he was the master of France and the Empire but, once at Saint Helena,
that was certainly not the case. This aspect of his life in captivity is only
very tangentially tackled in the profuse collection of period accounts.
Like many other facets of his intimate life at Longwood House only the
French chroniclers living there would have known details but if so, the
subject would have been muffled as unfitting to the egregious image
of Napoleon in captivity that they all were committed to project to the
world. As a result, there is here an ample field for speculation and...
fabulists.

Considering the facts it is quite obvious that his very limited
freedom of action would prevent him from having any affairs with the
privacy that was essential to him. Bringing women from the town into
Longwood was clearly out of the question, as they never could have
made their way into the house without being checked by the British
and, in any case, their silence and discretion couldn't be expected
either. Similar reasons stand for his household's feminine servants.
Consequently, the only remaining possibility to enjoy sexual relief

1.   *'Mémoires intimes de Napoléon 1er par Constant son valet de chambre'. Le Temps retrouvé.*
      Mercure de France 1967.

there would be the women in his inner circle; namely Betsy Balcombe, Fanny Bertrand and Albine de Montholon.

Betsy should be discarded at any rate, even though some alembicated, bad taste lucubrations can be found on the issue, they make no sense at all.

In the case of Fanny Bertrand, there are some foggy indications that the Emperor made some passes at her on 28th September 1819 followed by a harsh argument apparently because she refused these passes, which would keep him enraged even the day after... but whether she ever conceded favours to the Imperial solicitor has not yet been established[1].

The most likely candidate for being Napoleon's mistress at Saint Helena would be Albine de Montholon. References for such a liaison are explicit as quoted in prior chapters of this work. The striking resemblance to Napoleon of Albine's daughter born at Saint Helena on 18th June 1816[2] aroused some salacious remarks at the time and reinforced the suspicions of a long standing and surreptitious affair between this lady and the Emperor.

THE DEATH MASKS

Ce n'est pas la ressemblance qui compte, c'est l'image vive du génie![3] (It is not the resemblance that matters; it is the live image of genius!)

One of the most intriguing mysteries about Napoleon at Saint Helena is the question of his death mask –or better death masks– which, in turn, would be connected with another surprising fact in his life: the scarce reliability of his portraits produced during and after his death (see page 13). Other famous historical characters born long before Napoleon Bonaparte had a perpetual image cast in the collective imagination probably thanks to the mere scarcity of these images, which leaves little or no room to speculation or debate. That is not the case with Napoleon of whom a myriad of representations were made offering a variety, and sometimes even contradictory versions, of his

---

1.   *'Cahiers de Sainte-Hélène 1818-1819'. Général Bertrand. Editions Albin Michel.*
2.   *Charlotte Hélène Napoléone (1816-1907). Nothing was known of Hélène after she left Saint Helena, except that she died a nonagenarian in Aix-en-Provence.*
3.   *Quote as said by Napoleon to David by Rétif de la Bretonne. Bruno Roy-Henry, 'Anglais, Rendez-Nous Napoléon'.*

real looks. In addition, our man was not really interested in leaving to posterity a veritable, physical portrait, but rather emphasized the mythical –even propagandistic– aspects of his figure in a series of more or less institutional or official renditions.

In fact, he rarely was available to pose for a painting or sculpture the way he did for the famous Houdon bust in 1806 which, in any case, didn´t vary from the official nature of its predecessors and would be even used in a later work by the same artist exhibited in 1808. That showed the Emperor dressed in his beloved uniform of colonel of *Chasseurs de la Garde,* according to his own wishes. Very probably these two busts would be the closest Napoleon portraits ever done...

At Saint Helena things wouldn't be better regarding pictorial representations of the Emperor. There being no remarkable portraitist on the island at the time of Napoleon's stay, all surviving works have in common an amateurish nature –mostly burlesque sketches– coincidental in showing a short, fat man very far from the much more representative images Napoleon would have desired. In these circumstances, the existence of a faithful post mortem representation of his noble features would have been extremely desirable. Regretfully, it seems that the alluded elusiveness of his traits persisted beyond death. The story of Napoleon's masks could be regarded as a literary sub-genre by itself in the overwhelming Napoleonic bibliography. This is a rather obscure episode shrouded in mystery and scheming. Essentially, and for the sake of clarity, there are three basic death masks attributed to Napoleon of which none have yet achieved undisputed recognition:

ANTOMMARCHI'S MASK/S

This is the 'official' Napoleon's death mask, normally accepted as the real imprint of Napoleon face taken on May 7th 1821, about two days after his death. However, its authenticity is amply discussed today. Originally the Antommarchi mask would have been cast in association, or helped, by Dr Burton[1].

Apparently three moulds were taken for the face, top and back of the head[2].

---

1.   *Dr. Francis Burton, from the British 66th Regiment at Saint Helena. He was present at Napoleon's autopsy.*
2.   *The other two parts of this mask –top and back– are missing.*

Death mask reputed to be Antommarchi's first original casting. (KGM. ©Andrea Press).

Antommarchi and Mme. Bertrand are currently blamed for having stolen the mould of the face, from which the multiple variations of this mask existing today would originate. Once back in Europe Antommarchi gave to this mask ample diffusion and even got Napoleon's mother´s recognition of this work as the true representation of her illustrious son's face in death. However, it is a crude and poorly detailed piece of work, the fact that it is pretty much oversized for a man the height of Napoleon, or its thinness suggest that it is, by no way, an imprint of the Emperor's face. A lot has been –and it is being– written on the subject but, summarizing, there are two versions on how Antommarchi's mask could have been created:

– Antommarchi surreptitiously stole the mould or the first casting but, the plaster used being of very poor quality, or because of clumsy handling, the piece would have been seriously damaged at some point between the moulding and its arrival to Britain. The daring doctor would then have had the mask repaired by himself or by – or with the help of– some artist like, arguably, Canova; according to some sources.

– A more striking explanation concerns Rétif de la Bretonne[1] and Roy-Henry's theory of the substitution of Napoleon's corpse[2]. Once

1. *Georges Rétif de la Bretonne (1930-1999) was journalist and photographer who in 1969 published a book titled 'Anglais, Rendez-Nous Napoléon', so initiating a debate about the whereabouts of Napoleon's corpse.*
2. *Bruno Roy-Henry, born in 1956 is a writer specializing in the history of the French Revolution and the First Empire.*

the mould was performed Bertrand and the others, disliking the appearance of the real imprint, decided to ameliorate the real Napoleon mask by the simple procedure of exchanging it with that of Cipriani produced at the time of his death in 1818 (see page 113). Subsequent manipulations on this Cipriani mask would have resulted in the 'official' death mask of the Emperor, as it is (with slight variations) known nowadays.

Beyond the alembicated nature of these theories, the lack of veracity of this mask would still stand from mere dispassionate observation.

THE ARNOTT MASK.

(KGM. ©Andrea Press).

This is a mask reputedly taken by Dr. Arnott[1] with surgical wax on the night from the 5th to the 6th of May which has been sometimes

---

1.   *Archibald Arnott (1772-1855) was a British Army surgeon most remembered for being Napoleon's last physician at Saint Helena. He was present at the autopsy.*

credited as authentic, which is quite surprising as anyone familiar with human anatomy rarely could fail to notice that, if this is indeed a real casting taken from a death mask mould, it would have been so crudely and clumsily manipulated that any resemblance between this mask and the original casting would be merely coincidental.

THE RUSI MASK.

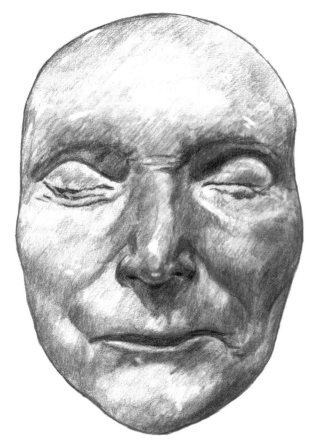

(KGM. ©Andrea Press).

So called because it was exhibited at the Royal United Service Institute from 1947 to 1973, this would be the original casting taken from the mould made by Burton/Antommarchi. This is a highly detailed mask that undoubtedly corresponds to a real dead man, with no apparent manipulation.

 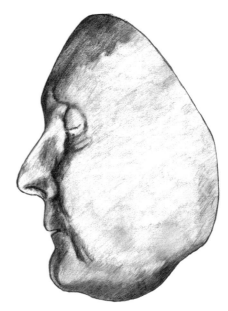

(KGM. ©Andrea Press).   *(KGM. ©Andrea Press).*

It emerged in 1935 from not very reliable sources, which has hindered its recognition as being the true Napoleon death mask. However, the fact that its size and features match pretty accurately those of Napoleon and some descendants, particularly Marie Walewska's son[1], sustains the idea that it is really the one and only real imprint taken from Napoleon's face in death. The existence of small facial hairs inserted in the mask ascertains that it would be a first copy and not a recast.

According to DNA tests performed in 2015 by professor Gérard Luccote comparing these hairs with Napoleon's DNA taken from descendants, he would have established that this would be the real mask of Napoleon... End of story?

---

1.   *Alexandre-Florian-Joseph Colonna, Count Walewski (1810 - 1868) was the illegitimate son of Napoleon and Maria Walewska.*

POISONED?

'I have been murdered lengthily with considerable detail and premeditation, and the infamous Hudson Lowe is the executioner of your ministers. You shall end up like the proud republic of Venice, and I, dying on this dreadful rock, I bequeath the shame of my death to the ruling house of England'[1]

These words pronounced by Napoleon shortly before his death could be regarded as a forerunner for the arsenic poising theories that flourished in the 1960's –coincidental with the last advances in scientific research– pointing to arsenic poising as the direct cause of the Emperor's death.

Sten Forshufvud, Ben Weider and H. Smith among others elaborated a poisoning thesis that, with slight variations, sustained that Napoleon didn't die from natural causes but as the result of premeditated and gradual poisoning with arsenic. The poisoner would be Charles de Montholon who, by taking advantage of his closeness to the Emperor would have been regularly doctoring Napoleon's wine with arsenic doses. Montholon on his side was thought not to be acting on his own account but as part of a scheme contrived by the Comte d' Artois on behalf of the interests of the Bourbon faction in France and possibly with the consent or collaboration of the British government. Among the reasons impelling Montholon to murder his master are commonly mentioned vengeance, jealousy and greed.

Doubtless a suggestive argument for a detective or mystery novel unless a supplementary element could be added giving historical dimension to the plot: proof.

However, proving a crime committed so long time ago is no small feat, but when a lock of Napoleon´s hair brought from Saint Helena was analyzed and contained a surprisingly high amount of arsenic, all the pieces seemed to fall into place. This finding really made an impression among scholars and even the general public. Unfortunately, subsequent analyses carried out by critical researchers showed that similar quantities of arsenic were present in pre-Saint Helena Napoleon's hair. In addition more period samples from members of his family, and even other contemporaries, showed similar traces of arsenic. In fact this substance was commonly used at the time for many different purposes

---

1. *Said by Napoleon to Dr. Arnott on April 20th 1821. Mémoires de Marchand. Paris Librairie Plon. 1955.*

ranging from rat killing to capillary tonics, dyeing, etc. That was a severe blow to the poisoning theorists that, all of a sudden, saw how the only conclusive 'proof' backing their thesis evaporated...

Nowadays the story of Napoleon being poisoned by his mistress' husband in connivance with the French and British governments at Saint Helena, even though still lingering in the collective imagination, is most critically questioned.

IS NAPOLEON AT LES INVALIDES?

In 1969 Rétif de la Bretonne[1] published his book titled 'Anglais, Rendez-Nous Napoléon', so initiating a debate about the whereabouts of Napoleon's corpse. His thesis, even though firmly disregarded by a majority of the, more or less, consecrated scholars and historians specialized in the Napoleonic saga, is still today subscribed to by a number of 'revisionists' headed by Roy- Henry, author of 'Napoléon L'Énigme de l'exhumé de Sainte-Hélène'.

In these books a conspiracy theory is thoroughly built that, in summary, claims that Napoleon's body was swapped some time between 1821 and 1840 for the corpse of his butler Cipriani (see page 113), which would be now occupying Napoleon's casket at Les Invalides. The real corpse would, on the other hand, be resting in an unmarked grave at Westminster Abbey, London. These conclusions are reached via a series of arguments and considerations in which the comparison of the state of the body at the moment of the interment in 1821 and its retrieval in 1840, by checking multiple testimonies, possibly plays a foremost role in the attempt to comply with the burden of proof:

THE HEAD

1821
The face and the head are completely shaved. The mouth closed. Features have been heavily altered and the face distorted and unrecognizable.

1840
Beard on the face and hair on the head. The mouth is open showing three very white teeth.

---

1. *Georges Rétif de la Bretonne (1930-1999) was a journalist and photographer who in 1969 published a book titled 'Anglais, Rendez-Nous Napoléon', so initiating a debate regarding the whereabouts of Napoleon's corpse.*

THE CASKET

1821

Three caskets: tin, lead and mahogany. No velvet lining on the bottom of the mahogany casket.

1840

Four caskets: one made of tin, a first one of mahogany, a lead one and a second one of mahogany. Bottom of the outer mahogany casket velvet lined.

THE DECORATIONS

1821

Légion d'Honneur, Couronne de Fer, Ordre de la Réunion, Grand Ribbon de la Légion de Honneur with cross over the tunic.

1840

Légion d'Honneur, Couronne de Fer, and Grand Ribbon de la Légion de Honneur without cross placed beneath the tunic.

THE BODY

1821

Advanced putrefaction. Limbs stretched.

1840

Perfectly conserved. Flesh mummified. Flexed legs.

THE SILVER VASES

1821

Placed at the lower corners of the tin caskets, they contained the heart and stomach.

1840

Placed between the legs, they would contain Cipriani's organs.

THE BOOTS AND THE UNIFORM

1821

Full dress order uniform, hat with cockade over the feet, silk stockings, silver spurs on the boots.

1840

Service order uniform, hat without cockade placed on the thighs, no stockings, visible toes, no spurs on the boots.

On 15th October 1840 the returning exiles, on opening the Emperor's casket, would astonishingly have noticed that the British had substituted Napoleon's body, but remained silent lest a serious diplomatic incident arose. This would have been a rather cumbersome plot involving quite a few personalities serving the purpose of surreptitiously whisking away the corpse from the French sending it to Britain, but why?

On assuming that Napoleon was poisoned, one of these purposes would have been avoiding any further autopsy showing that the Emperor had been effectively intoxicated. The other would be the pathological obsession of George IV[1] with Napoleon who, in connivance with Wellington would have had Hudson Lowe bring back the body of the great man to Britain as a war trophy in 1828, when he was once more at Saint Helena sailing home from Ceylon.

According with Roy-Henry[2] Gorrequer (see page 88), upon Lowe leaving the island in 1821, was ordered to keep the corpse at Saint Helena. That might suggest that there was a prior thought, or instruction emanating from the British highest authorities to keep the corpse. A decision possibly made after they knew about the affair of the substitution of the death mask.

It is of course a complex business full of contradictory testimonies and considerable political foul play scrutinized by Rétif and Roy Henry in their respective books, in which readers learn about how the British declare they are ready to send the Emperor's corpse back to France when they know perfectly well that Louis XVIII (then in power) wouldn't accept that, or how Antommarchi states in 1825 that Napoleon had lost a lot of weight in the last phase of his illness; which is in flagrant contradiction with his autopsy report, and so on until concluding that probably at a given time between 1821 and 1827, the English decided to substitute Napoleon's corpse for Cipriani's, which was exhumed being surprisingly well conserved, supposedly due to the fact that he had been poisoned with arsenic. Then Cipriani's heart, stomach and other organs would have been extracted (or perhaps they were by O'Meara at the time of Cipriani' s death in 1818).

The uniforms and decorations worn by 'Cipriani' at the moment of the exhumation in 1840 would be consistent with Napoleon's uniform

---

1. *George Augustus Frederic (1762-1830) was King of the United Kingdom of Great Britain and Ireland and of Hanover after the death of his father, George III in 1820. Due to his father's severe mental illness he was appointed Prince Regent from 1811 until his enthronization. Despite being a cultivated and handsome man in his youth, his flagrant way of life and psychotic personality earned him the contempt of his people.*
2. *Bruno Roy-Henry, born in 1956 is a writer specialized in the history of the French Revolution and the First Empire.*

seized by the British at Waterloo and used to dress the replacement body. Cipriani was taller than Napoleon, which would explain why the legs were flexed in 1840. Similarly, Cipriani's larger feet would explain the toes protruding from the boots...

Even though extensively refuted by more orthodox authors as being little more than a novelettish lucubration, this revisionist theory is coherent and well built. As requested by Bruno-Henry, the dispute would be definitively closed if a small piece from the corpse occupying the casket in 1840 and now at Les Invalides would be available for a DNA comparison with Napoleon's descendants, a request that has been repeatedly denied up to the time of writing these lines. However, if this refusal could be justified on the grounds of historical respect and bureaucratic impediments, that would be not the case for a tiny portion of skin retrieved as a memento from the corpse in 1840 and up to now exposed in a simple key-opened showcase at the *Musée de la Armée* in Paris but again Bruno-Henry's request has been denied to date...

THE RETURN OF THE ASHES

*ll eyes are fixed on the coffin. Everyone is holding their breath. There is nobody present in this scene indifferent to the Emperor that could be aware of the extraordinary effect on the faces when the Emperor was about to be uncovered. The lid removed; there is something resembling beaten egg white spread all along the coffin. It cannot be identified at first, but those who had placed the Emperor's body remembered that the tinplate coffin was lined with a light padding covered with white satin fixed with threads passing trough little holes on the tinplate and that these threads, burnt out or rotten, probably broke when doctor Guillard had the coffins drilled. The doctor raises the veil progressively and carefully from the feet upwards until the whole of the Emperor's body appears.*

Eyes are full of tears and hearts beat fast. Breathing accelerates. This is a sublime moment. The body is covered from feet to head by a thin mould that leaves visible only some portions of the green colour of the tunic and the red cuffs on the sleeves. The head still retains some resemblance with the mask, particularly the lower part of the face. The nose is deformed: the cartilage seems to have been creased by the lid. The hands are a little dried up, but still in a beautiful shape: they are whiter than the face and the skin is a little bit transparent. The nails are a little longer and slightly rosy. The boots, with detached soles leave the tips of the feet visible and the silk stockings had taken the colour of the skin. All that is gold, silver or copper presented a blackish hue. The vest, tunic and breeches seem to be well. Visible down the centre of the vest and breeches, is a greenish stripe five inches long and one inch wide. This marks where the autopsy was made.

The body is in a far better condition than could be expected. To have seen the two vases containing the heart and the stomach would have been desirable but, as these objects are below the legs which might be damaged when moved aside, it was preferred to leave things as they were.[1]

Napoleon's desire to be buried on the banks of the Seine would have to wait for almost twenty years before becoming a reality... Bertrand's requests to the British to be allowed to move Napoleon's

---

1. *'Journal inédit du Retour des Cendres 1840'. Mameluck Ali. Tallandier Éditions, 2003. Paris.*

body to France were plainly refused. At the same time the position of the government of Louis XVIII in France was rather ambiguous, afraid as they were that a return of Napoleon to France –even in death– might rekindle political unrest.

It would be only in 1840, under the rule of Louis-Philippe, that the idea of recovering Napoleon's mortal remains finally took hold as part of the king's policy to regain the past French glory. The legendary figure of Napoleon, was by then well established worldwide and undoubtedly reinforced by the dramatic final years at Saint Helena that the Emperor so cleverly had converted into a veritable enshrinement of his persona, now more than ever, able to excite the feelings and sympathy of many intellectuals, politicians and remarkable people like Thiers[1], who played a foremost role in the retrieval of Napoleon's body by boosting a vindication of the fallen Emperor in France.

But the attraction of this extraordinary man was of course not restricted to learned individuals, as it extended to the common people too in a more primary, emotional way. Thus, behind all the grandiose display of the '*Retour des Cendres*' was probably the idea of a political capitalization of the figure of Napoleon on behalf of the reigning monarchy in the understanding that his figure, once the great man was dead, could be assimilated as a general representation of more abstract values regardless of the inherent political principles of 'Bonapartism' that, as would be noticed in later years was still alive and vibrant. The British gladly consenting to the retrieval of the corpse on this occasion, the preparations for the recovery, including the transportation of the Emperor's mortal remains and the building of a splendid tomb at Les Invalides, begun with great splendour fuelled by a big budget...

On 7th July 1840 the frigate 'Belle Poule'[2], escorted by the corvette 'Favourite' set sail from Toulon towards Saint Helena. A considerable number of personalities boarded the Belle Poule under the command of the Prince of Joinville; Louis Philippe's son and naval officer. Among them was a good representation of Napoleon´s companions in exile: Bertrand, Gourgaud, Emmanuel de Las Cases[3], Ali, Noverraz, Pierron, Archambault, Coursot and Marchand; who sailed in the Favourite. Albine de Montholon also wanted to go but wasn't allowed to[4]. Also

---

1. *Adolphe Thiers (1797-1877), French politician and historian, he was prime minister 1840.*
2. *The 'Belle-Poule' –with 60 guns, 54 meters length, 14 meters beam and crewed by 300 men– was a fine cruiser class battle ship following the design of the USS Constitution.*
3. *Las Cases' son. His father, who would die two years later, was too ill by then to face this voyage.*
4. *'Journal inédit du Retour des Cendres 1840 '. Mameluck Ali. Tallandier Éditions, 2003. Paris.*

aboard was a splendid catafalque and funerary regalia in accordance with the occasion.

The crossing prolonged into about three months with most passengers enjoying a rather festive time aboard with stopovers of several days at Cadiz, Madeira, Tenerife and Bahía in Brazil before reaching Saint Helena on October 8th. The expedition was then informed that the Emperor's mortal remains would be finally handed over on Thursday 15th.

Early in the morning next day they set foot ashore at last and, without delay, made their way to the tomb finding it to be, after so many years, a forlorn and unkempt place. Things weren't better at Longwood House, now in depressive and decrepit shape. No furniture, ruined and smeared walls covered with drawings and inscriptions and, topping it all, Napoleon's bedroom converted into a stable. It was quite obvious that preserving these 'sacred places' had not been a major concern for the British authorities on the island during all those years...

The exhumation works, carried about by British soldiers, commenced at midnight on 14th October witnessed by French and British representatives. After the uncovering of the corpse described above, this would be protected inside a series of successive coffins weighing in total well over a ton; the last one being of ebony and sporting the sole inscription NAPOLEON in gold letters on the lid. It was raining heavily when the carefully staged funerary procession started the way back to the pier in Jamestown where the remains would be hoisted aboard the Belle Poule and placed into a candle lit chapel, always in keeping with the overwhelming pomp and panache shown all through the recovery process.

On 30th November the Belle-Poule reached Cherbourg. The coffin, after being transferred to inland navigation vessels went up the Seine reaching Paris amidst great popular acclaim and pageantry. But the plan put in motion by Thiers and Louis Philippe didn't work, as in 1848 the king's scarce popularity had collapsed and he was overthrown so clearing the way to Napoleon III and the coming of his Second Empire...

Finally, on 2nd April 1861, Napoleon's mortal remains would be moved to his definitive resting place under the dome of Les Invalides, by the Seine...

(Bombled. ©Andrea Press).

EPILOGUE

uman individuals of any kind can only be conceived inside and nurtured by groups that eventually evolve into societies or civilizations. This paradox between individuals and groups is ever present in all human development as a historical constant and it is especially evident in the mechanics of progress and social organization. Especially in religion and politics, any significant movement is always led by a particular individual followed by a mass of people eager to be guided –or conducted– through the uncertainty of life and the fear of living. A kind of dialectic which emanates from a basic fear: Death and the other subsidiary fears in life: illness, pain, hunger...

Fear is what basically makes mankind stick together in groups organized around myths. Myths of any kind as sublimations of an idea, a fact or a person are indispensable for the group development and its internal cohesion, in so far as they provide certainty and confidence regardless of a truth that, in any case, will always be unreachable. This could be a reason explaining how easily large groups of people follow –even to death– individuals invested with mythical proportions.

Napoleon Bonaparte was one of these men, belonging to the rarest breed of them all: those able to join thought and action in an overwhelming movement. This kind of men differs from the group because they are not afraid to die. Apparently, they serve a belief or an ideology: an imperial France leading Europe in the case of Napoleon but, in fact it is just movement as an end by itself that sets them in motion. Usually in terrible motion or, in other words: War.

War is of course an essential element in Napoleon's life and, according to known history something inherent to the human condition as, no matter how far men's scientific and technological progress goes, war is still there with increasing violence and misery. Napoleon's detractors blame him for millions of deaths during his rule, but it should be noted that this man was an outcome of the French Revolution, an especially bloody period in European history when the winds of war blew all across the continent.

For better or worse, perhaps the nearest we can get to an understanding of the personage would be by focusing on the paradoxical nature of his personality in the light of the dynamics between the individual and the group mentioned above and by assuming that the ultimate and unknown driving forces of history lie far beyond human capabilities.

So, the sharp contrasts existing between the young general fighting for the ideals of the French Revolution and the enlightened despot of later years; his fine wit and blind nepotism; his military sobriety and insatiable ambition; his exuberant personality and his cold inner void; his dazzling power and his pitiable end at Saint Helena could make some sense as the reflections of a man who, like any other human being, just couldn't escape his fate...

INDEX

BIBLIOGRAPHY

A Diary of St. Helena. The Journal of Lady Malcom. (1816-1817). Edited by Sir Arthur Wilson, K.CJ.E.

A Polish Exile with Napoleon. G. L. DE ST. M. Watson. Harper & Brothers, 1912.

Anglais, rendez-nous Napoléon. Georges Retif. Jérôme Martineau, éditeur. (1969)

Cahiers de Sainte-Hélène 1818-1819. General Bertrand. Albin Michel. 1959.

Dictionnaire Napoléon. Fayard. Paris. 1999.

Gorrequer's Diary. James Kemble. Heinemann. London 1969.

History of the Captivity of Napoleon at St. Helena. General Count Montholon. Henry Colburn. London, 1846.

History of the Captivity of Napoleon at St. Helena. Lieut. Gen. Sir Hudson Lowe. William Forsyth, MA. Harper Brothers. 1853, New York.

Journal de Sainte-Hélène 1815-1818. Général baron Gourgaud.

Journal inédit du Retour des Cendres 1840. Mameluck Ali. Tallandier Éditions, 2003. Paris.

Journaux de Sainte-Hélène. Docteur Verling & Capitaine Nicholls. Librairie Historique F. Teissedre. Paris.

La Vie quotidienne à Sainte-Hélène au temps de Napoléon. Gilbert Martineau. Tallandier.

Le Drame de Sainte Hélène. André Castelot. Perrin.

Le Manuscrit de Sainte-Hélène. Une Énigme Napoléonienne. Michèle Brocarde. Cabédita.

Le Mémorial de Sainte-Hélène. Le Comte de Las Cases. Garnier Frères. Paris 1895.

Les Derniers Moments de Napoléon. (1819-1821). Dr. Antommarchi. Paris. Garnier Frères, Libraires-Éditeurs,1898.

Letters of Captain Engelbert Lutyens. Edited by Sir Lees Knowles. 1915.

Letters Written on Board His Majesty Ship the Northumberland and at Saint Helena. William Warden. Ackerman. London 1816.

Marchand Memoirs. Proctor Jones's first English edition.

Mémoires de Marchand d'après le manuscrit original par Jean Bourguignon. Plon, Paris 1952.

Mémoires Intimes de Napoléon I. Constant. Le Temps retrouvé. Mercure de France 1967.

Napoleon and Doctor Verling on St Helena. J. David Markham. Pen & Sword, 2005.

Napoléon en Exil à Sainte-Hélène. Dr. Barry E. O'Meara. Plancher, Paris 1822.

Napoléon et Ses Soldats. L´Apogée de la Gloire 1804-1809. Paul Willing. Collections Historiques du Musée de L´Armée.

Napoléon, Dictionnaire Intime. Alain Fillion.

Napoleon. An intimacy account of the years of supremacy 1800-1814. Proctor Patterson Jones.

Napoléon. L'énigme de l'exhumé de Sainte-Hélène. Bruno Roy-Henry. L'Archipel. 2001.

Napoleon's Exile. F. Antommarchi. London. Henry Colburn, New Burlington Street. 1826.

Napoleon's Last Voyage. Rear-Admiral Sir George Cockburn. Simpkin, Marshall & Co. 1888.

Napoleon´s autopsy: New perspectives. A. Lugli MD, A. Koop Luigi, M. Horcic. Human Pathology. 2005.

Notes and reminiscences of a Staff Officer. Lieutenant-Colonel Basil Jackson. London, Harrison & Sons, 1877.

Sainte-Hélène. Île de Mémoire. Fayard.

Souvenirs du Mameluck Ali. Louis-Étienne Saint-Denis. Payot, Paris 1926.

St. Helena during Napoleon's Exile. Gorrequer's Diary. James Kemble. William Heinemann Ltd. London 1969.

The Drama of Saint Helena. Paul Frémeaux. New York. D. Appleton and Company, 1910.

The Last days of the Emperor Napoleon. Dr. F. Antommarchi. London 1825.

The Life of Napoleon I. John Holland Rose. George Bell and Sons 1902.

To Befriend an Emperor. Betsy Balcombe. Ravenhall Books.

With Napoleon at St. Helena. Dr. John Stokoe. John Lane the Bodley Head. London and New York, 1902.